THE INFLUENCE OF
IMAGINATION

THE INFLUENCE OF IMAGINATION

Essays on Science Fiction and Fantasy as Agents of Social Change

Edited by
LEE EASTON *and*
RANDY SCHROEDER

McFarland & Company, Inc., Publishers
Jefferson, North Carolina, and London

LIBRARY OF CONGRESS CATALOGUING-IN-PUBLICATION DATA

The influence of imagination : essays on science fiction and fantasy as
  agents of social change / edited by Lee Easton and Randy Schroeder.
      p.   cm.
  Includes bibliographical references and index.

  ISBN-13: 978-0-7864-3230-1
  softcover : 50# alkaline paper ∞

  1. Science fiction, American — History and criticism — Theory,
etc.   2. Science fiction, English — History and criticism — Theory,
etc.   3. Commonwealth fiction (English) — History and criticism.
4. Literature and society — English-speaking countries — History —
20th century.   I. Easton, Lee.   II. Schroeder, Randy, 1964–
PS374.S35I44 2008
823'.0876209355 — dc22
                                            2007037182

British Library cataloguing data are available

Cover images ©2007 Shutterstock

Manufactured in the United States of America

*McFarland & Company, Inc., Publishers
  Box 611, Jefferson, North Carolina 28640
  www.mcfarlandpub.com*

Acknowledgments

This volume partly originated at a symposium entitled *FutureVisions 6.0: SF and Social Change* held at Mount Royal College in Calgary, Canada, February 2004. The symposium received immense support from the Department of English at Mount Royal College. In particular, we would like to thank Sabrina Reed, chair of the Department of English, for her work. The Mount Royal Faculty of Arts Council provided generous grants to support the symposium; we want to specifically mention Alexandra Pett, associate dean of arts, who consistently supported our endeavors. The symposium would not have happened without the energetic efforts of Donna-Lee Ost. We also want to acknowledge the support the Department of English at the University of Calgary, the Faculty of Humanities at the University of Calgary, and the Calgary Public Library. Geof Bishop provided timely assistance in copy-editing an early draft. Janine Falck provided a close reading of the final draft on short notice. In addition, a grant from the Mount Royal College Scholarly Pursuits Fund provided needed time to prepare the final manuscript.

Contents

Acknowledgments   v

Preface: From *FutureVisions* to Critical Singularities   1

Introduction: Polarities at the Singularity   *(Randy Schroeder)*   5

1. The Continuum of Meaning: A Reflection on Speculative
   Fiction and Society *(Marie Jakober)* 27

2. Peter Jackson and the Deforestation of Middle Earth
   (David Hyttenrauch) 32

3. Seeking Stories: Possible Worlds Semantics in Greer Ilene
   Gilman's *Moonwise* *(Christine Mains)* 44

4. "Dancing on the Edge of the World": California and
   Utopia in Ursula K. Le Guin's *Always Coming Home*
   (Ken Simpson) 55

5. Passing Genes in *GATTACA*, or, Straight Genes for the
   Queer Guy *(Lee Easton)* 70

6. The Changing Role of Women in Science Fiction: *Weird
   Tales*, 1925–1940 *(Mary Hemmings)* 83

7. Storytelling and Folktales: A Graphic Exploration
   (Gail de Vos) 92

8. The Graphic Novel as New Testament: On Narrative
Progress, Cultural Change and the Heroic Story
(Richard Harrison) 99

9. Science Fiction, Religion, and Social Change
(Steven Engler) 108

10. Science and Science Fiction *(Todd C. Nickle)* 118

11. Olaf Stapledon's Americanized Planet *(Robert Boschman)* . . . 125

12. Nalo Hopkinson's Colonial and Dystopic Worlds in
Midnight Robber (Ruby S. Ramraj) 131

13. "Wartime Inventions with Peaceful Intentions":
Television and the Media Cyborg in C.L. Moore's
No Woman Born (Linda Howell) 139

14. The Fantasy of Gender/Sex: Angela Carter and
Mythmaking *(Darlene M. Juschka)* 160

15. In the Spirit of Process: A Braiding Together of New
Utopianism, Gilles Deleuze, and Anne Carson
(Jacqueline Plante) 174

16. Dystopia in a New Land *(Karyn Huenemann)* 183

17. Surfing the Singularity: Science Fiction and the Future
of Narrative Media *(Brian Greenspan)* 202

About the Contributors   221

Index   225

Preface: From *FutureVisions* to Critical Singularities

"Is science fiction finished?" pondered a headline in one of Canada's national newspapers, *The Globe and Mail.* Reporting on the 2004 Science Fiction and Fantasy World Con, Rebecca Caldwell observed, "Science fiction appears on the verge of getting beamed up to the great Enterprise in the sky, with sci-fi writers concerned that they are facing the unique irony of looking at a future where their writing could be a thing of the past" (R3).

Increasingly, observers such as Caldwell seem ready to pronounce science fiction a spent cultural force. The power of fantasy fiction is rarely even considered. In this gloomy portrait, speculative fictions are stuck in either a rut of medieval fantasy or a Möbius strip of *Star Trek* reruns. Science fiction, especially, seems able to move its focus "back to the future." In fact, SF critic Adam Roberts suggests science fiction has become primarily a historiographic mode for writing symbolically about the past (35). Has it? Although many emphasize that science fiction has a spotty record when it comes to predicting the future, Thomas Disch still contends that the "some of the most remarkable features of the present historical moment have their roots in a way of thinking that we have learned from science fiction" (12). For many commentators, science fiction and fantasy have become more than just popular genres that fill shelf space in mega bookstores; they *are* the world we inhabit. So are speculative fictions a spent force or a set of vibrant genres? Can speculative fiction only function as social commentary or is there still some visionary capacity as yet unrecognized?

1

With these questions in mind, we organized a symposium entitled
FutureVisions 6.0: SF and Social Change in 2004, at which we invited pre-
senters to explore the difficult relationships between science fiction, fantasy and social change. We attempted to create a hybrid conference, drawing
in diverse constituencies that rarely converse: writers, academics who study
SF, academics who do not, storytellers, librarians, other professionals, fans,
readers and the general public. We were fortunate to attract some of
Canada's top science fiction and fantasy writers, including Robert J. Sawyer,
Candas Jane Dorsey and Timothy J. Anderson, not to mention many fine
scholars, interested students and avid readers. The papers collected in this
book, including the essay by award-winning fantasy author Marie Jakober,
reflect that diverse collection of individuals and perspectives.

During the symposium, the conversations and debates often returned
to a question posed by Robert J. Sawyer: in light of the imminent technological singularity, where techno-science supersaturates culture and all bets
are off, can science fiction still anticipate the future as it did in its heyday,
or even influence society's political and social agenda? Sawyer mused that
science fiction might soon function exclusively as a form of social criticism,
but not as the force it was in the twentieth century, "Imagineering" the
future. Many participants disagreed, implicitly and explicitly; many sup-
plemented the discussion by arguing for the social vitality of fantasy fiction.
The optimism expressed at the symposium led us to think of publishing
the proceedings as a record of that discussion.

This collection is an attempt to consolidate and update the ideas
from *FutureVisions* and intervene in the debate of "whither SF and fantasy
now?" To that end, we turned to the notion that human cultures with
advanced technologies are arriving at a technological singularity, a point
at which we can no longer anticipate clearly the ways that AI, nanotechnology and genetics might reshape our existence. We wondered if there was
a corresponding *critical* singularity beyond which it is impossible to imagine the workings of culture itself, a point beyond which nothing is clear
and no "futurevision" possible. Coincidentally, however, the term "singularity" provides us with a clue. Among its meanings, a singularity also
suggests odd traits and peculiarities, a secondary signification that questions and even disrupts the totalizing sense of the first definition. There is
something inherently *not quite right* about the idea of a "singularity" that
excludes the possibility of imagining other futures. It is this queerness
that our contributors, working from a range of critical and imaginative
approaches, seize upon and play with to question the idea that speculative

fiction in all its forms has reached its creative end. As this collection shows, reiterating the lessons of theory, a move from the question of future visions to that of imminent singularity entails speaking of not one, but many singularities.

WORKS CITED

Caldwell, Rebecca. "Is Science Fiction Finished?" *Globe and Mail.* 8 September 2004. R3.

Disch, Thomas. *The Dreams Our Stuff Is Made Of: How Science Fiction Conquered the World.* New York: Touchstone, 1999.

Roberts, Adam. *Science Fiction.* The New Critical Idiom Series. New York: Routledge, 2000.

Sawyer, Robert J. "Reflections on Science Fiction and Social Change." Plenary Address at FutureVisions 6.0: SF and Social Change. Mount Royal College, Calgary, Canada. February 2004.

Introduction: Polarities at the Singularity

Randy Schroeder

"Deficiencies of language stand in the way inexorably."
— Alfred North Whitehead

In 1979, before Hawking's *Brief History of Time* went household, Disney Films premiered its spectacularly implausible *The Black Hole*. The final act featured evil robot Maximillian and equally evil creator Dr. Reinhart zipping through a singularity, getting the punishment they deserved, suddenly fused as a single devilish entity *en route* to Hell itself, in one of the most preposterous genre-bending resolutions in movie history. In 2005, inventor Ray Kurzweil released his doorstopping *The Singularity Is Near*, which took up the now-familiar argument that Big Science is about to reach a state of accelerated exponentiality — a *mathematical* singularity — in which technology will design itself and merge with us in ways that challenge all our assumptions about human nature. In 2006, political theorist Martha Nussbaum invited us to imagine a perfect science-fictional Being, as a way of recognizing that, by contrast, human imperfection must be acknowledged for any useful theory of rights, that pure rationality and self-reliance represent a practical singularity we will never encounter (132–33).

Do Maximillian, Kurzweil and Nussbaum share a planet? In their own distinctive idioms, all three examples introduce the theme of interconnection. Maximillian and Reinhart enact Kurzweil's post-human predictions in a manner he would probably find dire and phantasmagorical. Kurzweil imagines human/technology integration in optimistic ways that do not feature Hell or other mythical fancies. And Nussbaum uses the SF trope while rejecting the SF fantasy, in a sense casting her gaze backward rather than forward: she aims to heal the old "Kantian split between personhood and animality" (132), to favor "rich continuums" (133), to understand how enriching the lives of others simultaneously enriches our own. But, though all three idioms imply radical intersectionality, we might wonder if their terms are outstripped by their hopeful predictions, if adequate language exists to grasp genuine interconnectivity. Is the imagined actually *imaginable*?

The singularity is not new in mathematics, science, information theory or even the humanities. It was most famously argued by computer scientist, mathematician and SF writer Vernor Vinge in his 1993 paper "The Coming Technological Singularity," at a symposium sponsored by NASA and the Ohio Aerospace Institute. But the idea has a rich ancestry in the work of earlier mathematicians and statisticians, and made a dramatic appearance in the fermented eighties, in the posthumanist musings of Vinge himself, futurist Bruce Sterling, the Cyberpunks, and some of the more radical feminists. The singularity is an SF trope both delightful and enticing. But, ironically, if collisions between categories and entities are accelerating beyond our ability to measure and predict, we must wonder if SF is losing its ability to extrapolate and to diagnose the social. We will probably dismiss fantasy entirely as moribund and delusional. The key, philosophically, is a robust link between predictive power and social critique: one must know where society might go in order to suggest where it *should* go. But is such a link necessary? Or are there other, less linear means by which SF and fantasy narratives induce social change, pathways more subtle, sneaky and stochastic?

Our contributors remain optimistic, in varying degrees. Robert Boschman, for example, suggests that science fiction narratives succeed as social comment not through their literal accuracy, but through their symbolic relations with culture. He shows how the relevance of Olaf Stapledon's *Last and First Men*, published in 1930, is not "in the details," but in the anticipation of trends like resource exhaustion and urbanization. Christine Mains argues that fantastic narrative — in its deep structure — generates interactions between modal categories like possibility, obligation and knowledge, all of which are simultaneously operational in the real world. Literal accuracy, then, is again beside the point: fantasy authors are always necessarily "moral beings" situated within communities where morality is expressed and negotiated. Linda Howell examines narrative hybridity, which can never be commonsensically *literal*. Specifically, she explores the power of "cyborg writing" to engage wartime audiences in resistance to commercially dominated and conventionally gendered discourses of peacetime conversion.

Beginning with award-winning fantasy author Marie Jakober, all our contributors to some extent query the relations between speculative fiction and the conventions of realism. One major topic of this collection, then, is the old question of mimesis — whether narrative's power as ideological discourse lies primarily in its capacity for familiarization or defamiliarization. In either case, the dialogue is between the "real" and the "possible." But since the former term has always been problematic, the secondary questions proliferate. Who defines the "real"? And, whatever its definition, do we get from *real* to *possible* through the extrapolative and believable story, or the disjunctive and unlikely one? For that matter, is the possible only in the future, or, as Ken Simpson claims in his essay on Le Guin, also in the present?

These are turf-war questions. Their answers rank types of speculative fiction as to relative social vigor: if, for example, extrapolation is the key to social change, then high fantasy, with its atavistic habits, sparks more fun than flak as it tiptoes through the ideological fields. It confirms rather than questions stale routines of thought. Or does it? Once upon a time, in 1981's *Political Unconscious*, Fredric Jameson theorized that magical narratives —*especially* magical narratives — create social friction exactly by what they do *not* imagine. In Jameson's forensic model, fantasy can be probed and forced to blurt out its unstated assumptions and desires, driven to a libidinous aporia that exposes the very opportunities repressed by the story's familiar structure. Following Jameson, Marjorie Levinson and other New Historicists in the eighties examined the meaningful "silences" of texts, a mode now so familiar in cultural studies it has almost vanished to become its own silence. The model was, and is, heady stuff. But since it is doubtful that anyone will ever offer a quantitative model for ideology — given its escalating definitions, its contentious standing, its chaotic nature, its variables, its sensitivity to conditions initial and contextual, its sheer discursive *spookiness*— we have little way of knowing whether the relations between SF, fantasy and social change are better served by simple or complex explanations, or by both, or by neither.

Our contributors, read collectively, manifest this dialectic between high theory and received wisdom. They demonstrate that analyses of SF and fantasy are always situated within the zigzag history of cultural studies, still in dialogue with the contentious voices of post-structuralism and post-Marxism. Any serious discussion of SF or fantasy will necessarily resonate with the histories and futures of critical theory, as this introduction will suggest. Indeed, in the twenty-first century, speculative fiction studies must also tangle with the present: *post*-theory's wish to compensate for the constructivist excesses of theory! Simpson, for one, positions his argument within the postmodern moment of narrative exhaustion, where the critic must always question her tools and trade. Stephen Engler, questioning both science fictional and religious categories, examines the shifty relations between social change and social stability. Scientist Todd C. Nickle, more optimistically, suggests that SF might "model" the real world. But how? Ruby S. Ramraj, assessing the work of Nalo Hopkinson, suggests that politicized narrative offers models for alternative values and beliefs, creating, finally, a social "will for change." Her essay challenges the objection that popular narrative's sheer transience disables its social efficacy. Some critics, grounded in the original pessimism of the Frankfurt School, have wondered how many readers it takes to cause a threshold of social change, and despaired at the possibility that *The Da Vinci Code* is more potent than anything by Octavia Butler or Samuel R. Delaney. Librarian Mary Hemmings, exploring traditional representations of women in pulp fiction, implicitly questions these lines of causality: do available representations govern available worldviews, or do worldviews govern representations, or do both comprise a matrix of mutual feedback? Gail de Vos, examining the junctions between orality and the graphic novel, hints that narrative has always been promiscuous with ideologies, and that the two phenomena have co-evolved.[1] Richard Harrison, working in the same field, ponders whether stories are redemptive or wish-fulfilling, therapeutic or pathological, or — most likely — a complex interplay of both. His essay returns us to the center: when the social *real* presents us with problems, do stories intervene through symbolic solutions or formal disruptions, or through some dialectic where each is yin to the other's yang?

This problem will be numbing or invigorating, depending on one's theoretical temperament and tolerance for ambiguity. If there is an attendant *critical* singularity, beyond which this particular dialectic cannot be seized, there may be little reason for our anthology (or many reasons, depending on how one looks at it). So we remain as optimistic as Kurzweil and as cautious as Nussbaum, while hoping to avoid Maximillian's fate. But in order to remain optimistic, we must attempt the question: just how *do* nonrealist narratives prompt or produce social change?

Mirrorshades

The first answer views accurate mirroring of the *real* as the primary quality of socially potent narratives. In this answer, stories need to be *read*: they need to convince by reflecting the material conditions of culture as understood by most readers. The structure of such narratives will be reassuring, even if the content will be disturbing. Most stories will be characterized by verisimilitude and proximity to the conventions of realism; some will be characterized by predictive power, especially those that mesh social and technological change. All will probably be characterized by high levels of readership. In short, popular narratives will count for more than unpopular ones.

It is easy for scholars to dismiss the "mirror view," because it often assumes a transparency of perception and representation that has been thoroughly trashed in the twentieth century. Einstein certainly believed in an objective reality. But it was a deeply qualified belief. In 1930, on the three hundredth anniversary of Kepler's death, he claimed that "the human mind has first to construct forms independently before we can find them in things" (266); a year later, on the hundredth anniversary of James Clerk Maxwell's birth, Einstein reaffirmed that "our notions of physical reality can never be final" (266). Again, to the young Heisenberg, he claimed "it is the theory which decides what we can observe" (qtd. in Heisenberg 63). Ironically, Einstein was often echoed by his rival, Niels Bohr, who as late as 1961 wrote "all new experience makes its appearance within the frame of our customary points of view and forms of perception" (1). This introduction cannot supplement Bohr and Einstein with a full rehearsal of the Copenhagen interpretation of quantum phenomena, the history of structuralism, strong constructivism, ancient Indian metaphysics, or relevant Greek philosophers. Neither is it possible to recite the long qualification that many scientists still agree with Galileo that God speaks in the language of mathematics, that interpretations of quantum phenomena have been clawed back to more familiar materialist terrain, dropping the spooky category of *consciousness*— indeed, that Einstein famously disagreed with Bohr and the Copenhagen interpretation, and perhaps finally with himself. It is not even possible here to consider arguments against correlating "new physics" with the post-modern turn. What is clear is that any naïve correspondence theory of truth will not please the critical theorist. However, we should hesitate to dismiss the mirror view outright, because in the realm of popular representation, mimesis, however ironic, still counts. We are not dealing with reality *as it is*, nor with the best available paradigms for modeling reality, nor with the most equitable ideologies, but with popular conceptions of reality from limited standpoints of perception and investment. This is already an old problem for cultural studies. The advantage of the mirror view is that it takes consumption into account. We do not usually flock to the latest blockbuster surrealist film, nor download the best-selling e-books by French philosophers.

Many essays from this collection are useful on this point, because they examine utopian/dystopian narratives, invoking the genre's rich tradition of satire. The satirist's tools of ridicule, display and caricature often rely on mimetic assumptions, even when those assumptions are ironic or temporary. We might grant speculative satire extraordinary surgical powers: it becomes the theater in which to dissect and censure inequity while offering other, better power relations. It functions, in Ramraj's words, as proposition; its primary trope is unmasking, its primary effect persuasion. And if narrative works exclusively in the realm of rhetoric, then perhaps we need not ask epistemological questions, only questions about readers' epistemologies. One could argue credibly that *Uncle Tom's Cabin*, *Neuromancer*, *The Feminine Mystique*, and even the novels of Dickens and H.G. Wells have influenced the worldviews of their respective cultures in fairly straightforward fashion.

Still, this is a short list, and many critics socialized by post-structuralism will jump to invoke Donna J. Haraway. In "Situated Knowledges," Haraway decries the "god-trick," whereby the critic or scientist or diagnostician stands outside his field of observation, as the polemicist must necessarily do when a stable object of attack is assumed. Just who is *behind* those mirrorshades? Others will ask whether any narrative can exist in a linear equation with its readers, and its readers with their cultures. Causality itself is interpreted in multiple ways: linear and nonlinear, continuous and interrupted, incremental and episodic, gradual and catastrophic, stochastic and predictable. Of course, the second objection troubles the first by reprising exactly the epistemological assumptions at issue — again, an old and vexing problem for theory! But the question remains: why should real social change bear some identical relationship or literal equivalence with imagined social change? The most potent narratives might activate mutations in *how* we imagine, not *what* we imagine. "Important issue" stories might actually fritter the social energies vital for change, by safely displacing them in the ritualized spaces of page and screen.

Part of the post-structuralist enterprise has been to remove the mirrored lenses, indeed, to alternate lenses and screens as much as possible. The second answer to the question of SF, fantasy and social change involves not so much solving the conundrums of causality as exacerbating them. We do not replace conventional epistemology from the outside. We harass it from the inside.

Cracking the Mirror

If dystopian satires and other potent narratives unmask the social for display, the demons are loose: we are confronted with each quirk from the tortured lineage of the *referent*, disputed by materialists, idealists, pragmatists, linguists, mystics, not to mention other cultures — the list could fill this introduction. Feminisms have negotiated the problem since at least the early eighties, as neatly tweaked by Haraway in her insistence that "objectivity" is both curious and inescapable (183) and that ethically motivated theories, whatever their position along the constructivist spectrum, "would still like to talk about reality with more confidence than we allow the Christian Right's discussion of the Second Coming" (185). Haraway raises the crucial question: must one talk about reality by wholeheartedly and permanently affirming any particular version of it? Maybe it is just obvious that nonrealist stories specialize in *not being realistic*, whatever the current status of objectivity in any particular culture. What if— loosely following chemist Ilya Prigogene and philosopher of science Isabelle Stengers — prompting change is not a matter of predicting it, but of *failing* to predict it with mastery? The instruments of potent narrative might then be disruption, disjunction, dishevelment — all tools for injecting nonlinear turbulence into public discourse, now viewed as a complex and reciprocal matrix of chaos and order. The future would be heavy weather: truly open, exquisitely sensitive to initial conditions, impossible to specify. SF, fantasy and theory would be free to destabilize conventional narrative, free to view knowledge, in Prigogene and Stengers' striking paradox, as jointly "objective and participatory" (299). Such praxis has, among theorists, been the *One Ring* for decades: can we grasp a transitional epistemology and committed ethics where speculative narrative simultaneously deconstructs naïve materialism *and* naïve constructivism, *and* unmasks material social practices by unmasking itself, consciously *or* unconsciously? We're down the rabbit hole now, playing croquet with Derrida's ghost.

Our contributors hoist their flamingos and take up the challenge in various ways. Ramraj, thinking through Nalo Hopkinson, views narrative as a mode that can expose then normalize what is forbidden and hidden by dominant culture, where types of Otherness are, through positive feedback, continuously naturalized as absent exactly by their continued absence. De Vos, in a move that echoes the Reception Theory of Wolfgang Iser, wonders if the virtual language-space created between reader and text might hold the potential for ideological change. Shifts in language may kindle shifts in reader subjectivity, which may light more collective ideological shifts, which may finally ignite shifts in material social relations. Simpson takes it further and asserts that nonrealist narratives, by virtue of their nonrealism, work at de-naturalization: in a highly ironic sense, nonrealism unmasks realism's nonrealism. Karyn Huenemann, in an essay on James De Mille, provides an example. She suggests that 1888's *A Strange Manuscript Found in a Copper Cylinder*— sometimes mistakenly read as a batch of colonialist clichés — actually refuses to coalesce into tidy genre or idiom. Instead, it continues to repel our comfortable habits of thought and resists any "resolution to the ideological conflicts it creates."

Jacqueline Plante and Darlene M. Juschka assertively correlate the realism index with the ineffectiveness index. Plante, in her essay on Gilles Deleuze and Anne Carson, convincingly argues that utopias swing both ways. While utopias like *1984* or *Brave New World* are routinely understood as powerful prophecy, Plante de-links the "transformative potential" of narrative from mimesis or plausible extrapolation, suggesting instead that potent utopian narratives use highly experimental *bricolage* to sweep up reader, writer and context into a "variable state of *becoming*." For Plante, transformative literature is necessarily transgressive in its structural and representative modes: it must *get it wrong*, precisely because "wrong" takes its value from within the authorized and authorizing codes of dominant discourse. Juschka, in a complex and reflexive essay, theorizes a demystifying relationship between text and reader, where narrative displays its own limits to reveal ideological gaps and fissures. Juschka retains a qualified practice of unmasking, but stresses that "de-mythologizing" naturalized tropes does not simultaneously refresh the god-trick. No Gandalf the White rides forth to return the old magic.

Juschka's argument implies a particular paradigm, argued most famously by Raymond Williams, where current, dominant ideologies jostle
with emergent and residual ideologies in a busy field of representation.
Further, her argument favors *discursive* ideology, the swirl of language that
saturates material culture in order to constrain and condition consciousness. This paradigm has been a talisman for cultural studies. If ideologies
are latticed and braided, cultural products will manifest ideology in contradictory patterns of resistance and reinscription, which the theorist can
carefully untangle. To use a March Hare's metaphor, pop culture has its
cake, eats it too, gets indigestion, and is forced by the theorist to burp. But
cultural studies is sticky business: in this model, shifting ideologies interact not only with each other, but with the material conditions of production, distribution and consumption, and with the structural and formal
constraints of various media. Narratives and representations do not then
reflect those configurations — how could they? — but embody them. In this
hall of mirrors, the scholar is always situated: if the god-trick means "seeing everything from nowhere" (Haraway 189), cultural studies means seeing a few things from somewhere. And the vision from *somewhere* remains
uncertain. The mirrors are always curved.

De Vos agrees that narrative can be exquisitely layered, able to hold
multiple and disparate meanings. She reminds us that readers and viewers
are not passive consumers, but active participants in the field of ideological distortion, at once taking and making meaning. In this reciprocal context, contradictions proliferate. Hemmings, for example, finds a predictably
limited range of roles for women in historical pulp SF, but also notes the
dissonance between stories and their attendant visuals, and between the
more sexist covers and the woman undercover who produced them. Lee
Easton demonstrates how *GATTACA* internalizes the very representations
it seeks to criticize. The film nervously crosses and un-crosses its legs while
performing a magic show with queer and straight props. Dominant concepts of gender, sex and disability vanish in one hand only to reappear in
the other, suggesting that for pop narrative, structure is stricture: stories
that are popular *and* political work against themselves in order to work at
all.

Clearly, light bends at this horizon. The complexity and reflexivity of
cultural studies sometimes distorts its conclusions — has since Derrida —
and the celebration of that distortion as the antidote to Enlightenment
might finally make knowledge too diffuse and prismatic to connect with
material social change. Haraway and Jean-François Lyotard presented par-

tial solutions in the eighties, when they imagined highly particular knowledges linked in more global, pragmatic webs. But this corner-painted paradox is on par with light understood as both particle and wave. Decades on, it still seems that post-structuralism has handed us a ten-dimensional universe and a pair of 3-D glasses, so the further we pull from the singularity, the closer it gets. So we must ask, with Alice, what happens when we come to the beginning again.

Now, the Tea Party

Juschka performs the tics of theory in her deft rehearsal of the "binary" problem, perhaps the oldest riddle of all. Politicized theories have always suspected the toxicity of binary thought, especially in its various configurations of self/Other, center/margin and power/powerless. The binary problem, polarized, is the reification problem — the addiction to monadic *thingness*, the compartmentalizing of self, the failure to see Otherness as convention or even delusion. Reification simultaneously creates and naturalizes absolute demarcations where there is actually flux and flow; the Other, in whatever form, becomes resource, antagonist, succubus, invisible man — disappeared, derogated, demented. Reification is neatly described and rejected in a quotation often attributed to Einstein, phrased in the idiom of his time: "A human being is part of the whole.... He experiences himself, his thoughts and feelings as something separated from the rest — a kind of optical delusion of his consciousness" (qtd. in Weber 203). Stephen Batchelor, discussing eighth-century Indian scholar Shantideva, explains with more subtlety: the subjective sense of self is not grounded in "isolated personal essence," but instead manifest in "myriad and unrepeatable relationships" (33). Both Einstein and Shantideva anticipate and even exceed the post–Lacanian deconstruction of subjectivity, without giving language dubious and excessive privilege as explanatory model and therapeutic mode.

Meantime, post-structuralism and its scions have tried to defang binarism and reification by valuing fluidity and hybridity while demonstrating social construction and performing uncertainty. But the challenge now is not to pull the rug out from under Enlightenment, but to pull the rug out from under the rug. As the thoughtful theorist concedes — tugging at the rug while standing on it — post-structuralism is talented at problematizing binaries, but fearful of erasing the whole *category* of binary. Boundaries and distinctions are necessarily binaristic, and, so far as we can understand, the rhetoric of theory has neither clarity nor continuity without distinctions and boundaries.[2]

Queer theory, to take one example, willingly engages this paradox or parasitism (a paradox already identified by Derrida in the mid-sixties). Queer theory invests in fluidity, the deconstruction of fixed, essentialized subjectivities. Yet, in order to argue fluidity, the theorist must prize apart the conflation of sex, sexuality and gender that is so deeply naturalized in hetero-normative discourse. So necessary distinctions and reified categories — in other words, binaristic tools — are used in service of their opposite: a provisional fixity in service of fluidity. This contradiction is old news, and to point it out is to confuse one dimension with another, since a good theorist will readily admit to the sparks between her political commitments and necessary residual logics, and since objections to the contradiction are always-already infected with the Enlightenment virus. But the point is that we have been waiting a long time to ditch Hegel's version of the dialectic. As we wait, we can only understand fluidity as distinct from the reified *things* necessary for *flow* to move through, over and around. We cannot get rid of our old prepositions.

As Juschka implies, this circle has never been squared from within theory.[3] De-binarizing strategies continue to originate from within the force-field of binarism, and, in doing so, continue to strengthen that field. Ethically committed theories need to erase the boundary between self and Other while simultaneously recognizing that boundary's relative truth. We need to honor both and neither at once. But this maneuver requires an ontology and set of commitments we cannot yet grasp: a critical singularity.

Plante moves us close to the event horizon, taking cues from Deleuze. She is determined to un-reify *things* by shifting nouns into verbs and releasing them into a radical, relational flux. But even at the expanding borders of the post-structuralist universe, the final frontier is always the simple, simplistic, indissoluble boundary between binary and *not*-binary. Try solving that one. Attempting the binary problem makes one feel like a child loose in a laboratory, enthusiastic and overwhelmed, finally humbled. One response to the critical singularity, as many feminists and neo-Marxists have pointed out, is to apprehend an emergent paradigm collectively, not as monads or as communities of monads, but from somewhere altogether outside the inherited terms of individualism (indeed, outside the residual geometry of "outside"). But we have yet to accomplish such rich intersubjectivity, partly since theory is often in business with its own conundrums, its own reinvention, forever going back to the future to move the past forward into the present. And what would the solution be? To discern some kind of full-force non-binarism, which is simultaneously one and many, and neither, or — misusing Orwell — to claim all binaries as equal, but some as more equal than others? Even the question is a nest of either/or propositions. And so — misusing Uncle Remus — theory keeps punching the tar baby.

A Mirror Up to Nature

What about narrative itself? SF and fantasy have long wrestled with the binary while dreaming of realms beyond the binary — the dimension of pure bliss, the somewhere over the rainbow. In SF, the standard Other is the alien; in mythic and high fantasy, the role is filled by the Orc, the necromancer, the witch, the stepmother. As far back as 1884, Edwin A. Abbott imagined singularity in *Flatland: A Romance of Many Dimensions*. In this curious novel, a sphere tries to get a square to understand three dimensions, for which the square, obviously, has no available terms. In 1969, Ursula K. Le Guin's famous *Left Hand of Darkness* grappled with the polarities of gender and the possibility of grasping a porous and fluid sociosexual interaction. More recently, in *Ptolemy's Gate*, Jonathan Stroud imagines the nondual world of the Djinn, "a ceaseless swirl of movement" where "nothing is fixed or static," yet forms exist (377). In this novel, humans are distressed by the bare notions of fluidity and interconnection, and incapable of understanding any dance between *one* and *many*.

Robin Hobb, in her popular *Farseer, Liveship Traders*, and *Tawny Man* trilogies, further explores radical questions of intersubjectivity and *intra*-subjectivity. Her sentient ships, for example, negotiate their plural "selfness" as they demonstrate consciousness that is prismatic and contradictory. The ships are mirrored in two human characters. The pirate captain, Kennit, demonstrates a multiple subjectivity in that his sexuality is not fixed anywhere along the gender spectrum, making his identity amphibious and his behavior contextual. The Fool/Amber takes queer even further, performing a complete fluidity of gender that baffles other characters — and perhaps readers — through all nine books. Since the series *is* popular narrative, most of these relatively radical moves are finally clawed back into dominant ideological terrain: Kennit's queerness is finally linked to his childhood rape, while the liveships must become "whole" and integrate their subjective multiplicities in an almost Jungian sense. But Hobb's narrative, for moments at least, tears gaps and reveals contradictions in dominant ideologies of gender and identity.

Hobb's successful failure prompts us to wonder: can story truly imagine beyond the dualistic singularity, or merely imagine *about* such realms? Le Guin is well known for her fascination with paradox and alternate dialectics, and claims, in the introduction to *Left Hand*, that "the novelist says in words what cannot be said in words." Again, in her essay "Text, Silence, Performance," she insists that writing "fixes the word outside time, and silences it" (180). Indeed, of Le Guin's obsessions, the relation between naming and unnaming is the most fascinating, explored in many works, including "The Rule of Names" and "A Trip to the Head" from *The Wind's Twelve Quarters*, and especially "She Unnames Them" from *Buffalo Gals*. But her teasing aphorisms are rather hopeful, and say less about narrative than her own preoccupation with reconciling story and Taoism. If anything, such riddling claims shade into mystical poetry, closer to Rilke, Rumi and Basho than to Asimov or Tolkien.

We might expect Cyberpunk to most fully engage questions of radical subjectivity. Think of three generations: Gibson's *Neuromancer* (1984), Greg Bear's *Queen of Angels* (1990), and Richard Morgan's *Altered Carbon* (2002), all of which explicitly disconnect identity from the body. Each work actually tends to reintroduce residual concepts of selfhood. Identity becomes a transportable phenomenon that can jump from body to body, organic to digital, "meat" to AI. But even in transit, the self remains the Self— coherent, stable, monadic, reified — loosely analogous to a soul. Gibson's first novel, especially, complicates the question. Decades after its publication, *Neuromancer* continues to engage emergent tropes even as it collapses the binary between SF and fantasy. But the novel achieves both through a contradictory use of residual distinctions: on its surface, the story is at once an extrapolative tour de force and an SF museum, opening room after room of science fiction knick-knackery; upon closer inspection, it yields that its foundations are pure romance and its basement a gallery of dusty mythic tropes and fantasy curios. Will popular narrative always remain stuck within the overlapping layers of residual, dominant and emergent representation? More importantly, can story ever unzip reification where theory cannot? Can story move beyond the critical singularity?

Thinking in a structuralist mode, we might see narrative as distinct from other linguistic forms in its unique constraints and compulsions. As

Engler argues, conventional story is hardwired with ideologies of human agency: in narrative, characters make decisions under pressure, act on those decisions, create consequences. Those consequences usually have reciprocal effects on the characters' motivations, which, in turn, influence further choices along the rising action. Even at narrative's experimental, high-hedged borders, beyond which there are no elves or aliens, story thresholds apply, as we will see with Le Guin.

An "issue story" will typically comment on injustice by demonstrating the effects of a social system on individual characters, who make choices under pressure of those effects. The consequent actions might defeat the system, change it, lose to it, draw even with it, or create unforeseen ironies. But they will not fail to generate non-trivial consequences. Even Winston Smith, in Orwell's *1984*, worsens his own situation within the all-seeing and encompassing ideological regiments of the Thought Police by trying repeatedly to free himself. There is little sense in which conventional story can present intersectionality *as* intersectionality and remain conventional story. As Harrison suggests in his structuralist essay, narrative's hardware is programmed to generate moral boundaries, which, at some level, always generate attendant binaries of protagonist/antagonist. Conventional story is a reification engine.

The dilemma deepens when nature becomes the Other. As Simpson demonstrates, Le Guin imagines a suspension of fixed binaries and thus a "state of consciousness interconnected with all things." But while Le Guin's orientation is emergent and her art postmodernist, her trajectory is residual, as it gathers energies from the very creation myths so deeply problematized by Juschka. Radical intersectionality exceeds story structure: it manifests like a sphere to a square — distorted and flattened to image, metaphor and paradox. Each works against narrative momentum, latching uncomfortably within the fractal folds of plot. Thus Simpson's argument focuses on Le Guin's tricky sense of *place*, which appears in narrative but can never be fully articulated in narrative terms, except as an othered realm of mystery, hostility, or potential resource. Le Guin gets us further than most popular writers, and covers herself wittily: "it's unsafe to say anything about narrative, because if a poststructuralist doesn't get you a deconstructionist will" ("Thoughts" 37). Still, as Peter Nicholls has implied, Le Guin's most intriguing gestures beyond the singularity work at the expense of story, in fiction that increasingly seems "a little static" and places "quixotic demands" on readers (704). If anything, her best moments point at the Taoist enigmas so silent and present in all her work, suggesting that what can be spoken is essentially untrue, in ways that have nothing to do with the boundaries between truth and falsehood. At her subtlest, despite her protests, Le Guin joins her beloved Lao Tzu beyond gate and gatekeeper.

David Hyttenrauch most fully takes up the problem of nature representation in his essay on Tolkien and *Lord of the Rings* filmmaker Peter Jackson. Tolkien understood that, within story, nature can never be allowed to speak for itself because its voice would immediately reconfigure all narrative elements in non-narrative relations, indeed, speak itself into those relations. Nature is beyond agency, anatomy and category, yet entangled vine-like with all of them; it is ineffable in ways that resist even the comforting polarity of "ineffable" and "understandable." Nature devours verbs and prepositions, and so, by necessity, nouns. As Hyttenrauch demonstrates, Tolkien knows this, and releases mildly non-narrative tropes into his story: song, trees, the characters of Tom Bombadil and Goldberry so absent in Jackson's films and so puzzling to many readers. But *LoTR* is still story, of course, and quest to boot. The story precepts overshadow these tropes for most readers — including, apparently, Jackson — and liminal nature becomes liminal narrative. We remain, with the disappointed Tolkien, at the edge of the forest.

Through the Looking Glass

Where now? It seems we must decrease language's privilege and shift our myths so that unnaming holds more power than naming. We have little problem identifying discrete things as parts of process, but we have no way to grasp every thing *as* process, dropping the noun "thing" altogether so it erases then replaces itself with a noun that does not exist. But this would appear more nonsensical than anything encountered by Alice in Wonderland: which words would encourage us to give up words? This introduction has examined two basic modes by which nonrealist narrative might provoke social change — verisimilitude and defamiliarization — and bumped against the limits of both. But what if we neither resisted nor indulged the distinction, but simply gave up on it?

In *The Dharma of Dragons and Daemons*, International Studies scholar David R. Loy and English professor Linda Goodhew offer accessible and intriguing insights to help address the binary problem through an analysis of Tolkien, Le Guin, Philip Pullman, German writer Michael Ende and Japanese filmmaker Hayao Miyazaki. Loy and Goodhew's ethically charged book commits to "interpermeation" (117), the authors' term for the radical intersectionality beyond the singularity of boundary and reification. Their investments are with subjectivity "understood not as a thing but as an ongoing *process*" (69), against the self that is "mental construction" built of "habitual intentions and automatized responses" (105). Surprisingly, while respecting the darkened paradoxes of interpermeation, they remain optimistic that popular narrative can illuminate the necessity of seizing those paradoxes, indeed, that narrative presents the best medium by which to do so. Their work is deliberately populist and does not tangle with needless complexities or theorize story as anything more than a set of representational "lessons." But, extrapolating strenuously from their analyses, we might redeem narrative by temporarily dropping the binary argument of mimesis versus transgression in favor of a loose dialogic that embraces both.

Since narrative remains binaristic, it can never itself seize, enact, perform, present or represent interpermeation. It *can* present the consequences of failing to grasp interpermeation, because those consequences are themselves painfully binaristic and are experienced by monadic and reified characters who, in some qualified way, represent our own subjectivities. For example, narrative will always be a temporal art form, separating its characters, events and other props, then inserting them *into* time in an almost Newtonian sense. Story will never capture the intersectional hunch that "*objects are time*" and that "*time is objects*" (60). However, as Loy and Goodhew show, novels like Ende's *Momo* can easily demonstrate the toxic consequences of characters who, captured by ideologies of separated and "spatial" temporality, commodify then hoard time at the expense of others. To use another of Loy and Goodhew's examples, Saruman, Wormtongue and Gollum demonstrate in exquisite detail how reification leads to the desire for power and domination. But, taking Loy and Goodhew's argument and braiding in a second strand, *LoTR* can only speak *about* the antidote to reification; it cannot grasp or manifest genuine insight into interpermeation, as Tolkien himself suspected. Characters easily represent subjectivities of constriction, and, in doing so, point at what they can never represent—subjectivities of openness, which always incarnate in gestures beyond or outside language (neither preposition will do, but the page and screen are always hungry).

Narrative, then, might succeed strictly through failure, its impotence its potency. Neither map nor vehicle, but challenge and impetus, story is the candle that burns itself in order to illuminate. In a sense, it is both mimetic and transgressive, and neither: it represents and embodies the toxicity of dualism while whispering of the release of its own dualistic structures. For the reader or viewer, the representation might occur at a cognitive level, the whisper at a less conscious level. Metaphorically, and borrowing from Jameson, the most socially potent stories might consist of a "mimetic" consciousness and a transgressive unconscious. Unlike Jameson's analysis, here the conscious would be as therapeutic as the unconscious, because they would be inseparable, and contradictory only in a relative sense.

We could take it further into Mirkwood. Perhaps the most effective narrative will offer three magicks at once. First, story might reinforce and pacify reification, in the ideological sense so familiar to the critical theorist and especially the old-fashioned Marxist. Looking to reassure ourselves that we are Selves, and to rationalize our behavior within a world of others, we greedily consume narrative to perpetually reproduce its naturalizing and legitimating effects. But second, story might simultaneously and more subtly aggravate the sense of reification and its affinitive alienations, because at some level we know that story is construction. At some level, story accentuates the constructed nature of its own reifications. Third — most paradoxically — story might tempt our repressed desires for relief, our contradictory drives to unreify and let go our monadic delusions. Nonrealist story might untell itself, and so inspire us to untell ourselves.

A Garden of Live Flowers

It is ironic and inevitable that intersectionality, an insight beyond the linguistic singularity, has many names: interpermeation, interconnectivity, interdependence, interbeing, ecosystemic thinking, radical consilience, pure collectivity, morphic resonance. A further irony is that the names are generated from so many reified disciplines and movements, all seeking to recognize intersectionality from isolated standpoints, working within their own economies and trading in their own currencies. It is especially weird that cultural studies so often preaches hybridity to a purebred choir. If boundaries are the trouble, why do we still cast vicious protective spells at our academic borders? We have little chance to wake from our theoretical slumber unless we are willing to kiss the frogs — embrace those sources considered SF or fantasy from within academe and hybridize in ways no scholar has been able to get away with. Those of us who theorize SF and fantasy need to start taking our own advice and open more directly to the "other voices" we so often invoke, become more porous to and fluid with the whole chorus of attempts to move beyond the singularity.

First, and most easily, we need to consider a fuller spectrum of academically sanctioned voices, including the flawed but genuine attempt by Martha Nussbaum to imagine new relations with non-human animals in *Frontiers of Justice*, and the more radical attempt by sociologist Ted Benton in *Natural Relations*; the "pollutions" of post-theory, still groping its way through the residual oppositions of *theoretical* and *empirical, constructed* and *essential*; the continuing feminist projects to think beyond the binary; the boundary-crossing and dialogical "ethnocriticism" of Arnold Krupat; the nuanced ecology of Edward O. Wilson, who suggests we cannot separate issues of poverty from issues of biodiversity in *The Future of Life* (189); the lineage of paradigm-shifting scientists from the early twentieth century, and, more recently, the controversial propositions of Prigogene, David Bohm and Paul Davies. Second, we need to treat seriously the academically suspect or forgotten movements, including Ecofeminism, especially the self-consciously socialist stream; the dicey process philosophy of Alfred North Whitehead, which attempts to seize a radically contingent and relational universe; the continuation of Whitehead's work at the Center for Process Studies in Claremont, California; the worldwide movement of "Green" articulated in many contradictory voices, from vegan to feminist to engineer. Third, and most vital, we need to sit quietly and listen to the knowledges mocked or "studied" from our ivory Isengard, including the radical proposals of Deep Ecology; the border-jumping of transpersonal psychology; the controversial and questionable "Integral Post-Metaphysics" of philosopher Ken Wilber, a continuing project most famously articulated — in nascent form — in *No Boundary*; the neo-Pagan movement; the species-boundary work of authors like Susan Chernak McElroy (especially her "Strange Relations: Repulsion, Romance, and Befriending"); the tricky and decidedly non-Hegelian dialectics of Medieval Indian scholars such as Nagarjuna and Shantideva; the "Kirk/Spock" fantasies of slash fandom. The list could go on and on, deep into Mordor and beyond: as theory has sometimes realized, genuine hybridity is also recovery and rearticulation of hostile ideas. We might even recover and redirect the suspiciously residual hope of Ray Kurzweil to see technology "saturate the universe with our intelligence" (366).

The last irony is that Kurzweil's technological singularity may help dissolve the critical and narrative ones. In language, an emergent relation of opposites can be processed only through an appeal to what is *not* present — balance, equality, reciprocity, opposition, recursion, complimentarity, interchangeability. We need some means to strip away the relational nouns and modifiers we currently possess. We need some means to deny the usual spatial and temporal relations imagined between structuralism and post-structuralism, so there is no supersessionism, no prioritization, no "post," but a complex dynamic in which the binary of certainty and uncertainty is denied altogether, as incoherent. We need some means to tell stories that are wildly multidimensional, whose geometries we can hardly anticipate.

Language will not by itself pull off this cognitive magic. But at some point, a densely networked, holographic and fractal intermedia platform may provoke us to seize intersectionality *qua* intersectionality. The connections between digital media already suggest a supersaturated interpermeation that erases inherited concepts, a situation eerily anticipated by Jean Baudrillard in the early eighties. Brian Greenspan, in a wide-ranging essay that concludes this collection, explores current forms of extreme narrative hybridity that implode not only genres and the category of *genre*, but also the enabling technologies and preferred media of those genres, and the very polarities of reader/writer, story/software and public/private that are simultaneously felt as natural and monstrous within "network society." His essay leans into the resultant paradox: we imagine futures that are always already here, yet can never exist, and will be neither memorized nor memorialized. But as such intermedia evolve, will they still *be* narrative, with narrative's oppositions and resolutions? And if they erase the received truth of reification and trouble false boundaries, will they, in an ironic conflation, be a kind of unreal realism? These are stories no one will ever tell or read, since presumably telling and reading will no longer function at each other's boundaries. Still, these are stories whose untelling we eagerly await. Contemporary Bön Master Tenzin Wangyal insists that if we can drop our deepest dualistic preconceptions, we can grasp stories that are "truer than fact" (11). In context of this introduction, this collection, this legacy of criticism, this industry of scholarship, can Wangyal's pith statement mean anything? Of course not. But perhaps it is not fantasy to hope that it will.

NOTES

1. To the casual observer, the inclusion of essays on the graphic novel may seem unusual in a collection of articles on speculative fiction; however, the field and range of speculative fiction demonstrates that, in 2007, the *exclusion* of graphic novels

would be even more unusual. Since one of the basic arguments here is that realism is an attenuated mode defined primarily by what it ignores or leaves out — namely, tropes and story structures that are extrapolative, magical, liminal, disruptive and extra-mundane — then the graphic novel has never, by definition, been anything other than speculative fiction. To take the obvious example, Superhero narratives have always engaged readers in the slippery interstitial space between "soft" SF, fantasy and myth. Many writers in comic-book history have entered from or exited to SF and fantasy, including Harlan Ellison, Margaret Atwood, Michael Chabon and Neil Gaimon. More importantly, if speculative fiction is the set of defamiliarizing narrative modes by which dominant ideologies can be questioned and social change imagined, then the graphic novel, as an intertextual phenomenon, is currently one of the most significant examples of speculative fiction: it fully takes up such imagined defamiliarizations and disseminates them widely. As librarian Stephen Weiner notes in *Faster Than a Speeding Bullet*, the graphic novel is the most recently accepted and fastest growing form of publication in North America. Bookstores reserve entire sections for the form. Librarians are taking a keen interest. And mainstream film is sweeping through the history of the comic book and graphic novel, raiding for stories both obvious — *X-Men, Spiderman, Batman, Superman, Fantastic Four*— and less obvious — *Ghost World, Road to Perdition, Ghost in the Shell, Sin City*. The graphic form now has a hundred-year history in Europe and North America; its intersections with and inputs into other forms of speculative fiction are indisputable.

2. Ironically, post-structuralism hexed itself through its own post–Saussurian linguistics, all along depending on *différance* to levitate distinctions, while hoping that *différance* would not endlessly levitate. The unnamable proclaims itself, said Derrida, conjuring a magic circle where the act of *unnaming* dissolves boundaries while proclamation reconstructs them. Or is it the other way around?

3. This introduction, in its discussion of boundaries and distinctions, does nothing *but* boundarize and distinguish. In the case of binaries, the back door is always open.

WORKS CITED

Abbott, Edwin A. *Flatland*. 1884. New York: Buccaneer, 1976.

Batchelor, Stephen. *Verses from the Center: A Buddhist Vision of the Sublime*. New York: Riverhead, 2000.

Baudrillard, Jean. *Simulations*. Trans. Paul Foss, Paul Patton, and Philip Beitchman. New York: Semiotext(e), 1983.

Bear, Greg. *Queen of Angels*. New York: Warner, 1990.

Benton, Ted. *Natural Relations: Ecology, Animal Rights and Social Justice*. New York and London: Verso, 1993.

The Black Hole. Dir. Gary Nelson. Perf. Maximilian Schell, Anthony Perkins and Ernest Borgnine. Disney, 1979.

Bohr, Niels. *Atomic Theory and the Description of Nature*. London: Cambridge University Press, 1961.

Derrida, Jacques. "Structure, Sign and Play in the Discourse of the Human Sciences."

1966. Trans. Alan Bass. *Modern Literary Theory* 4th ed. Eds. Philip Rice and Patricia Waugh. London: Arnold, 2001. 195–210.

Einstein, Albert. *Ideas and Opinions.* Trans. Sonja Bargmann. New York: Bonanza, 1954.

Gibson, William. *Neuromancer.* New York: Ace, 1984.

Haraway, Donna J. "Situated Knowledges: The Science Question in Feminism and the Privilege of Partial Perspective." 1988. *Simians, Cyborgs and Women: The Reinvention of Nature.* New York: Routledge, 1991. 183–201.

Heisenberg, Werner. *Physics and Beyond: Encounters and Conversations.* New York: Harper and Row, 1971.

Hobb, Robin. *Assassin's Apprentice.* New York: Bantam, 1995.

_____. *Assassin's Quest.* New York: Bantam, 1997.

_____. *Fool's Errand.* New York: Bantam, 2002.

_____. *Fool's Fate.* New York: Bantam, 2004.

_____. *Golden Fool.* New York: Bantam, 2003.

_____. *Mad Ship.* New York: Bantam, 1999.

_____. *Royal Assassin.* New York: Bantam, 1996.

_____. *Ship of Destiny.* New York: Bantam, 2000.

_____. *Ship of Magic.* New York: Bantam, 1998.

Iser, Wolfgang. *The Act of Reading: A Theory of Aesthetic Response.* Baltimore and London: Johns Hopkins University Press, 1978.

Jameson, Fredric. *The Political Unconscious: Narrative as a Socially Symbolic Act.* Ithaca, NY: Cornell University Press, 1981.

Krupat, Arnold. *Ethnocriticism: Ethnography, History, Literature.* Berkeley: University of California Press, 1992.

Kurzweil, Ray. *The Singularity Is Near: When Humans Transcend Biology.* New York: Viking, 2005.

Le Guin, Ursula K. *Buffalo Gals and Other Animal Presences.* New York: New American Library, 1990.

_____. *The Left Hand of Darkness.* New York: Ace, 1969.

_____. "Some Thoughts on Narrative." *Dancing at the Edge of the World: Thoughts on Words, Women, Places.* New York: Grove, 1989. 37–45.

_____. "Text, Silence, Performance." *Dancing at the Edge of the World: Thoughts on Words, Women, Places.* New York: Grove, 1989. 179–187.

_____. *The Wind's Twelve Quarters.* New York: Harper and Row, 1975.

Levinson, Marjorie. *Wordsworth's Great Period Poems: Four Essays.* Cambridge: Cambridge University Press, 1986.

Loy, David R., and Linda Goodhew. *The Dharma of Dragons and Daemons: Buddhist Themes in Modern Fantasy.* Boston: Wisdom, 2004.

Lyotard, Jean-François. *The Postmodern Condition: a Report on Knowledge.* Theory and History of Literature 10. Trans. Geoff Bennington and Brian Massumi. Minneapolis: University of Minnesota Press, 1984.

McElroy, Susan Chernak. "Strange Relations: Repulsion, Romance, and Befriending." *All My Relations: Living with Animals as Teachers and Healers.* Novato, California: New World Library, 2004. 144–54.

Morgan, Richard. *Altered Carbon.* London: Golancz, 2002.

Nicholls, Peter. "LeGuin, Ursula K(roeber)." *Encyclopedia of Science Fiction*. Eds. John Clute and Peter Nicholls. New York: St. Martin's Griffin, 1995.

Nussbaum, Martha C. *Frontiers of Justice: Disability, Nationality, Species Membership*. London: Belknap, 2006.

Orwell, George. *Nineteen Eighty-Four*. London: Martin Secker & Warburg, 1949.

Prigogene, Ilya, and Isabelle Stengers. *Order out of Chaos: Man's New Dialogue with Nature*. New York: Bantam, 1984.

Stroud, Jonathan. *Ptolemy's Gate*. New York: Hyperion, 2006.

Vinge, Vernor. "The Coming Technological Singularity." *Acceleration Studies Foundation*. 1993. 1 June 2006. <http://accelerating.org/articles/comingtechsingularity.html>.

Wangyal, Tenzin. *Healing With Form, Energy and Light: The Five Elements in Tibetan Shamanism, Tantra, and Dzochen*. Ed. Mark Dahlby. Ithaca, NY: Snow Lion, 2002.

Weber, Renée. *Dialogues with Scientists and Sages: The Search for Unity*. London and New York: Routledge and Kegan Paul, 1986.

Weiner, Stephen. *Faster Than a Speeding Bullet: The Rise of the Graphic Novel*. New York: NBM, 2003.

Whitehead, Alfred North. *Process and Reality*. New York: Macmillan, 1929.

Wilber, Ken. *No Boundary: Eastern and Western Approaches to Personal Growth*. 1979. Boston: Shambala, 2001.

Williams, Raymond. *Marxism and Literature*. Oxford and New York: Oxford University Press, 1977.

Wilson, Edward O. *The Future of Life*. New York: Vintage, 2002.

1

The Continuum of Meaning: A Reflection on Speculative Fiction and Society

Marie Jakober

Before we ask "What sort of fiction has the greatest potential to promote social change?" we must ask whether any fiction has such potential. A significant number of people would suggest that it does not, that only fact-based knowledge has practical value in understanding and organizing matters in the real world. Fiction is "made up," and is therefore presumed to have no legitimacy beyond idle entertainment; indeed, there are people who will defend absurd lapses of internal credibility and simple common sense in a piece of drama or fiction on the grounds that "it is just a story," thereby implying that story, by definition, is indifferent to rational coherence or sense. Speculative fiction is even more suspect, judged by many to be silly or even dangerous. Such dismissive views of storytelling are not universal, of course, but they are by no means rare.

Yet throughout human history, storytelling has been one of the strategies by which we have tried to understand the world, and to communicate our understanding to others. We can understand nothing without a foundation of facts; that much is given. But facts, however carefully collected, however brilliantly displayed, are still only part of the truth; the meaning of those facts to ordinary human life is also part of the question. Thus, if

27

we can somehow *experience* these facts, we are likely to understand them better. Realistic fiction has the potential to give us such experience in one way; speculative fiction can give us the experience in a different but equally valuable way. It is the premise of this essay that factual works, realistic fictions, and speculative fictions all lie along a continuum of meaning, each fulfilling a function the others cannot, each adding to the total of human understanding.

Let us look, for example, at the phenomenon of racism, which has left a brutal legacy across so much of human history. We could make a lifetime study of it — colonialism, slavery, American ghettoes, European ghettoes, the Holocaust, Nanking, Kurdistan, Rwanda — to say nothing of the many small bits of nastiness that pass on the streets of our own cities, and everyone else's, every day. But can any amount of history or number of statistics convey the meaning of racism — that is, racism as people actually experience it — as effectively as a well-constructed narrative? We read the statistics and the news accounts and feel sadness or despair. We do not feel oppressed; we do not feel silenced, or tortured, or raped. We do not walk a mile in the shoes of another with our intellects; we walk with our emotions and our imaginations. We walk *in* their stories. We walk, for example, in the novels of Peter Matthiessen's *Mr. Watson* trilogy, where life proceeds with a surface calm while the absolute power of racial domination lies like a cobra in the shadows, barely noticed by the reader until it strikes. And then we realize: "My God. *That* is what it was like."

That is what it was like to be a black person in the nineteenth century American South, a Jew in a concentration camp, a native child in a Canadian residential school. The gift of realistic fiction is to take a particular time, a particular place, a particular manifestation of racism or some other human phenomenon, and compel the reader to understand it better by living it through story. But this gift is also a limitation: realistic fiction is about one time, one place, one set of economic and cultural circumstances. Everything Matthiessen shows us about American racism is shaped by American history — by early colonialism, by the economics of slavery, by the Civil War, by the experience of the frontier. It is not necessarily transferable to Nazi Germany or Rwanda. In some situations, racism is actively cultivated, sometimes with considerable pretense of scientific or intellectual legitimacy, in order to justify injustices like slavery or aggressive war. In other situations, racism has other, more varied roots, and the accompanying economic and social problems seem to be its effects rather than its cause. So we might ask: can we tell a story about racism that transcends a particular time and place, which transcends familiar social and cultural contexts and simply asks, "What *is* this thing?" Does it have an essential *thingness* of its own? Can we look at it in some way where we are not distracted by a particular cultural context, where we can consider it for itself, simply as a phenomenon of humankind, or, at least, of humankind at this point in time?

This is where speculative fiction can add to the continuum of meaning. Just as realistic fiction can help us to understand an aspect of human life in all the complexities of a particular context, speculative fiction can help us to understand it in a different way, by lifting it *out* of its familiar contexts and searching for the elements that might be universal. In John Wyndham's *The Chrysalids*, we see a future society, sufficiently separate and different from our own that obvious cultural contexts no longer apply. But that society suffers from familiar obsessions. In Wyndham's narrative, a centuries-old and wholesale nuclear war has worked massive devastation and left a planet in which plant, animal and human life have all been affected by mutations. To the inhabitants of Waknuk, all deviations from what is presumed to be the "true image" of a living thing are blasphemy, and dealt with accordingly: crops are burned, animals killed, and human deviants sterilized and driven out to the Fringes to survive as best they can. But centuries have passed since the war, and communities are isolated; as we soon discover, no one actually knows what the "true image" is, or ever was; beyond the boundaries of Waknuk , each region or community defines the matter for itself. Everyone is someone else's mutant, someone else's enemy. Even those who, through positive mutations, have evolved into more capable and gifted beings look upon the others as valueless and expendable:

> The lands down there aren't civilized. Mostly they don't have any sense of sin there so they don't stop Deviations; and where they do have a sense of sin, they've got it mixed up.... There's one tribe where both the men and women are hairless, and they think that hair is the devil's mark.... In one place they don't think you're properly human unless you have webbed fingers and toes.... There are even said to be some islands where both the men and women would be passed as true images, if it weren't that some strange deviation has turned them all completely black — though even that's easier to believe than the one about a race of Deviations that has dwindled to two feet high, grown fur and a tail, and taken to living in trees [73].

Thus *The Chrysalids* lays bare, with exceptional clarity, what one might call the phenomenon of Othering — the process by which humans decide that another is an Other, both different and inferior, deserving of abuse or even death. In any society it is imperative for us to understand our social and cultural history through factual study and realistic portrayals. At the same time, all cultures and all histories encourage us to accept certain givens — certain assumptions, certain beliefs, certain ways of thinking. We forget that some of those assumptions and beliefs are based on nonsense. We forget to wonder why two colors of skin should matter so much, when two colors of hair do not. A novel like *The Chrysalids* exposes the underlying nonsense, demonstrating not only the capacity of humans to "other" their fellows over trifles, but also the strategies we use to do so.

Speculative fiction also contributes to social change in a second way. As noted, the sharing of experience through fiction can deepen our understanding of the world, and such understanding is a basic requirement for social change. We rarely concern ourselves with entrenched patterns of behavior until we are persuaded that there is something wrong with those patterns. While facts can persuade us, sometimes emotions and shared experience can persuade us more effectively. However, even if we wish to work for change, we cannot move in directions we do not see. We cannot work for a future we have not imagined.

Here again, speculative fiction can add significantly to the continuum of meaning. By inventing alternate or futuristic worlds, such stories can suggest other ways of organizing societies — ways we have never tried — other modes in which families, religions, divisions of labor, and political structures can function. It does not matter if some of these imagined alternates might still be impossible in our own world, or if they might *always* be impossible because the circumstances of the invented world are too different from our own. These stories still make us think, make us question, make us wonder what is, and what is not, changeable. To take an example: for much of our history, sex roles have seemed immutable. Men were men, women were women, and transsexuals never entered the discussion. But what if we encountered a fictional world where sex was mutable? What if its people were both male and female at different times in their lives? What if sex roles were simply something learned, like a new job? Might that not make us wonder, just a little bit, about our own beliefs?

Here, I think, is the great gift of speculative fiction: it makes us think, and, specifically, it makes us think *differently*. It makes us examine things we have never examined. Even better, it makes us *re-imagine* things we thought we knew. We may change our perspectives through the reading of speculative fiction, or we may not. What is important is that we have had fresh ideas; we have engaged reality with our minds open. We have become more comfortable with the idea that little, if anything, is written in stone.

So what kind of narrative contributes most to social change? Will any speculative work ever equal the impact of Harriet Beecher Stowe's abolitionist novel *Uncle Tom's Cabin*? Perhaps. Perhaps not. What we can say is that Stowe's novel, however great its impact, was a product of its time and place; its meanings are not transferable to other times and places. By contrast, the possibilities explored in speculative fiction, precisely because they are speculative, are fluid. In this they are much like myths, with the potential to move from culture to culture and from age to age. Indeed, one might suggest that myths are simply the oldest form of speculative fiction. They were the stories humans told — often by inventing things that did not exist in their ordinary lives — to explain the unknown, the mysterious, the very good, the very evil, the very odd. Most importantly, they were — and are — the stories that cause us to wonder about all the things that have been lost in the world, and all the things that might yet be.

WORKS CITED

Matthiessen, Peter. *Bone by Bone*. New York: Random House, 1999.
_____. *Killing Mr. Watson*. New York: Random House, 1990.
_____. *Lost Man's River*. New York: Random House, 1997.
Wyndham, John. *The Chrysalids*. London: Michael Joseph, 1955.

2

Peter Jackson and the Deforestation of Middle Earth

David Hyttenrauch

"No, it was only a glimpse then," said the man; "but you
might have caught the glimpse, if you had ever thought it
worth while to try."
— Tolkien, "Leaf by Niggle"

As Peter Jackson released *The Return of the King* in 2003, a standard
media question for academic and other observers was whether Jackson's
films are true to Tolkien's work. The emotional power of the story on screen
is indisputable, the outlines of the plot are accurate, and the films capture
both the epic and individual heroic scales of *The Lord of the Rings* (*LoTR*).
Despite the visual majesty and cinematic sweep of the films, though, this
is a disorienting landscape. The hobbits speak, feel, act and surprise us
appropriately, yet they seem fundamentally severed from their relationship
with environment, whereas Tolkien's hobbits are our guides to the comfortable, disorienting, threatening and wondrous landscapes (and their
intrinsic cultures) they encounter, with us, for the first time. The richness
of Middle Earth is grounded in Tolkien's method of composition, in the
constant tension inherent in a choice between apocalyptic defeat and quiet

sorrowful decline, and in his own deeper love for *The Silmarillion*. Granting the impossible challenge of bringing any reader's imagination to film, and Jackson's profound achievement in bringing the project to the screen at all, his vision lacks truth in one essential aspect. Jackson systematically weakens the spirit of Middle Earth, its animist soul, in his treatment of nature and landscape, and commits a deforestation on a par with Saruman's.

The Hobbit establishes an elemental and animist conception of Middle Earth. The unexpected sentience of predatory animals like the eagles and wolves, and their location within a moral order, is part of this. Tolkien's subtle animism connects to his very first description of hobbits. He represents them as though they are creatures of our own world, just as the Norse and Anglo-Saxon *middlegeard*, Middle Earth, is a later and further fallen development of his own. He sets the opening of the novel "one morning long ago in the quiet of the world, when there was less noise and more green, and the hobbits were still numerous" (*Hobbit* 5) and offers a necessary description of hobbits because "they have become rare and shy of the Big People, as they call us" (*Hobbit* 4). He makes it clear that if humans were to walk more quietly and love nature better, they might still find, in the fields and woods, hobbits: not tiny or invisible fairies, but a real people still existing on the diminishing natural fringe. When Tolkien turns to describing hobbits outside his fiction, he crystallizes many of their traits and even identifies himself with them. In 1951, he wrote

> The Hobbits are, of course, really meant to be a branch of the specifically
> *human* race.... They are entirely without non-human powers, but are ...
> much more in touch with "nature" (the soil and other living things, plants
> and animals), and, abnormally for humans, free from ambition or greed of
> wealth [*Letters* 158].

Professionally, Tolkien repudiated biographical criticism, but he did answer one correspondent by identifying, as the only significant biographical facts affecting the composition of *LoTR*, his birth "in a pre-mechanical age" (*Letters* 288) and his Roman Catholicism. He goes on, however, to write

> I am in fact a *Hobbit* (in all but size). I like gardens, trees and unmechanized
> farmlands; I smoke a pipe, and like good plain food (unrefrigerated), but
> detest French cooking; I like, and even dare to wear in these dull days,
> ornamental waistcoats. I am fond of mushrooms ... [and] I do not travel
> much [288–89].

This identification is so consistent throughout the secondary materials that it even creeps into a description of hobbits offered by Billy Boyd, discussing his role as Pippin in Jackson's films: "Hobbits are a lot like Scots. It's all about nature and enjoying their land, which is a very Scottish thing." The question, obviously, is whether the films truly express the values Boyd articulates.

Autobiography does inform two of Tolkien's mountain episodes, one in *The Hobbit* and the other in *LoTR*. In his letters, Tolkien describes a hiking expedition through Switzerland in his youth, where rocks came crashing down across the hikers' path, with several near misses (*Letters* 392–93). The Stone Giants seen and heard by Bilbo (*Hobbit* 54–55), and the rage of the mountain Caradhras, take Tolkien's random and meaningless experience and give it, respectively, a dangerously playful and a malevolent will in the two books. In both instances, Tolkien attaches the agency to animate nature.

Caradhras becomes explicitly a nemesis of the Fellowship, harassing them and driving them back from the slopes with blizzard and avalanche: "They heard eerie noises in the darkness ... shrill cries, and wild howls of laughter. Stones began to fall from the mountain-side, whistling over their heads, or crashing on the path beside them" (*LoTR* I: 275). Gimli even ultimately blames the mountain's cruelty for Gandalf's fall in Moria (*LoTR* I: 316).

And Caradhras provides a nearly perfect example of Jackson's disruption of Tolkien's animism. In his *The Fellowship of the Ring*, Jackson uses Caradhras first as an opportunity to interpolate character development for Boromir when Frodo drops the Ring, and second as an example of the long, malevolent arm of Saruman, not Sauron, whom Gimli blames in the text (*LoTR* I: 275). Jackson contrasts the ice of Caradhras with the fires of Isengard in shots alternating between the two locations. Jackson's Saruman anticipates and amplifies the fear of Moria, saying, "So, Gandalf—you seek to lead them over Caradhras. If the mountain defeats you, will you risk a more dangerous road?" As the blizzard scene develops, Saruman's voice is heard chanting in the wind, and the Fellowship begins to respond:

> Legolas: "There is a foul voice on the air."
> Gandalf: "It's Saruman!"
> Aragorn: "He's trying to bring down the mountain!"

We might see this choice as simply artistic license, a use of compression and rationalization to advance the story and simplify its motivations. Yet Tolkien, both inside and outside the text, explicitly condemns the impulse to attribute the events to Sauron or Saruman. In *LoTR*, the experienced travelers in the Fellowship disagree over how to interpret the blizzard and the voices, with Gimli persistently noting the Mountain's hostility, especially to Elves and Dwarves (I: 276, I: 278–89); Boromir arguing that the stones are aimed by an intelligence (I: 276); and Gandalf acknowledging the possibility that the storm, if not the rocks, comes from the Enemy (I: 275). The ambiguity ensures that the Fellowship cannot comprehend or rationalize Caradhras' hostility and violence. Aragorn's conclusion, though, resonates: "There are many evil and unfriendly things in the world that have little love for those that go on two legs, and yet are not in league with Sauron, but have purposes of their own" (I: 276). Caradhras here becomes a complex expression of the numinous, of animism, something Jackson collapses to an unequivocal and less interesting certainty.

Jackson's handling of "The Flight to the Ford" collapses to a similar binary conflict. In Tolkien's work, Frodo rides Glorfindel's horse to the Ford, and turns to defy the Nine himself. Tolkien describes Frodo's invocation to Elbereth as he draws his sword, then shifts the narrative to Frodo's point of view:

> Dimly Frodo saw the river before him rise, and down along its course there came a plumed cavalry of waves. White flames seemed to Frodo to flicker on their crests and he half fancied that he saw amid the water white riders upon white horses with frothing manes [I: 209].

A number of the Ringwraiths are overwhelmed and the others retreat as we share Frodo's view of the event. Note how this is framed, though, especially Frodo's initial uncertainty: "seemed" and "half fancied" become the operative words. Are there really horses and riders? What is the nature of Bruinen's rising? Is Frodo's invocation of the goddess Elbereth effective?

Now Tolkien does resolve some of the uncertainty, and reveals that Bruinen, like Galadriel's Lothlórien, has an affinity for the Elves who love and protect it. Hearing that Glorfindel knew the flood would appear, Frodo asks who made it, and Gandalf replies

> "Elrond commanded it.... The river of this valley is under his power, and it will rise in anger when he has great need to bar the Ford.... I added a few touches of my own: ... great white horses with shining white riders and there were many rolling and grinding boulders. For a moment I was afraid that we had let loose too fierce a wrath, and the flood would get out of hand and wash you all away. There is great vigour in the waters that come down from the snows of the Misty Mountains" [I: 216].

The question of Gandalf's and the Elves' relationship to nature is a complex one. As Hood points out, "Environments which have been preserved from near the beginning by Elvish care still have a kind of numinousity which sympathizes with the elves and cooperates with them" (6), yet the One Ring, as the ultimate expression of technological domination, is a temptation and threat even to Elves because they are not pure environmentalists, having made Rings, Palantiri, and other such technology of their own. Even the Silmarils, which perfectly blend nature and craft, are a beautiful and disastrous creation precisely because the pride in the craft crosses immediately into the desire to possess their nature. Note the details of Gandalf's language above (not forgetting that Tolkien was a philologist, dictionarist and linguistic purist): the *OED* defines vigor as "Active physical strength as an attribute or quality of living things; active force or power; activity or energy of body or constitution" (*OED* sv. "vigour"). Vigor implies life and an autonomous force. The references to the river's anger and too-fierce wrath belie the certainty of Elrond's command and Gandalf's influence. If the river is a servant, it is a willful one.

Contrast this with the film's handling of the episode. Frodo, nearly unconscious, is carried on horseback by Arwen, dodging Black Riders for a day and a night. At the Ford, it is Arwen who challenges the Riders, daring them to come and claim Frodo. As the Riders enter the Ford, she begins an incantation that has the direct causal effect of raising the river. The riders are swept away by watery horses crashing down upon them. As Frodo falls unconscious, Arwen performs a literal act of Grace, offering a prayer out of her own being to protect Frodo's life. There is a reasonable argument that the enhancement of Arwen's role is necessary to address a gendered critique of the book, and that it has a functional purpose in establishing a precedent and a motivation for Arwen's eventual surrender of her immortality. Intensifying Frodo's suffering and vulnerability may have further dramatic purpose (though it dismisses the indomitability of will that allows him to bear the Ring into Mordor). But Arwen's invocation, and the collapse of the original description's potentials to a single visual reality, again oversimplify to a binary. Arwen becomes a redemptive figure, and precisely by taking on a mystical and spiritual function here obliterates the animism behind Bruinen's sudden surge. Notice too that this is another case of attribution error: the force of nature becomes merely a tool of Arwen's goodness.

Tolkien elsewhere reinforces the message that these attributions cannot be made so simply. In 1955, responding critically to a BBC radio adaptation of *The Fellowship of the Ring*, he wrote:

I think the book quite unsuitable for "dramatization" ... I thought Tom Bombadil dreadful — but worse still was the announcer's preliminary remarks that Goldberry was his daughter (!) and that Willowman was an ally of Mordor (!!). Cannot people imagine things hostile to men and hobbits who prey on them without being in league with the devil! [*Letters* 228].

Tolkien here rejects exactly Jackson's rationalized, binary conflict: Saruman is by now the servant of the devil, as Arwen may be the servant of the gods. Tolkien's animism, in sharp contrast, allows for an Other, a poorly understood intelligence in the liminal spaces of (loosely) human experience.

It was the treatment of Tom Bombadil, Goldberry and Old Man Willow that provoked Tolkien's outrage at the BBC production. Like Caradhras, these three figures sit in an uncomfortable position in Tolkien's cosmology. The creation stories of *The Silmarillion* predate the composition of both *The Hobbit* and *LoTR*, and Tolkien argued consistently that the Third Age they describe only has meaning in relation to the First and Second Ages of *The Silmarillion*. The cosmology there is clear and linear, if disrupted by the willfulness of various gods: "There was Eru, The One, who in Arda is called Ilúvatar; and he made first the Ainur, the Holy Ones" (*Silmarillion* 15). Eru is the Creator and outside Creation. The Ainur divide into the greater Valar and lesser Maiar as immortal powers. Eru decrees the creation of the Firstborn (Elves) and the Followers (Men) (*Silmarillion* 18). Aulë, craftsman of the gods, in his arrogance creates the Dwarves and conceals them in the earth (*Silmarillion* 43), but Eru permits their survival. Melkor Morgoth, the rebel Ainu, creates Orcs by enslaving and corrupting elves (*Silmarillion* 50); Morgoth further corrupts and raises other creatures to hostility and intelligence. Figures like Gandalf, Saruman, Radagast ("the friend of all beasts and birds," *Silmarillion* 300) and even Sauron are of the ranks of the Maiar, lesser angelic powers within creation. This is the sum total of the sentient beings accounted for in the creation stories, and it leaves out many animist spirits.

Old Man Willow represents the animist presence of the Old Forest bordering the Shire. Goldberry remarks that "The trees and grasses and all things growing or living in the land belong each to themselves" (I: 126). In consequence, the Old Forest, like Greenwood and Fangorn, also has its own memory and will; it leads the hobbits off their track and into its depths where it has sufficient presence and malice, centered around Old Man Willow, to act against them. In an extended description of the hobbits' creeping somnolence, Tolkien notes that "[S]leepiness seemed to be creeping out of the ground and up their legs, and falling softly out of the air upon their heads and eyes" (I: 118) while Frodo notices the tree's "sprawling branches going up like reaching arms with many long-fingered hands" (I :119); Merry and Pippin recline against the tree and look up "at the grey and yellow leaves, moving softly against the light, and singing. They shut their eyes, and then it seemed they could almost hear words, cool words, saying something about water and sleep" (I: 119). Notice that, as with the Fellowship's varied theories about Caradhras, there is a suggestive and thus ambiguous quality to the description of the tree and its actions. The repeated use of similes rather than direct assertions lures the hobbits to fall under the tree's spell; as readers we cannot be certain whether there really are words and singing in the air, or whether sleep is creeping up from the earth and falling like pollen or spores. Curry describes Tolkien's characteristic use of "as if" and "it seemed" as "plainly a sop to rationalists" (134) but these constructions also have a quite different effect of generating real uncertainty about the hobbits' perceptions, and thus of the tree's capability of forming intention and action. Sam, from whose point of view we discover Frodo trapped under water by a root, and Merry and Pippin confined by the cracks in the trunk, does not witness the critical moment of action and even he dismisses Frodo's initial account as a dream (I: 119–20); at this point the text simultaneously resists and encourages an animist understanding of the event.

The uncertainty only lifts when Frodo and Sam resolve to set fire to the tree, and it speaks to Merry (I: 120); that is, it finally speaks directly out of its memory, and its source of hostility, the original encroachment on and burning of the margins of the Old Forest. Frodo and Sam stray toward equal culpability with the other peoples of Middle Earth (including Orcs) for the trees' resentment. Tolkien writes

> In all my works I take the part of trees as against all their enemies. Lothlórien is beautiful because there the trees were loved; elsewhere forests are represented as awakening to consciousness themselves. The Old Forest was hostile to two legged creatures because of the memory of many injuries. Fangorn Forest was old and beautiful, but at the time of the story tense with hostility because it was threatened by a machine-loving enemy [*Letters* 419–20].

This awakening to consciousness does not fit easily into his cosmology, at least in the Human and Elvish understanding of it. Tolkien, though, through characters like Old Man Willow and later the Ents, seems to ask how our world would differ if nature had the capacity to speak and act for itself in the face of senseless destruction. All of this subtlety is sadly lost when Peter Jackson transplants this particular tree to Fangorn Forest, where (only) in the extended version of *The Two Towers*, it captures Merry and Pippin in a bare and unmotivated comic sketch, and they are rescued by Treebeard.

Tom Bombadil, who performs the rescue in Tolkien, was initially conceived independently of Middle Earth. He is described by Tolkien as "the spirit of the (vanishing) Oxford and Berkshire countryside" (*Letters* 26). Tolkien uses him to personify "Botany ... Zoology ... and Poetry" (*Letters* 179) and, in response to a question from his editors, argued that

> Tom Bombadil is not an important person — to the narrative. I suppose he has some importance as a "comment" ... I would not, however, have left him in, if he did not have some kind of function. I might put it this way. The story is cast in terms of a good side, and a bad side ... but both sides ... want a measure of control. But if you have as it were, taken "a vow of poverty," renounced control, and take your delight in things for themselves and without reference to yourself ... then the question of the rights and wrongs of power and control might become utterly meaningless to you, and the means of power quite valueless [*Letters* 178–79].

That is, Bombadil has achieved a sort of Zen state unburdened by ego or any sense of utility, at peace and in perfect empathy with his surroundings. At the Council of Elrond, Erestor asserts that Bombadil "has a power even over the Ring" (I: 254), but Gandalf replies, "Say rather that the Ring has no power over him. He is his own master. But he cannot alter the Ring itself, or break its power over others.... And if he were given the Ring, he would soon forget it, or most likely throw it away. Such things have no hold on his mind" (I: 254).

His real power is evident in the two rescues he performs. In the first, he says to the Willow "I'll freeze his marrow cold, if he don't behave himself. I'll sing his roots off. I'll sing a wind up and blow leaf and branch away. Old Man Willow! ... You should not be waking. Eat earth! Dig deep! Drink water! Go to sleep! Bombadil is talking!" (I: 122). His warnings are elemental, and he encourages not oblivion but a peaceful and natural sleep (not an extinction of consciousness) for the tree. He brings order and containment to nature without denying its essential spirit; where he tends it, the Old Forest is (very deliberately) like an English romantic garden, a blend of the wild and the orderly. In Goldberry's words, released in hesitant fragments, "He is.... He is, as you have seen him.... He is the Master of wood, water and hill" (I: 126). And in an elaboration of his natural empathy, Bombadil says of the rescue, "Just chance brought me then, if chance you call it. It was no plan of mine, though I was waiting for you"

(I: 127). This statement speaks to the paradox of a primeval consciousness that both anticipates the future and is surprised by its arrival, and plays around the edges of spiritual questions of will and predestination, synchronicity and salvation.

The second rescue, when Bombadil leaves the Old Forest for the Barrow-Downs and rescues the hobbits from the Barrow-wights, opens a new understanding of the character. Bombadil is a fertility symbol reminiscent of the medieval Green Man, associated with plenty and regeneration, and his role is reinforced by his consort Goldberry's water symbolism as river-daughter or naiad. When Frodo invokes Bombadil, who opens the Barrow and drives out the Wight with his song, we see another instance of chance in the instantaneous response and intervention. Bombadil's song ends, "Lost and forgotten be, darker than the darkness / Where gates stand for ever shut, till the world is mended" (I: 143). Bombadil then revives the hobbits with a further verse that defies the dead hand, Night and the closed Gate. In essence, he asserts the timelessness of his own natural power and pits it against death and darkness, as the Wight is banished into nothingness until the world's end. Bombadil is an adjuster of balances: where death begins to encroach prematurely on life, he controls it, just as he controls the Willow when its animism/animosity encroaches on travelers through his demesne.

So what is the value, then, of the Bombadil/Goldberry episode? It becomes the first real expression of the complex spirituality of Middle Earth and the relationships among its powers throughout nature and over time. The hobbits have some little awareness of the complexity, but we discover this essential knowledge along with them in an environment that is largely isolated from the book's central conflict. Bombadil embodies Middle Earth's animism: ambiguous, nuanced, powerful, inexplicable. Yet Peter Jackson elects to omit entirely the character and, with him, his symbolic weight.

Instead, Jackson shifts the problem of the use and destruction of nature from a thematic and spiritual undercurrent to a plot device and thumbnail sketch of the character of Saruman. Tolkien was no admirer of technology. In 1944 he wrote

> It is not the *not-man* (e.g. weather) nor *man* (even at a bad level), but the *man-made* that is ultimately daunting and unsupportable. If a ragnarök would burn all the slums and gas-works, and shabby garages, and long arc-lit suburbs, it c[oul]d for me burn all the works of art — and I'd go back to trees [*Letters* 96].

Saruman is unequivocally the advocate of technology in the book, but Jackson's conception lacks subtlety. Tolkien's own response to technology was complex and thoughtful (Hood 6; Curry 128). For example, he saw no real difference between magic and technology, both being labor-saving devices that duplicated the functions of cheap or slave labor, and both lending themselves to an instrumental need for control, both as likely to destroy the physical landscape to build human monuments (*Letters* 200). This is precisely why Gandalf cannot accept the Ring from Frodo; it is a technological tool; tools exert force; force may and will be misused; the original intention, and the user, may and will become corrupted.

Jackson's Saruman, however, drifts towards caricature. In *The Two Towers*, he turns to an Orc and, in an extended sequence as the camera tours his forges, says "The old world will burn in the fires of industry. The forests will fall." Faced with the news that there is not sufficient fuel to run the forges, he says "The forest of Fangorn is on our doorstep. Burn it." This is melodrama, not the subtle seduction of technology. A recently broadcast Canadian public service video captures this subtlety; produced by the Sustainable Forest Management Network, it praises the work of university forestry researchers (who are funded significantly by commercial forestry interests) without managing to show a single felled tree. Jackson's version of nature is leaden and blunt, and at times confused. Who, after all, would be in favor of shooting elephants? An Orwellian distortion of Legolas, apparently, fighting (rare and wonderful) Oliphaunts, swashbuckling and killing and killing. And who lives above cloud level on distant mountain tops for centuries, waiting to light the stratospheric beacons that summon Rohan to Gondor's aid? Someone, apparently, as the beacons are lit in Jackson's spectacular special effects sequence.

It would be difficult to overstate Tolkien's affinity with nature and particularly with trees. As Curry writes of *LoTR*, "It is in fact a work in which a deeply sensual appreciation of this world is interfused with an equally powerful sense of its ineffability" (135). This ineffability is perhaps best captured in Tolkien's "Leaf by Niggle," written during the composition of *The Lord of the Rings* and best reflecting his anxieties about completing and publishing his works. The story also explores the spiritual value of art and its relationship to salvation; Niggle's exquisite and painstaking painting of the tree becomes an Edenic refuge after death.

The Silmarillion establishes as its central image and source of conflict the Silmarils, which capture the light of the Two Trees of Valinor, associated with sun and moon, male and female, life and heat. Greed for their light becomes the engine of the Fall in Tolkien's world; Morgoth's destruction of the two trees is one of his primary purposes. Tolkien, through the "Quenta Silmarillion," the "Akallabêth" and *LoTR* scrupulously tracks the movement of each sapling of the two trees, from Valinor, to Númenor, to Gondor, to Minas Tirith. After the War of the Ring, Gandalf leads a despairing Aragorn up the slopes, where he discovers a last descendent of the Trees; "Already it had put forth young leaves long and shapely, dark above and silver beneath, and upon its slender crown it bore one small cluster of flowers whose white petals shone like the sunlit snow" (III: 220). At each planting, the tree is the symbol of preservation of good, of hope, of connection to the Blessed Realm. By means of their spiritual significance, the Two Trees and their descendants thus take on many external associations: with the Biblical Trees of Knowledge and Life; with the Rood-Tree of Tolkien's beloved Anglo-Saxon; with Yggdrasil, the world-tree of Norse myth. But in Jackson's *The Return of the King*, Gandalf, leading Pippin through Minas Tirith, says of the dead white tree there, without context or comment, "That is the Tree of the King."

Responding at great and angry length to a film treatment of the books proposed to him in 1958 by Forrest J. Ackerman, Tolkien said of the screenwriter "He has cut the parts of the story upon which its characteristic and peculiar tone principally depends, showing a preference for fights" (*Letters* 271). He continues, "I have already suspected [the writer] of not being interested in trees: unfortunate, since the story is so largely concerned with them" (275). We can only surmise whether he would regard Jackson's treatment (of Old Man Willow, Bombadil, and nature) more highly.

There are a number of ironies in considering the intersection of Tolkien's and Jackson's landscapes. First, it is difficult to fault Jackson for emphasizing technology over nature in the films when Tolkien himself doubted the ability of any dramatic medium other than animation to capture his story. Second, the films do seem to have sparked an interest in landscape — New Zealand's — with all the accompanying ironies of exhausted jet fuel and intensive tourism. Third, Tolkien himself, increasingly concerned about money as retirement approached, ultimately said that he would accept a film of his works either if it was art (defined as his retaining total creative control) or if it paid him well enough (*Letters* 261). Finally, since the films lack the crucial matter of "The Scouring of the Shire," and the reassertion of a natural balance there, Peter Jackson has not himself cut down the Party Tree. In implicitly leaving this one tree standing, he denudes an animist landscape, the hobbits' horror at its destruction, and thus their inspiration to us to set the world right.

WORKS CITED

Boyd, Billy. Interview. Retrieved 19 January 2004 <http://www.theonering.net/movie/cast/boyd.html>.

Curry, Patrick. "'Less Noise and More Green': Tolkien's Ideology for England." *Mythlore* 21 (1996): 126–38.

Hood, Gwyneth. "Nature and Technology: Angelic and Sacrificial Strategies in Tolkien's *The Lord of the Rings*." *Mythlore* 19 (1993): 6–12.

Jackson, Peter. *The Lord of the Rings: The Fellowship of the Ring*. Extended Edition DVD. Los Angeles: New Line, 2002.

_____. *The Lord of the Rings: The Return of the King*. Los Angeles: New Line, 2003.

_____. *The Lord of the Rings: The Two Towers*. Extended Edition DVD. Los Angeles: New Line, 2003.

Sustainable Forest Management Network. *About the SFM Network* (promotional video). Edmonton, AB: Sustainable Forest Management Network, 2003.

Tolkien, J.R.R. *The Hobbit*. 1937. London: HarperCollins, 1999.

_____. *Letters*. Ed. Humphrey Carpenter. London: Unwin, 1981.

_____. "Leaf by Niggle." *Tree and Leaf*. 2nd ed. 1964. London: Unwin, 1988. 74–95.

_____. *The Lord of the Rings*. 2nd ed. 1966. London: Unwin, 1974.

_____. *The Silmarillion*. Ed. Christopher Tolkien. London: Unwin, 1977.

3

Seeking Stories:
Possible Worlds Semantics in
Greer Ilene Gilman's *Moonwise*

Christine Mains

In his 1947 essay "On Fairy-Stories" in which he describes the art of Sub-creation, of creating imagined worlds out of words, renowned fantasist J. R. R. Tolkien argues that "Fantasy remains a human right: we make in our measure and in our derivative mode, because we are made: and not only made, but made in the image and likeness of a Maker" (85). In these words, Tolkien is responding to complaints that works of fantasy are a means of escaping the world's woes rather than illustrating and addressing the problems of society, as realistic and thus more serious fiction presumably does. By claiming a parallel between God the creator of the real world and fantasists as creators of imagined secondary worlds, Tolkien not only affirms the inherent connection between reality and fantasy, but also asserts the importance of authors, particularly fantasists, and by extension all who follow them into fantastic narrative worlds, as moral beings with a responsibility to the community of which they are a part.

The perception by its critics that fantasy is escapist or frivolous literature is not the only complaint lodged against it; works of fantasy are also condemned for being "formulaic," as though fantasists were checking off a list of required characters or plot events. This specific complaint may be valid in some individual instances, and it is true that patterns can be traced

44

in terms of plot events and character types in certain subgenres of fantasy, such as quest fantasy, in which the motif of the hero's quest is predominant. The recognition of these patterns lies behind the critical interest in structural approaches to fantastic literature and its root texts in folktales, myths, and legends. The quest motif as it appears in the myths and legends of many diverse cultures is analyzed by Joseph Campbell in his book *The Hero With a Thousand Faces*, in which the ritual journey followed by the hero is structured as a circular Pattern (245). The hero leaves his or her community and crosses the Threshold into the unknown, into an Otherworld often represented by caves, a great forest, or the sea. The hero undergoes a time of testing, marked by battles and other trials, and eventually, with the magical aid of helpers, achieves the treasure or elixir which is the object of the quest, and returns to share this boon with the community. Another structural analysis of the hero's quest is described in Vladimir Propp's *Morphology of the Folktale*. Propp's examination of one hundred Russian folktales suggests that the seemingly almost infinite variety of characters and events can be reduced to an underlying fabula, which contains only seven actants and thirty-one related functions. As in Campbell's Pattern, the Proppian structure includes the hero, magical helpers, the opponent, and an object of value (categorized by Propp as the princess-bride) (79–80).

A growing interest in the logic and semantics of possible worlds suggests another fruitful approach to the study of the underlying structures of fantastic fiction, which is, after all, more than philosophically concerned with the construction of imaginary worlds. Campbell's Pattern and Propp's framework are attempts to answer one of the fundamental problems facing scholars of narrative semantics, a question posed by narratologist Lubomír Doležel: "how is a sequence of narrated events organized into a coherent story?" ("Narrative Worlds" 543). Narrative semantics is defined by Doležel as "the study of the narrative structures which underlie stories manifested in narrative texts" (NW 543). Doležel describes the Proppian structure[1] as a "functional" kind of global constraint, and proposes another approach in the form of a "generative" structure ("Narrative Semantics" 141) based on the philosophical concepts of logical semantics, especially the notions of modal logic. Doležel outlines the four systems of modal logic that generate narrative worlds:

1. The *alethic* world in which the narrated actions are subject to the restrictions of the "classical" modalities — possibility, impossibility and necessity.

2. The *deontic* world in which the narrated actions are governed by the modalities of permission, prohibition and obligation (see von Wright, 1963; 1968).

3. The *axiological* world in which the narrated actions are dominated by the modalities of goodness, badness and indifference (see Ivin, 1970; Rescher, 1969).

4. The *epistemic* world in which the narrated actions follow the course given by the modalities of knowledge, ignorance and belief (see Hintikka, 1962). (NW 544)[2]

Alethic modalities govern what is considered possible or impossible within the fictional world, while deontic modalities shape normative values, what is prohibited or prescribed. Epistemic modalities deal with knowledge and its lack, and axiological modalities determine what is valued in the fictional world, what is desired or, conversely, feared.

While Doležel states that most fictional worlds are primarily generated by a single modal system, he acknowledges that "in the formation of fictional worlds modal systems can be manipulated in many different ways" (*Heterocosmica* 114). It is obvious that quest fantasy, for example, is the product of the intersection of all of these modal systems: the narrative world in which the story is set contains such impossibilities as magic and magical creatures; the quest arises because some object of value is desired by the hero, the seeker on a quest, who is willing to undergo prescribed trials to achieve that object, in the course of which he or she gains knowledge of the self and of the community in which he or she lives. Since magic, impossible according to the natural laws of the primary world, the real world inhabited by authors and readers, is recognized as a controlling principle in works of fantasy fiction, to the extent that many critics define the genre according to the presence or absence of magical agents and events, the alethic modality is the dominant generating force behind the narrative structure governing quest fantasy; magical forces mediate the alethic transformation between possible and impossible that is the defining feature of the narrative worlds of quest fantasy.

Among the possible variations in the structure of narrative worlds produced by the interaction of the modal systems is the dyadic world, Doležel's term to describe any fictional world in which are operative two distinct domains, marked by opposing values in any of the four modalities. His example of a dyadic world generated by the alethic modality, for instance, is that of mythology: the natural domain, closely resembling the real world in terms of what is and is not possible, co-exists with the supernatural, containing agents and events that would be considered impossible according to the natural laws of the real world (*Heterocosmica* 128–9). Given that the tales of the world's mythologies are root texts for quest fantasy, it is not surprising that many of the narrative worlds of quest fantasy can be described similarly, as alethic dyadic worlds. In many works of fantasy, particularly the subgenre of quest fantasy, characters inhabiting what can be termed the Primary Narrative World (PNW), the world of the possible reflective of the primary world, undertake a quest which involves encounters with or journeys through a Secondary Narrative World (SNW) in which magic is not impossible and beings out of myth and legend reside. In some works of quest fantasy, the very act of sub-creation is foregrounded; the characters are storytellers inhabiting a version of the real world, transported by magic to the narrative worlds created out of their words.[3]

One example of such a work is Greer Ilene Gilman's novel *Moonwise* (1991), which won the Crawford Award for best first novel for its author. Ariane and Sylvie are old college friends, both imaginative and creative artists and writers. At their first encounter as college students, Sylvie asks Ariane "Do you think writing about, like, other worlds creates them? Or are they *there?*" (23–4). Thus begins a long partnership, during which the two friends collaborate in the creation of fictional worlds. Through games, tarot card readings and other rituals invented by Ariane, who cannot imagine creating without such aids, Sylvie spins stories about their imagined worlds which Ariane records. Sylvie and Ariane, through their acts of storytelling, "set the cosmos in its order, and cast the blind and labyrinthine fortunes of its kings" (25); they are sub-creators, with the power of Makers over the agents and events of their imagined worlds. Ariane envies Sylvie's ease of entry into the worlds of imagination; she feels weighted down by the rituals and records which she believes necessary to the creative process, and longs for Sylvie's natural writing abilities.

Eventually, they separate, Ariane off to graduate studies where she feels her creative energies wasting away, stifled, while Sylvie works from her grandmother's home as an artist and poet. They do keep in touch with postcards, but their paths diverge. Once, they were "as close and contrary to each other as the dark and light of one moon ... as Sylvie had walked farther, lost and found herself amid her green and ancient wood, Ariane had spiraled inward, spellbound by her own intensity of patterning" (24). Finally, in the cold and wet of winter, Ariane arrives at Sylvie's home, full of questions, doubt, uncertainty, feeling that "She had no place here. Time, that had changed nothing in this house, had estranged her; yet she knew no other haven" (4). Yet Sylvie happily welcomes her, and they quickly fall into their old habits, reading Ariane's tarot cards — a traveler wielding a sword, a stone child in winter — and fashioning prophecies out of the fall of the cards.

When Sylvie vanishes into the woods during their solstice ritual, and an elf-child appears on the doorstep in her place, Ariane sets off on a quest to find her friend. She enters the fictional world they have named Cloud, afraid and awkward and uncertain.[4] Meanwhile, Sylvie, who is exhilarated and very much at home in the world that she has often visited in dreams and imagination, although never before in the flesh, has been assigned the task of restoring the balance of the fictional world. Cloud is governed by the renewing cycle of full and dark moon, and of seasonal change, which is halted when the witch-goddess representing the dark and winter refuses to yield her place in the spring. Separated for much of the narrative, each aided by a group of magical helpers, Ariane and Sylvie eventually reunite; their quests come together; they solve the riddles, defeat the witch and restore the natural balance. They return to the physical world, now celebrating early summer, where Ariane finds she no longer needs her rituals to contact the creative forces around her: "I've my witch's eyes, thought Ariane" (356). Their actions in the Secondary Narrative World, the world of Story that they have created, are echoed, reflected, in the Primary Narrative World that to them is the real world, the community from which they departed on their quest; magic mediates their movement across the alethic border between reality and fantasy, between possible and what has seemed to them impossible.

The structural analyses of narrative worlds focus primarily on the interactions of the characters at the surface level of the text in order to trace the relationship between actants or character types at the underlying structural level. Each character or agent is the center of what Doležel terms the "agential domain" "constituted by his property set, his relation network, his belief set, his action scope, etc." ("Mimesis" 487); he later uses the term "agential constellation" to describe the hierarchical interaction of characters, noting that such agential constellations are not only interlinking (as each character has his or her own) but also "arranged in compositional patterns such as symmetry, parallelism, contrast" (*Heterocosmica* 97). The structural constellations described by Campbell and Propp, describing the relationship between the hero, magical helpers, the opponent, and the object of value, center on the character or agent who fulfills the function of the hero, "taking the relationship to the 'hero' as the partitioning criterion," in Doležel's words ("Extensional" 197). Furthermore, the narrative structure generated by the four modalities governs the properties attributable to each agent and the ways in which the agents act and interrelate; there are distinct differences in the agential domain of the subjects of axiologically generated quests and deontically generated quests, for instance.

In *Moonwise*, it is Ariane's agential domain that is dominant; the narrative begins and ends with her, and the reader has access to Ariane's thoughts on people and events more often than those of other characters. It is also Ariane who undergoes the most significant changes, from feeling out of place and homeless when she arrives on Sylvie's door to finding a sense of her place in the community at journey's end. More importantly, Ariane is the subject of an axiologically-generated quest;[5] when Sylvie vanishes into the fictional world, Ariane lacks not only her friend who resolves her lack of a home, but also the agent who represents her desire for natural and easy access to the worlds of imagination. Ariane has always felt "ill at ease in her inheritance ... afraid of losing herself in it, afraid of trespass and of loss. Coming late and anxiously into her kingdom, she had then hung back, a stranger, longing and unsure.... It was Sylvie, holding light her great dominion, who had met her at the door" (23). Ariane values both Sylvie and what Sylvie represents to her; lacking her friend and her creative energy, Ariane sets out to liquidate that lack, despite her fear and discomfort. In the agential constellation centering on Ariane as the axiological hero, her object of value is Sylvie. She is aided by several magical helpers: a raggedy man she thinks of as a tinker, Craobh, the elf-child who guides her into the SNW, and an owlish witch named Mally, who provides the group with food and shelter before sending them on their way. Her opponent is Annis, the raven-witch who hunts the souls of the lightborn, the elf-children, and Ariane's protection of Craobh brings her into dangerous confrontations with Annis and her followers.

Sylvie is not only the object of value in Ariane's agential constellation; she is also the hero of her own quest, undertaking a task assigned to her by the witch Mally, whom she learns is also Malykorne, the goddess of the full moon, who has been denied her turn in the dance of seasons and requires Sylvie to restore the balance of the SNW. Sylvie's quest is thus deontically-generated; Doležel notes that "deontic marking of actions is the richest source of narrativity; it generates the famous triad of the *fall* (violation of a norm — punishment), the *test* (obligation fulfilled — reward), and the *predicament* (conflict of obligations)" (*Heterocosmica* 121); the test forms a significant component of the hero's quest for both Campbell and Propp. Although Doležel separates the norms of prohibition and obligation, implying that each generates autonomous story structures, it is common in quest fantasy for the hero to be both promised a reward if the assigned task is fulfilled, and also threatened with punishment if he or she fails at the task. Sylvie's quest is governed by norms of obligation, in that her fulfillment of the task will be rewarded with the return of the natural balance; and by norms of sanction, since, if she fails to achieve the quest, spring will not succeed winter, light will not replace dark, and the lightborn, the elf-children, will continue to be hunted down by the dark witch's ravens. In Sylvie's agential constellation, her object of value is the restoration of balance and creative energy to the SNW; her helpers are the witch Mally, who provides her with tools and advice with which to accomplish the task, and an elf-child, a lightborn who names himself Cobber and informs Sylvie that he has given his soul into the tinker's safekeeping, much as Craobh has given hers to Ariane. Sylvie's opponent is Annis, the goddess of winter and the dark of the moon.

One intriguing result of taking a structural approach to analysis is to emphasize the "compositional patterns" noted by Doležel, such as parallelism and contrast (above). The shared features of helpers — the lightborn Craobh and Cobber as well as Mally — and opponent in the separate quests of Ariane and Sylvie suggest a parallel connection between them, as do repeated references to them as the "Silly Sisters" or as a "dyarchy" ruling their imagined worlds (24). Both are heroes, seemingly on separate quests. But their separate quests are not actually separate, but instead differing surface expressions of the same underlying structure; Ariane and Sylvie are separate characters at the surface sharing the same structural role. Such interweaving of separate quests, such doubling and splitting of roles and functions, is not unusual in narrative, where the correspondence between the characters at the surface level of the text and the actants at the structural level is seldom one to one. Narratologist Mieke Bal, describing this feature of narrative, uses the term "numerical inequality" to refer to "the possibility of the coalescence of two actants into one actor [character] or the reverse, the concretization of one actant" into several actors (199). Sylvie and Ariane are two characters, but they fill one actantial role, that of the hero, facing the same opponent, aided by the same magical helpers. As Ariane's agential domain is dominant, the deontically-generated quest of which Sylvie is the subject is subordinate to Ariane's axiologically-generated quest; Sylvie's quest is a part of Ariane's testing. By this logic, Sylvie's object of value, the restoration of the natural balance of the SNW, is also, at a structural level, Ariane's object of value: the natural access to imagination that Sylvie seems to possess, a restoration of her own creative power of imagination and her identity as a creator of fictional worlds.

Ariane and Sylvie, the Silly Sisters, and their lightborn helpers, Craobh and Cobber, are not the only instances of doubling in *Moonwise*. Both Sylvie and Ariane are aided in their quests by Mally, the witch who sends each of them further into the SNW, into "the wood [that] was all the tales that were"(158). Mally is an embodiment of Malykorne, a creator-goddess present from the beginning of time in the SNW, symbolized as thorn tree and owl and moonlight; her sister is Annis, stone and raven and dark of moon, and the opponent in both quests. Malykorne and Annis are also doubles, twinned aspects of one being: "bound each in the other, changing yet unchanged: the journey and the tower.... Two sisters and one being, turn and turn. One dance" (48). Their dance creates the changing seasons, the lunar cycle, the path of life from birth to death, an ever-moving circle defined by balance and harmony, each taking their turn and sharing in power. Until, as Mally explains to Sylvie when she assigns to her the task of restoration, Annis refused to yield her turn in the dance. "Thinks she: why journey, sint end is dark? Why make, sin t'soul is marred, becoming such carrion as earth?" (163). In other words, why create what must some day end? Why waste the power? Hating and fearing change, desiring unending sameness for eternity, wishing to keep everything for herself forever, Annis denies the coming of spring, and sends her ravens to hunt down the lightborn, elf-children whose souls are the stars, in order to trap them in rings of stone and thus end the dance of the constellations. "When the ring was closed, no dance would be, nor turn of year. No leaf nor moon, no starry carol nor the quick brave sun, but cold unchanging death" (50). No more creation, no more Making.

Such a division between light and dark, what would seem to be good and evil, something valued and desired and something rejected and feared, is a common narrative practice that Bal references when she notes that the power, her term for the force, human or otherwise, that proves a help or hindrance in achieving the goal (198), can sometimes be concretized as two actants, "a positive and a negative one" (204); Northrop Frye suggests a similar structural motivation behind the depiction of the doubled heroine in romance narratives, one dark and one light, or one who remains virgin and one who weds, as a representation of "the separation or polarizing of the action into two worlds, one desirable and the other detestable" (83).

That is, the technique of doubling might suggest two different paths, two possible outcomes of the hero's decisions and actions, one to be valued and one to be rejected. If Sylvie's task is part of Ariane's testing, the contrast between Annis and Malykorne, between Sylvie and herself, illustrates two paths for her to choose between on her quest to achieve what she desires: a renewal of her creative energy and easier access to the worlds of imagination. Sylvie has taken a different approach than Ariane's both to the task she has been set and to her artistic endeavors; where Ariane is frightened and even miserable to find herself in the SNW, Sylvie is delighted, "laugh[ing] out loud for joy" (156). When their paths cross and they face Annis together armed only with a brooch belonging to Mally, Ariane tries desperately to invent a ritual by which to restrain her; Sylvie, following instinct and revelation, simply closes up the brooch (289). Their success leads Ariane to realize that she has been following the wrong path: "She'd had it wrong, the fretting after words on tape, the riddling with the cards; the dance is in the taking hands" (297). For Ariane, Annis and Malykorne symbolize opposing values within her own mind: "I am Annis, I am Malykorne...Dark and light of one moon. Weird sisters. I child and I devour; I am grave and lap, annihilation and O reborn.... I am Cloud and Law. It's Sylvie who is other. She's the traveling, the sword, the falling star; she's now and elsewhere" (269). Sylvie, the initial object of value in Ariane's agential constellation, who possesses the talent and imagination that Ariane so much desires, has always taken Malykorne's path, has chosen change and movement, the dance, the journey, sharing with the community over aloofness and isolation.

Malykorne represents what is to be desired; Annis what is to be feared, the hoarding rather than sharing of energy, of emotion, of life. As Cobber explains to Sylvie: "She cares for nothing in itself, only for knowing it. Having it all to herself" (191). This knowledge is the true object of value, the boon which the hero wins through the successful completion of the tests and trials. Ariane the axiological hero is also the subject of the epistemic quest, the search for knowledge, of the self and of a recognized place in the community. The search for identity, for self-knowledge, is a well-recognized theme of quest fantasy, as acclaimed fantasist Ursula Le Guin notes in *The Language of the Night*, about her employment of Jungian archetypes in her fiction and Jungian terminology in her critical essays. All individuals, says Le Guin, but especially those who desire to enter the House of Beauty and speak with the Muse of Poetry, must undertake a journey into their own psyche, must confront the shadow within themselves and accept its guidance, and only then will they grow "toward true community, and self-knowledge, and creativity" (64). Ariane's journey through the SNW, her encounters with Malykorne and Annis, her reflection on Sylvie's approach to the tasks and responsibilities of becoming a sub-creator, lead her to the knowledge she needs in order to realize her potential and find her place in the community.

The task successfully completed, Ariane and Sylvie watch as the dance of spring returns to Cloud, as the natural balance is restored and the SNW is renewed. Their quest over, they are returned to the PNW, to the woods behind Sylvie's grandmother's home, where it is early summer, and friends and neighbors are celebrating a wedding with food and flowers, music and dancing, and children at play. It was a hard winter at home, they learn, implying that their actions have had an impact in the real world as well as in the world that they created. Watching the fireflies, the dancers, the summer stars above her, Ariane feels a sense of home, a responsibility to the world around her as well as to the worlds "of stone and soul and thorn within her, the green wood and the starry heavens" (373). It is this kind of recognition of the need for balance and harmony between self and Other, between people and the environment of the natural world, so familiar a theme in quest fantasies like *Moonwise*, that critic Brian Attebery has in mind when he speaks of the "ecological treatment of humankind's place in the natural world" (35) common to the genre of fantasy, which is, as Attebery asserts in defiance of those who would condemn it, far from "silent on the problems of the human community" (31). Indeed, it may be that the fantasist, more than any other author, best understands the power of narrative to create a world in which all desire to live together rather than live apart in fear.

NOTES

1. Elsewhere, Doležel acknowledges not only "the Proppian system" but also "Lévi-Strauss' system of myth analysis, the Jungian system of 'archetypes' (as well as other archetypal systems) [including Campbell's]" as similar methods to his own of abstracting a system of narrative semantics from analysis of myths and folktales ("Extensional" 199).

2. Doležel states that "a modal system can be said to define a *narrative world* in which only some courses of narrated actions are admissible" (NW 543). Since it is a critical convention to speak of the "world" of the text, and all four modal systems can be operative within one textual world, Doležel's use of "world" is misleading and somewhat limiting; it would seem preferable, therefore, to speak in terms of modalities rather than worlds.

3. The craft of storytelling in particular and the production of art more generally, especially the metaphorical magic performed in creating worlds out of words, has been a familiar theme explored by many fantasists, among them Charles de Lint in *Memory and Dream*, Sheri Tepper in the short story "Prince Shadowbow," and Patricia McKillip in many of her works, as discussed in "Bridging World and Story," an article published in the *Journal for the Fantastic in the Arts* which examines similar structural concerns (Mains).

4. The relationship between Ariane and Sylvie's primary world and the narrative worlds through which they wander is depicted as a much more complex structure, more like nested dolls, a Chinese-box structure. For the purposes of this essay, however, it is simpler to focus on the alethic dyadic world and ignore further complexities.

5. For more on the primacy of the axiologically generated quest over deontically generated quests, see Mains, "Bridging World and Story."

WORKS CITED

Attebery, Brian. *Strategies of Fantasy*. Bloomington and Indianapolis: Indiana University Press, 1992.

Bal, Mieke. *Narratology: Introduction to the Theory of Narrative*. 2nd ed. Toronto: University of Toronto Press, 1997.

Campbell, Joseph. *The Hero with a Thousand Faces*. 1949. Bollingen Series XVII. 2nd ed. Princeton: Princeton University Press, 1968.

Doležel, Lubomír. "Extensional and Intensional Narrative Worlds." *Poetics* 8 (1979): 193–211.

_____. *Heterocosmica: Fiction and Possible Worlds*. Baltimore and London: Johns Hopkins University Press, 1998.

_____. "Mimesis and Possible Worlds." *Poetics Today* 9 (1988): 475–496.

_____. "Narrative Semantics." PTL: A Journal for Descriptive Poetics and Theory of Literature 1 (1976): 129–151.

Frye, Northrop. *The Secular Scripture: A Study of the Structure of Romance*. Cambridge and London: Harvard University Press, 1976.

Gilman, Greer Ilene. *Moonwise*. New York: ROC-NAL-Penguin, 1991.

Le Guin, Ursula K. "The Child and the Shadow." *The Language of the Night: Essays on Fantasy and Science Fiction*. Ed. Susan Wood. New York: G.P. Putnam's Sons, 1979. 59–72.

Mains, Christine. "Bridging World and Story: Patricia McKillip's Reluctant Heroes." *Journal of the Fantastic in the Arts* 16.1 (Spring 2005): 37–48.

Propp, Vladimir. *Morphology of the Folktale*. American Folklore Society Bibliographical and Special Series 9. Trans. Laurence Scott. 2nd ed. Rev. and Ed. Louis A. Wagner. Austin, TX: University of Texas Press, 1968.

4

"Dancing on the Edge of the World": California and Utopia in Ursula K. Le Guin's *Always Coming Home*

Ken Simpson

The relationship between utopian fiction and social change has always been strained despite the prominence of detailed political experiments in the genre. Already associated with wishful thinking and, therefore, with impractical speculation on the one hand, and the nightmare of Stalinist Russia on the other, utopian writing, according to Fredric Jameson, now faces further challenges because of the convergence of postmodern skepticism and late capitalism, under which imagining a radically different political system has become nearly impossible. In *Archaeologies of the Future*, a phrase borrowed from Ursula K. Le Guin's *Always Coming Home*, Jameson still manages to find a positive political role for utopias, despite these suffocating conditions: "this increasing inability to imagine a different future enhances rather than diminishes the appeal and also the function of Utopia" (232) because its purpose today is not to render a complete political blueprint but to demonstrate the impossibility of utopian representation, shifting the emphasis to utopian form and its signification of disruption, difference, and discontinuity. At the same time as he reminds us of the continuing political role of utopian form, however, Jameson underestimates the importance of feminist writers in developing critical utopias, for in writing within the hegemonic patriarchal assumptions of the genre, they rehearsed important oppositional strategies that could be taken up more broadly during the era of "full-blown globalization and postmodernity" (216).

At the same time as the "twilight of utopia" (Manuel 21) was being announced, American feminists of the 1970s and 1980s, including Marge Piercy, Joanna Russ, Joan Slonczewski and Ursula K. Le Guin, were rediscovering the social force of literary utopias: the opportunity to create worlds that called contemporary political realities into question offered an indispensable strategy for social change. Because many of the targets of feminist political critique, such as patriarchal authority, isolated subjectivity, and technological progress toward a predetermined end of history, were also features of utopian fiction, feminist utopias were often "ambiguous" or "critical" (Moylan 10). To subvert the patriarchal assumptions of the genre while taking advantage of the juxtaposition between a vivid, imaginary, alternate world and the stark reality of oppression that makes the literary utopia such a powerful force for social change, it became necessary to assert and deny utopia at the same time. The well-known irony of utopian fiction — that the ideal or good place (eutopia) is no place (outopia) — helps to define the imaginative space in which utopias can effect social change in an anti-utopian context. In the contrast between the utopian and the real, once apparently natural or essential conditions are shown to be only selected possibilities among many others, ideologies of gender, race, class, and nationality can be transformed into whatever form the utopian vision recommends.

In her essays and novels, and especially in *Always Coming Home*, the focus of this paper, Ursula K. Le Guin registers similar reservations but also optimism about the social and political dimensions of utopian fiction; however, her narrative strategies and her unique relationship to the utopian setting of the novel, in this case California, make significant contributions to both the theory and practice of feminist utopian writing. Jameson's too facile account of Le Guin's use of Taoism and "Native American social forms" (96) blunts his appreciation of her development of the very strategies that he claims are essential for the survival of utopian writing. On the one hand, unlike the utopias of Russ, Piercy, and Slonczewski, Le Guin's utopic California is a rigorously concrete place, even though California is also metaphorical, a thought experiment in representing the state of mind and being that is most likely to lead to utopian political formations. While other utopias use the contrast between the present and utopian worlds to show how women's present realities fall short of what is possible, the utopian world is often only vaguely related to physical setting, whether the action takes place on another planet (Slonczewski), in another time (Piercy), or in a parallel dimension (Russ). By presenting California in such rich and abundant detail, Le Guin is able to locate utopia not only in the here but also in the now; she shows that the incomplete realization of place both in contemporary culture and in utopian writing has been a serious deficiency. The state of mind in which we are always coming home is the present, fully imagined world of the Kesh, and the utopian social formations in which women can live full lives follow from dwelling in this place that she calls home. At the same time, this utopian vision is inseparable from its opposite: the dystopian world of the Condor and of twentieth-century California.

Le Guin, as a specifically Californian writer, is ideally placed to explore this new kind of skeptical utopia. As Charles Crow argues, like many other Californian writers Le Guin constructs a myth in which California represents the last chance to attain "a fully realized life in harmony with an inviting and nurturing landscape" (3). California is at the brink of the world where the dream of progress and opportunity succeeds or fails; there is no frontier over the next horizon, and California is literally and figuratively the end of the road for Western progress and expansion. For Le Guin, as for so many Californian writers, California also represents the failure of and disillusionment with such dreams of utopian progress, but she fails to rest there for the new utopia is more concerned with renewal than progress. In *Always Coming Home*, her most experimental and successful attempt to write utopia, California is the place where no-place finds a home in the renewal of the moment rather than the march to the future. The myth of California as a place where utopian ideals are destroyed and renewed, a myth informing the concrete place realized in *Always Coming Home*, develops in several of Le Guin's works (Cummins 153–98). Many of her science fiction novels and short stories are marked by the geography of the West Coast, the settings of distant planets or future societies often strongly reminiscent of her familiar territory. Fog and mist, important images of a reality outside of conventional boundaries in many of Le Guin's works, are also, as everyone knows, prominent features of Portland, where she lives, and the coast of northern California, where she grew up. As important as the West Coast is as a setting that links the future and the present in Le Guin's fiction, the coast also plays an important mythical and metaphorical role in her works, especially in *The Lathe of Heaven* and "The New Atlantis," both set in Portland, and *Always Coming Home* and the stories in *Searoad: Chronicles of Klatsand*, both set in Northern California. For Le Guin, the coast is an epistemological space and a mythic region, a state of consciousness in which binary opposites, boundaries, and frontiers that enslave perceptions and actions are overthrown, allowing a creative response to reality's flux to emerge. Between the borders of land and sea, reason and intuition, objectivity and subjectivity, the West Coast is a metaphor of creativity and renewal in response to the destructive death wish of the larger West — the "Westward ho!" imperialism of male, technological, object-oriented reason. As she commented in 1981, on the West Coast we are compelled to dance "on the brink of the world":

> This place where I was born and grew up and love beyond all other, my world, my California, still needs to be made.... To find a world, maybe you have to have lost one. Maybe you have to be lost. The dance of renewal, the dance that made the world, was always danced here at the edge of things, on the brink, on the foggy coast ["World Making" 48].

Le Guin's construction of the West Coast as a state of consciousness interconnected with all things, made possible by the suspension of fixed binary opposites and boundaries, is also part of a creation myth of loss and renewal, apocalypse and creation in which the coast is associated with birth, creativity, and the possibility of a utopian future. The apocalypse, on the other hand, takes place further up the coast in Portland in both *The Lathe of Heaven* and "The New Atlantis." Le Guin acknowledges this in a 1982 interview:

> One thing I've noticed about my settings is that when I have something I really don't want to say but which insists on being said I set it in Portland. *The Lathe of Heaven* and *The New Atlantis* are among the saddest things I've written, the nearest to not being hopeful, and they're both set right here [qtd. in Cummins 154].

While creation and apocalypse are present in the myths of both California's and Oregon's coasts, these can be seen as stages in Le Guin's thinking of utopia, for they are ultimately both part of the process of always coming home, the process of being made and unmade, that she eventually identifies with California in *Always Coming Home*.

Le Guin's myth of the West Coast as an epistemological region suspended between customary binary opposites is evident in the smallest details as well as the mythic pattern of creation and apocalypse that links her stories and novels of the West Coast. Critics have noticed the importance of antithetical imagery in Le Guin's novels before, emphasizing the influence of Taoist philosophy (Bain 211–13) or of "wholeness and balance" (Barbour 39), but these views tend to reduce the play of opposites and binaries to a complementarity or resolution. Even in *The Left Hand of Darkness* and *The Dispossessed*, the two novels most often cited in discussions of this imagery, oppositions are used not to emphasize their harmony and mutuality, but to underline that the oppositions are culturally constructed in the first place, restricting the authentic, human relationship between Estraven and Genly Ai, on the one hand, and the values of Anarres and Urras realized in Shevek's contradictory character, on the other. The imagery of walls throughout *The Dispossessed* also indicates how important the demystification of binary opposites is for Le Guin. The first words of the novel describe a physical, but also cultural wall that Shevek believes he has or will overcome, but near the novel's conclusion, he warns Ketho about the wall he will need to walk through when he reverses Shevek's journey and travels from Urras to Anarres. As the narrator comments, "walls" are "ambiguous, two-faced," indicating the difficulty, if not the impossibility of dissolving them in harmonious balance.

If in the Hainish novels Le Guin's antithetical imagery is somewhat static, suggesting that balance between opposites is desirable, in the West Coast stories she complicates the pattern of imagery, developing it in ways already present in her more famous novels. In *The Lathe of Heaven*, set in Portland in 2002 when the world has been reduced to chaos by melting ice-caps, overpopulation, pollution, and war, Le Guin "continues her concern with boundaries in a more cryptic fashion: they become doors, walls, and windows which separate inside from outside" (Selinger 75). George Orr, whose dreams become reality, is a particularly good example of this interplay between objective and subjective reality, but images of the coast also figure importantly here: the aliens who come to offer rebirth are sea turtles who are at home in the sea and on the land; while part of the coastal area is threatened by rising water, Portland's water level is falling; while Orr sees the ocean's depth, Heather hears a "roaring creek" of "unborn children singing"; and at the end of the first chapter, mist surrounds Orr, suggesting that frontiers and boundaries are not conflated or resolved but fluid and permeable (Selinger 75). In response to the apocalyptic future, utopian rationalists like Haber, the psychiatrist who tries to turn Orr's dreams into reality in order to build a planned utopia, create a world that is "half wrecked, half transformed" (*Lathe of Heaven* 168), but the sea turtles can at least offer consolation in words foreshadowing *Always Coming Home*: "There is time. There are returns. To go is to return" (175). Similarly, in "The New Atlantis," the title suggesting the ancient utopia, Portland descends into the sea as a new city arises in the ocean, but the imagery of renewal is muted because the new city never really materializes in a concrete way. The voices of the reborn, however, emphasize the imagery of the play of opposites associated with the coast in Le Guin's mythology:

> When we break through the bright circle into life, the water will break and stream white down the white sides of the towers, and run down the steep streets back into the sea. The water will glitter in dark hair, on eyelids of dark eyes, and dry to a thin white film of salt [38].

The combination of rising and falling, light and dark patterns reiterates that the coast is an epistemological and mythical region as well as a natural one in which conventional categories of reality often portrayed in opposition or balanced harmony are, for Le Guin, inconstant and always in the process of becoming. The emphasis in the Portland stories, however, is on apocalypse rather than renewal.

In *Always Coming Home*, Le Guin once again develops antithetical imagery, but here it is more varied and nuanced than in her previous novels, and creation rather than apocalypse myths are prominent, creating an apocalypse/creation pattern within the West Coast stories as well as within the novel itself, for the Kesh inhabit a world poisoned and polluted by the "backward-head people" of the distant past that is clearly our present. There are at least twelve creation myths told, all of which are different, reflecting the culture of the storyteller. For the Condor, the embodiment of patriarchal values, "One made everything out of nothing [;] ... he made it [the universe], and gives it orders" (212). The Kesh, Le Guin's utopian society, prefer creation myths of people dancing on the water, of sacred eggs in the wombs of animals, or of "waters mixed up with the sands of the beach and the air so that there were no edges, no surfaces, no insides" (175) until the sand begins to dance and sing, bringing shapes into being. In another version of the same myth, the narrator explains that

> the sands of all the beaches of all the coasts, the grains of sand of all the beaches of all the coasts of all the world, are the lives of the unborn, who will be born, who may be born. The waves of the sea, the bubbles of foam of the waves that break on the coasts of the seas of the world, all the flashes and gleams of light on the waves of the seas of the world, the flicker of sunlight on waves of the ocean, those are the lives of the Nine Houses of Life without end vanishing without stay forever [492].

This use of antithetical imagery in creation myths associated with the coast is continued in the life story of Flicker, visionary of the Serpentine House. Flicker's name suggests the mystical bird but also, as the previous quotation suggests, neither dark nor light but the play of both, and her vision is of the interconnection of all things in which divisions between subject and object lose their permanence:

> It was the network, field, and lines of the energies of all the beings, stars, and galaxies of stars, worlds, minds, nerves, dust, the lace and foam of vibration that is being itself, all interconnected.... [This world is] one momentary glitter of light on one wave on the ocean of the universe of power, one fleck of dust.... No image can contain the vision which contained all images ... [but] foam, and the scintillation of mica in rock, the flicker and sparkle of waves and dust, the working of the great broadcloth looms, and all dancing [reflect the vision temporarily] [308].

Foam, dust, glittering light, dancing at the edge of the world all allude to the impermanence and play of the sea and land, light and dark, vision and power and imply that this is the way to the world's renewal. The Kesh themselves live close to the "inland sea," an ambiguous landscape formed by earthquakes that buried cities of the past, but our present, underwater, while their religious vision is symbolized by the "heyiya," a word meaning sacred, or sacred thing that refers to two contrasting spirals or gyres joined by a hinge or center that cannot be located in space. Le Guin's creation myths of the West Coast, then, are stories of creation without beginning and apocalypse without end, both of which occur simultaneously in an abundant and undivided present. To return to this present means to be always going home by overturning fixed polarities of perception and thought that obscure the sacredness and interconnectedness of the cosmos, the source of the utopian social organizations of the Kesh. The future world of California is a fully realized present made out of the past, a vision of utopia that celebrates renewal and process rather than planning and progress. As important as the mythical and epistemological dimensions of Le Guin's California and utopia are, however, it is the specificity of the setting of *Always Coming Home* that sets it apart from other utopias.

Le Guin has stated that "the book [she] wrote about the [Napa] Valley is called *Always Coming Home* (*Way of the Water's Going* 1), and this involves, as I have argued, a myth of California and the West Coast, but the Valley of *Always Coming Home* also consists of a carefully realized present. Although set in a future world in which California's coast has been transformed by earthquakes that form an inland sea, shift the Valley to the

Coast and submerge a toxic industrial society reminiscent of our own, *Always Coming Home* also includes minute geographical, geological, anthropological, and botanical details of today's Northern California landscape — the manzanitas and oaks, severe foothills and shaded valleys, the small creeks and streams, the flickers and woodpeckers, grasses and shrubs, coyotes and rabbits, and the lives and stories of the Kesh creating a sense of potential for renewal within the present rather than a purely speculative future world.

The Kesh — the peaceful inhabitants of the Valley — "might be going to have lived a long time from now in Northern California" (*Always Coming Home* 1), but they also resemble what Le Guin knew about the native peoples of northern California's past — the Coast Miwok, the Pomo, the Wappo, the Wintun, the Yuki, the Yurok, the Costanoan, the Karok. Familiar with her father's *Handbook of the Indians of California* (1925), her mother's *Ishi in Two Worlds* (1961), and Walton Bean's *California: An Interpretive History* (1968), Le Guin transformed anthropological details about California's native peoples to create in the Kesh not so much an idealized past projected into the future, but a metaphorical people who embody the spirit of the land itself, a people who know the names and stories of every bird, flower, mountain peak and patch of grass, a people who live in the fullness of their present as an extension of the land. This contrasts starkly with "our culture, which conquered what is called the New World, and which sees the world of nature as an adversary.... We are the inhabitants of a Lost World.... Even the names are lost" ("World Making" 47). California in Le Guin's novel is utopian not because it represents a future goal toward which rational thought marches, sacrificing the present by planning and plotting, but because it is where she experiences being-at-home to the fullest extent. As she wrote in 1981,

> If utopia is a place that does not exist, then surely (as Lao Tzu would say) the way to get there is by the way that is not the way. And in the same vein, the nature of the utopia I am trying to describe is such that if it is to come, it must exist already.... I believe there are people there. They have always lived there. It's home. There are songs they sing there; one of the songs is called "Dancing at the edge of the world" [quoting, while changing "on the brink" to "at the edge," A. L. Kroeber 471] ["A Non-Euclidean View of California" 93, 98–99].

For Le Guin, the Valley is home, home is utopia, and utopia is a temporal dimension outside of time, re-created in time by always returning to the moment of creation. As one of the narrators, Stone Telling, relates, and the symbols of hinges, spirals, and ritual dances remind us throughout the novel, "I have come where I was going" (*Always Coming Home* 7).

In the early 1980s, Le Guin began publishing essays in which we now know she was beginning to imagine the utopian California later explored in *Always Coming Home*. In 1981, her contribution to a symposium at Stanford called "Lost Worlds and Future Worlds" included reflections on "the people who lived here, in this place, on these hills, for tens of thousands of years" but who were named by their Spanish conquerors ("World Making" 47), reflections based on the anthropological research of her father, A. L. Kroeber. She uses a line, slightly modified, from a Costanoan dance song in *Handbook of the Indians of California* as the title of her collection of essays, *Dancing at the Edge of the World*, in itself a brilliant image of her California, and she also cites a song found in her father's book first sung by the wood rat:

> I dream of you,
> I dream of you jumping,
> Rabbit, jack rabbit, and quail.
> [A. L. Kroeber 471; qtd. in "World Making" 48].

She may have even had her father's research in mind when she was considering the discontinuous structure of the book, for as A.L. Kroeber notes, the "deliberate or artistic incoherence, both as regards personages and plot, is...a definite quality of the mythology of the southern California tribes" (625). Ursula Le Guin herself, however, attempts to overcome the charge of appropriation that could be leveled against her father, and what seems now the naïve objectivity of his viewpoint, by constructing multiple narrators, some of whom admit to being unable to understand the artifacts they record and describe, and by emphasizing the metaphorical nature of fiction and the subjective nature of observation.

Le Guin was carefully considering her father's book, then, while she was bringing the new world of *Always Coming Home* into being. She must have been overpowered by the rich cultural traditions of California before European conquest and especially by the songs, dances, and rituals that were repeated to mark each season, and each milestone in a person's life, bringing the participants into harmony with natural and human events and with the dream time when the songs were sung in the beginning to commemorate the acts of coyote, wood rat, quail, flicker, and a host of others. While A.L. Kroeber observes the various rituals, Le Guin gives them imaginative life, not by copying them but by inventing new ones for situations that the Kesh shared with many of the cultures described by Kroeber for blessing the house, for traveling across boundaries, for initiation, menstruation, and the harvest or the hunt.

Of greater importance for Le Guin in creating utopian California, though, was the style of the songs and myths recorded by her father. The concrete, rhythmic style of incremental repetition and parallelism found in the song cited above can be seen throughout the examples of poetry and prayer in the *Handbook of the Indians of California*. A Yokut bear doctor's song is as follows: "Again he comes,/ Again the grizzly bear comes to me" (515). And Coyote says, "What am I?/ I am coyote./ I am of the water./ What am I?/ I am coyote" (515). Le Guin re-creates several creation myths involving coyote, but her real achievement is in capturing the poetic texture and rhythm of the original songs translated by A.L. Kroeber. The one that opens the book especially recalls the song of the quail:

> In the fields by the river
> from the meadows by the river
> from the fields by the river
> in the meadows by the river
> two quail run
>
> Run two quail
> rise two quail
> two quail run
> two quail rise
> from the meadows by the river.
> [*Always Coming Home* 1].

From suggestions in anthropological records, Le Guin made a world of the present-future from the past.

Already looking ahead to the California of *Always Coming Home,* she suggests in "A Non-Euclidean View of California as a Cold Place to Be" that her emerging idea of California is inseparable from her revision of utopia. This essay, the most sustained and thoughtful in the *Dancing at the Edge of the World* collection, was first prepared as part of a series of lectures honoring Robert C. Elliott of the University of California, San Diego. Le Guin refers to Elliott's study, *The Shape of Utopia,* several times throughout the essay, and in particular to Elliott's acknowledgement of "our distrust of utopia" since it implies the belief that "through the exercise of their reason men can control and in major ways alter for the better their social environment.... One must have faith of a kind that our history has made nearly inaccessible" (Elliot qtd. in "A Non-Euclidean View" 86). About this kind of utopia Le Guin is unequivocal:

Utopia has been euclidean [rationalist], it has been European, and it has been masculine.... It is a monotheocracy, declared by executive decree, and maintained by willpower; as its premise is progress, not process, it has no habitable present, and speaks only in the future tense.... I am trying to suggest ... that our final loss of faith in that radiant sandcastle may enable our eyes to adjust to a dimmer light and in it perceive another kind of utopia ["A Non-Euclidean View" 88, 87, 88].

California has been a victim of rationalist, utopian thinking in two ways: first, the march of progress by Europeans was made possible only by the slaughter of California's native people; secondly, having lost or forgotten the only people who knew the land and its deep past, California's people are rootless, cut off from the land they inhabit and therefore from understanding their place in the cosmos in any significant way.

In *Always Coming Home*, this vision of utopia is represented by the war-like Condor. Most significantly, the Condor, as Stone Telling's grandmother warns her, are "Men of No House" (16), lacking any relationship to the natural world except one of domination and willpower. They are linked to the technological West by advanced engineering applied to bridges and weapons, but also by their misuse of the Exchange, a system of computer terminals containing all known information (204), a remnant of the same civilization that polluted the land and built the enormous cities now under the water. Their society is monotheocratic, driven by an ideal of purity to imitate the One and dominated by a caste of warrior priests. Only "True Condor[s]" warriors read and write, although no writing is allowed in public since the One has written all there is to say; the women are trained to keep an orderly household and to please their husbands.

On the other hand, Le Guin also presents her true utopia, her California, both in her essay "A Non-Euclidean View of California as a Cold Place to Be" and in *Always Coming Home*. Utopia, she argues, must now include diverse voices, religious and literary imagination, participatory festivals, and especially, an emphasis on the present moment made intelligible by turning and returning to significant moments of the past. The guiding spirit of this utopia is not Urizen, but coyote, the trickster who "falls into things, traps, abysses, and then clambers out somehow, grinning stupidly" ("A Non-Euclidean View" 98). This utopia will be non-linear, incomplete, always in process, disorderly. It will resemble an improvised song or dance rather than a blueprint.

Always Coming Home embodies this utopia in the lives of the Kesh and their relationship to the natural world. At the same time, Stone Telling's dual origins — her mother is Kesh while her father is Condor — underline the dialectical nature of utopias. The novel's title echoes her earlier emphasis on the need to return and relive the past in the present, not as a reaction but as a subversion of future-oriented, technological reason. Stone Telling has returned home after each journey of discovery that has formed her life: as a child she goes to Kastoha and returns; as a young woman she goes to the mountains and returns; she goes with her father, a Condor, marries and returns to her home village; and finally, as Stone Telling, she returns to these journeys in her narrative. The relationship of the Kesh to the cosmos is also developed through figures of turning and returning: the "heyiya" is a sacred symbol that pervades the novel, appearing in such diverse arrangements as patterns of birds, dust, musical notations, and instruments in the novel's illustrations.

The heyiya is most apparent, however, in the structure of Kesh society. Every individual belongs to a lodge, each with its own rituals and economic activities. There are nine lodges in each village, five belonging to the earth and four to the sky, and all are built along contrasting arms of two spirals, radiating from a center marked by a well, surrounded by a space for ritual dances and ceremonies that take place according to natural and human cycles. The hinge not only joins two contrasting spiral arms representing the earth and sky; it also swings back and forth in constant movement, as people turn and return to the centers of the world. The rituals of the Kesh enact an eternal return of the same: the sacredness of the world is renewed each time the ritual is danced at the hinge even though the people dancing are always changing. California, Le Guin implies, is such a place where the dance of renewal at the edge of the world needs to occur.

Le Guin's emphasis on utopia as always in process, always incomplete, but also intimately connected to the cosmos reveals the extent to which she was influenced by her father's depiction of northern Californian aboriginal cultures, but equally important was her mother's book, *Ishi in Two Worlds* (1961), the story of the last surviving Yahi man discovered in 1911 and placed in A. L. Kroeber's care at Berkeley. Le Guin must have known about Ishi and her mother's account of his contact with twentieth-century America as well as anyone could have, and this could account for the many similarities between her portrait of the Kesh and Theodora Kroeber's account of Ishi's lost world. The following description of Ishi's community could also describe the Kesh:

Life proceeded within the limits of known and proper patterns from birth through death and beyond. Its repetitive rhythm was punctuated with ritual, courtship, dance, song, and feast, each established according to custom going back to the beginning of the world, an event which, along with subsequent events having to do with setting the way of life, was well known and fully recounted in the peoples' oral but elaborate and specific histories [23].

Ishi's culture, like the Kesh's fictional one, marked the coming of age of its members with great ceremony and known boundaries were crossed with great reluctance. Ceremonies of naming were important for both worlds as well. As a child, Stone Telling is named North Owl; with her father she is Ayatu, "woman born above others" (*Always Coming Home* 86); when she is returning to Sinshan she is Woman Coming Home, and as she tells her story she is Stone Telling because she goes "nowhere, sitting like a stone in this place, in this ground, in this Valley" (7). Names also had power for Ishi; this is why he never revealed his real name to anyone, but accepted Kroeber's name for him. Finally, the Yahi, like the Kesh, live in "a small world, intimately and minutely known" (Theodora Kroeber 18), each inhabiting an isolated ecological island for the most part, as occurs often in utopian fiction, the natural boundaries of California protecting them from invasion from the south, east, and west for thousands of years.

The intimately known world of California is what has been lost by most of today's inhabitants, but which Le Guin painstakingly re-creates in her novel: the songs, poems, myths, rituals, languages, and personal narratives conveyed in the diverse voices of the Kesh as well as their names for plants, trees, animals, and geographical features are all included to create a thick, vibrant world. Le Guin's later comments on the novel reveal her own need to create the spirit of her valley:

> When I began to write about the place I have loved the longest, the Napa Valley of Northern California, I found that I wanted to describe it as closely and truly as I could — more closely and truly than is possible: stone by stone.... I wanted to know and tell the trees and shrubs and grasses native to that stony earth, and the looks and lives of all the creatures that live in the Valley, in its river and creeks, on the wild hills above it and in the air above the hills [Introduction *Way of the Water's Going* 1].

The intimacy between the Kesh and their Valley is also conveyed in the body metaphor often used to describe the landscape. Stone Telling sits like a stone "in the ground, in this Valley" (*Always Coming Home* 7), and later she calls dirt, the "mother of my mothers" (20). Kastoha is called "Granny's Twat" because "it is between the spread legs of the Mountain" (16), and when she leaves the Valley with her father, North Owl feels like she is leaving her body behind:

> I began to feel the Valley behind me like a body, my own body. My feet were the sea-channels of the River, the organs and passages of my body were the places and streams and my bones the rocks and my head was the Mountain. That was all my body, and I here lying down was a breath-soul going farther away from its body everyday [201].

It is no coincidence that this disembodiment occurs while she is traveling toward the dystopic home of the Condors. During her first introduction to the Condors, she has a vision of vultures pecking at her mother's mouth and body; conversely, while thinking of having children of her own she imagines "that a child would be like the Valley. It would be a part of me and I a part of it; it would be beloved home" (371).

Ursula K. Le Guin's beloved home is northern California and especially the Napa Valley. The depth of her feeling for her place and her understanding of its influence on her can be seen in her decision to write California as a utopia. California, and especially the West Coast, is, first, an epistemological space in which conventional boundaries, opposites, and frontiers are always being transformed. When she began developing the idea of California as utopia in the early 1980s, and by the time she published *Always Coming Home* in 1985, however, she had created a detailed future world based on her minute and intimate knowledge of northern California's ecology and anthropology, the latter due in part at least to her familiarity with the work of her parents. But this is a utopia with a difference. The strategy for social change used in traditional utopias, in which details of the writer's present are juxtaposed with details of the utopian world in order to show how the future must change, is also used by Le Guin, but the richly detailed world of the Kesh, itself based on the past, is presented as a response to the present; here the alternate, utopian world, despite its dialectical dependence on its own opposite, is a richly named present rather than a rational blueprint of the future to be followed at all costs. Californians have already tried that, and the result has been disastrous: in *Always Coming Home* we are told of the "Backward-head people" who pollute the land, poison the streams, and contaminate the air with radioactivity, and it is clear that they are us. Le Guin offers the lives of the Kesh in the world of California as a chance of renewal, a dance at the brink of the world, giving utopia a local habitation and a name in the here and now.

WORKS CITED

Bain, Dena C. "The 'Tao Te Ching' as Background to the Novels of Ursula K. Le Guin." *Ursula K. Le Guin: Modern Critical Views.* Ed. Harold Bloom. New York: Chelsea House, 1986. 211–13.

Barbour, D. "Wholeness and Balance in the Hainish Novels of Ursula K. Le Guin." *Science Fiction Studies* 9 (1982): 39–52.

Bean, Walton. *California: An Interpretive History.* New York: McGraw Hill, 1968.

Crow, Charles L. "Homecoming in the California Visionary Romance." *Western American Literature* 24.3 (1989): 3–19.

Cummins, Elizabeth. *Understanding Ursula K. Le Guin.* Columbia: University of South Carolina Press, 1990.

Elliott, Robert C. *The Shape of Utopia.* Chicago: University of Chicago Press, 1970.

Jameson, Fredric. *Archaeologies of the Future: The Desire Called Utopia and Other Science Fictions.* London and New York: Verso, 2005.

Kroeber, A. L. *Handbook of the Indians of California.* Bureau of American Ethnology #78. Washington: Government Printing Office, 1925.

Kroeber, Theodora. *Ishi in Two Worlds.* Berkeley: University of California Press, 1961.

Le Guin, Ursula K. *Always Coming Home.* New York: Harper & Row, 1985.

_____. *The Dispossessed.* New York: Avon, 1974.

_____. *The Lathe of Heaven.* London: Victor Gollancz, 1972.

_____. *The Left Hand of Darkness.* New York: Ace, 1969.

_____. "The New Atlantis." *The Compass Rose.* New York: Harper and Row, 1982. 12–14.

_____. "A Non-Euclidean View of California as a Cold Place to Be." *Dancing at the Edge of the World: Thoughts on Words, Women, Places.* New York: Grove, 1989. 80–100.

_____. *Searoad: Chronicles of Klatsand.* New York: HarperCollins, 1991.

_____. Introduction. *Way of the Water's Going: Images of the Northern California Coastal Range.* Photographs by Ernest Waugh and Alan Nicholson; Text from Ursula K. Le Guin's *Always Coming Home.* New York: Harper & Row, 1989. 1–3.

_____. "World Making."*Dancing at the Edge of the World: Thoughts on Words, Women, Places.* New York: Grove, 1989. 46–48.

Manuel, Frank E., and Fritzie P. Manuel. *Utopian Thought In The Western World.* Cambridge, Mass.: Harvard University Press, 1979.

Moylan, Tom. *Demand the Impossible: Science Fiction and the Utopian Imagination.* London: Methuen, 1986.

Piercy, Marge. *Woman on the Edge of Time.* New York: Fawcett Crest, 1976.

Russ, Joanna. *The Female Man.* Boston: Beacon, 1975.

Selinger, Bernard. *Le Guin and Identity in Contemporary Fiction.* Ann Arbor: UMI Research Press, 1988.

Slonczewski, Joan. *A Door into Ocean.* New York: Avon, 1986.

5

Passing Genes in GATTACA,
or, Straight Genes
for the Queer Guy

Lee Easton

"Consider the work of God. Who makes straight that which
God has made crooked?"
— Ecclesiastes 7:13 (qtd. in *GATTACA*)

"On the whole, science fiction is an overwhelmingly *straight*
discourse, not least because of the covert yet almost completely
totalizing ideological hold heterosexuality has on our culture's
ability to imagine itself otherwise."
— Veronica Hollinger

Representation matters. And it particularly matters in science fiction
films. This is because, however much we may enjoy these movies' special
effects and swashbuckling narratives, the representations are not simple
pleasures without ideological significance. As Laura Briggs and Jodi Kelber-
Kaye have aptly stated, "science fiction narratives are simultaneously arguments about how science should (or shouldn't) be done, what should
happen in the realm of business and technology" (93). Being neither
simply social commentary nor precise scientific prediction, science fiction films nevertheless actively help to constitute the available fields of

discourses in which science, technology and cultural relations operate in our vernacular reality. More importantly, science fiction films shape the available ways we can conceptualize our "projected reality," a term that scientist Ursula Franklin uses to denote the vernacular reality of the future. As Franklin points out, we plan how projected reality based on our currently available ideas of technology (38). Given science fiction film's constitutive role in molding how we imagine such futures, it seems crucial that we interrogate closely the social possibilities that how such films *project* technologies and science in the future. To what extent do they posit futures that might be otherwise different from what we already know today? Do these films contribute to social change and, if so, in which ways?

The 1997 film *GATTACA* offers an exemplary opportunity to explore such questions especially as they relate to the emergent technology of genetic engineering. Set in a dystopian future where geneticists routinely manipulate an embryo's genes in order to eliminate diseases and to adjust specific physical and intellectual characteristics, *GATTACA* attempts to show how such a society quickly comes to oppress any who fail to pass their tests of genetic purity. Using advanced computer processing technology to monitor its citizens — the same technology that makes genetic engineering possible — the world *GATTACA* portrays uses this information to discriminate against those who are deemed genetically inferior. The offspring of couples who still opt for natural conception or "faithbirths" are a particular focus of this discrimination. *GATTACA's* narrative takes up the story of one such faithbirth, Vincent Freeman (Ethan Hawke), whose natural conception has given him a congenital heart condition that will see him die before he turns thirty. A "degenerate" in a world of human perfection, Vincent is condemned to live as an invalid — pointedly pronounced "invalid" — ostracized from school, family and society. Despite his dreams of space travel, Vincent is deemed unfit for such heroics and is left to languish. Subject to his father's reproving gaze and his brother's disdain, Vincent leaves home and drifts about the country until he eventually gains employment as a janitor at GATTACA, the command center of the nation's manned space missions and the film's setting. Relying solely on his ingenuity and inherent plucky human spirit (for which, the movie's promotional spots remind us, there is no gene), he locates Jerome (Jude Law), a genetically perfect athlete, whose accident has left him an embittered alcoholic paraplegic. In an unusual and illegal exchange, Vincent and Jerome conspire to give Vincent access to Jerome's perfect genetic patterns in order for Vincent to bypass the genetic scanning arrangements that ensure security at GATTACA. Through a series of inventive procedures that become a daily routine, Vincent uses the genetic information contained in Jerome's blood, urine and skin flakes in order to secure and keep a position as a topflight programmer/navigator in GATTACA's space training program. Things fall apart, however, when a murder investigation leads the police to discover that Vincent has in fact been passing as Jerome. The film's suspense lies in determining whether Vincent/Jerome will be revealed for the degenerate trespasser his society deems him to be.

As a work of science fiction, the film actively seeks to shape how we think about genes, family, gender, race and sexuality now and in the future (Briggs and Kelber-Kaye 93). In fact, what is most interesting is how the film has been framed as an explicit intervention in the popular discourses of genetic determinism. This intervention has been noted: *GATTACA* has elicited a range of critical responses and not only from the usual academic circles. Science fiction critic David Kirby has shown how the film received a lukewarm reception in scientific circles, and he argues that this reception partly rests in the fact that "*GATTACA*'s approach is not only unique among bioethics texts, it is virtually alone among recent popular-culture narratives in its rejection of the genetic-determinist ideology" (212). Kirby sees *GATTACA* as an important statement against the way that "genes" discourse has been popularly framed in biological determinist terms. He argues the fact that "human genetics researchers felt the need to confront GATTACA attests to sf cinema's capacity to provide a venue for discourse about the prevailing 'social forces' of science" (211–212).

Although we might applaud the film's interventionist impulses, we might require more skepticism about its politics than Kirby appears to maintain. For example, Briggs and Kelber-Kaye caution that "there are important and very conservative, anti-feminist stories at work beneath the cultural silence about women in the discourse of genes" (94). Films such as *GATTACA* are particularly dangerous because they continue the silence about the relationship between women and genetics. Briggs and Kelber-Kaye view *GATTACA* as "a genetic reworking of the Cold War themes of 'Third World' overpopulation, Communism and homosexuality as threats — not to the State in this iteration but to the white nuclear family" (94). Elsewhere Susan George notes rather dryly that the focus of GATTACA's society and its reproductive technologies is not "to make the birthing process easier or safer for the mother but to improve the product — in this case, produce the perfect son" (George 178). Indeed, *GAT-*

TACA offers little to assuage women's concerns about how genetic tech-nologies might — and in fact are — already used to favor the conception of male instead of female children. Critics looking at representations of dis-ability have also taken exception to the film. Kathleen Ellis highlights how Eugene's representation (Jude Law) supports a number of stereotypes about people with disabilities, including the "widely held belief that disability is an individual's problem" (113). Ellis criticizes the film and its problematic ending for reassuring able-bodied audiences of their privilege while isolat-ing the disabled and reminding them that they are not valued (114). With so many caveats and problems, perhaps the film is a 21st century rework-ing of Cold War themes. Far from showing how science fiction may yet critically intervene in popular scientific, moral and technological discourses, perhaps *GATTACA* illustrates precisely how science fiction has reached its imaginative *cul de sac*.

However, and perhaps fortunately, there might be a way through these concerns that would allow us to account for the film's conservatism and still see it as having the potential to project both a progressive social cri-tique and futures with a difference. To navigate this course, we might consider the important but somewhat neglected trope that structures the film: passing. David Kirby has noted that passing is used to call into question "the assumption that minority individuals are not capable of performing as well as others' (202). Recently Jackie Stacey has adeptly demonstrated that Vincent's determination to pass as a genetically valid Jerome underscores the performativity of masculine identity revealing its claim to singularity and mastery as a ruse. However, both Kirby and Stacey's analyses can be pushed further when we look at the film as a story of the perils and possibilities that adhere to passing which is an inherently disruptive act that highlights and questions the social, political, economic and cultural forces at work to maintain specific forms of identity (Squires and Brouwer 287). Passing's doubled operation , a doubling echoed in the film's narrative and imagistic patterns, enables readers to critically under-stand how heterosexuality and patriarchy produce and sustain white het-erosexual masculinity even while it questions and destabilizes the idea of essential biological identities. These contradictory meanings suggest that possibilities for social change in science fiction texts rest not in deciding whether or not a given text works for or against social change, but in under-standing that both progressive and reactionary readings co-exist within the text.

Pass 1—*v.* *(p.p.* passed) discharge from the body as or with excreta

GATTACA ostensibly focuses on the murder investigation of the manned space center's flight director. However, the real story focuses on Vincent's illegal use of Eugene's blood, skin, hair, and urine to impersonate genetically perfect Jerome and the possibility that this deception will be discovered. To pass off this arrangement as simply an economic one (Kirby) underestimates the complexity of the relationship. To be sure, Vincent and Eugene's economic arrangement underscores the point that in *GATTACA*'s projected future genes have become another commodity for sale to the highest bidder. But there is something not only deliberately icky but also very queer about all this "body stuff" being passed between Vincent and Eugene. To note that the relationship itself partakes of the abject, with which the homosexual is always associated, is draw attention to how the film identifies this connection as aberrant yet also makes it the object of investigation and fascination. From the opening sequence which reveals itself gradually not as snow but as the skin Vincent sloughs each day, like a snake shedding its skin, to the final scene with Eugene assuring Vincent that he has left him a life time supply of body fluids, this exchange forms the film's homo heart.

Given the homoeroticism involved with exchanging such intimate body discharges, Vincent and Eugene's relationship can be figured as cryptogay. Add in Eugene's fussing about dyes as well as the dinner sequence where Vincent takes Eugene out for an evening on the town and tenderly puts him to bed drunk and the homoeroticism blurs further in the realm of the homosexual. Certainly Eugene fits the pattern of the "sad young man" that Richard Dyer has identified as typical of gay representations in the post-war period (Stacey 1870), but Vincent's sexuality is less clear. Given the flashback scenes that reveal him to be a housebound bookish momma's boy, he too fits the stereotypical codes of homosexual representation, especially when compared with his brother, the robust Anton. Although this paper is not ultimately interested in outing Vincent as gay, the possibility that Vincent *is* gay gains additional traction from a deleted sequence at the gene center where Vincent's parents go to arrange for their second son's birth. In this scene, later re-shot and edited, Vincent's parents discuss with the African-American geneticist the genetic modifications they want to make *in vitro* to their second son. Looking somewhat guilty, Vincent's mother says, "We would like to have grandchildren," to which the doctor replies, "I have already taken care of that." The sequence links Vincent's mother, Vincent and her frustrated desire to have grandchildren, to Vincent's inability to reproduce. His brother Anton in contrast has been "fixed" so that he will be a healthy reproductive male, one whose sexuality will undoubtedly be heterosexual, not homosexual. In linking reproduction and heterosexuality, the film engages the popular notion of the gay gene which is posited to account for male homosexuality.

Briggs and Kelber-Kaye contend that in coupling Vincent's secret genetic identity with gayness, the film's ambiguous politics are revealed as antifeminist (106). According to their reading, Vincent's apparent "gayness" is the consequence of maternal coddling, which re-inscribes a conventional natural versus unnatural opposition: heterosexual, non-technological motherhood as natural, and homosexuality, communism and genetic technology as unnatural (202). While it is certainly anti-feminist and regressive to suggest that bad mothering produces homosexuality, it is not so certain that the film necessarily reads as homophobic. First, several gay scientists have made concerted attempts to locate a 'natural' basis for homosexuality in men and women. These gained particular prominence in the 1990s when Simon LeVay published his research on gay male brains and Dean Hamer and his team produced studies suggesting that male homosexuality was linked to an area on the mother's X chromosomes (Terry 284). Such studies have been greeted with some excitement, for as Vernon Rosario notes, finding a "gay gene legitimizes a homosexual metahistory that transcends conventional genealogies" (11). These findings also created a sense of gay brotherhood with other homosexuals in history (Rosario 11). More important, the existence of a gay gene enables gay rights activist to use the dominant discourse of genetic determinism to support their claims that sexual orientation is inherent given and not, *contra* right wing commentators' assertions, a choice. Far from being homophobic, equating Vincent's *natural* faithbirth with homosexuality deploys the very discourses that gay activists have used to argue that since sexual orientation is genetically determined (natural), gays and lesbians cannot be denied human rights. While it is correct to suggest that genetic deterministic arguments recapitulate the old Freudian approach of blaming Mom, which does speak to the anti-feminist bias of genetic determinism, the film also seeks to position homosexuality as a genetic trait in order to question it.

The geneticist's benign assurance that he has already "taken care" of any possibility that Anton might be anything than heterosexual is central to contesting the discourse of genetic determinism. Read in the context of the "gay gene" findings, this mild statement is a loaded reminder to gays and lesbians that adopting genetic determinist perspectives presents considerable danger in a homophobic culture that has repeatedly attempted to eradicate homosexuals and homosexuality. In fact, much of the initial research about homosexuality and genetics came via Franz Kallmann, who approached the gay question from "a largely medical and eugenical point of view" (Allen 249). As Jonathon Tolin's play *Twilight of the Golds* makes abundantly clear, a genetic "cause" for homosexuality makes it possible to screen for its presence and then follow the all-too-familiar path of gender selection which sees girls routinely aborted in favor of boys. Reading Vincent as genetically gay takes GATTACA into similarly cautionary terrain. Positioning orientation along the same axis as other disabilities and defects, GATTACA assumes that aberrant sexualities will be screened out along with other disabilities creating a race of able-bodied heterosexuals.

This subtle conflation of gayness with disability is foreshadowed in the film's opening epigram from *Ecclesiastes*, which admonishes, "Consider the work of God. Who makes straight that which God has made crooked?" Seemingly addressing the problem of disability, the epigram also warns equally against the eugenics agenda that initially motivated the search for biological origins of homosexuality. Having suggest the outcome of genetic determinism for both gays and the disabled, the film goes on to recode both as occurring naturally. Since Vincent is a "faithbirth," his crooked — dare we say 'bent'? — sexuality is now recast as God-given, and therefore not be to set "straight" as is the wont in GATTACA's heterosexist world. Ironically re-deploying the self-same religious texts that are often cited against gays and lesbians, GATTACA mobilizes them as a defense of a natural homosexuality against the godless technologies of genetic engineering.

Pass 2 — *v.* to be accepted for

Successful passing is ultimately predicated on the assumption that the visual (outward) appearance is a guarantor of knowledge and identity. As race critics have shown, successful passing depends on mastering regimes of visual identification, which the act of passing then highlights and subverts. In GATTACA, however, identification is rarely authenticated visually or through social interactions. Photographs are passé; interviews are conducted with a blood test. The reliance on biometrics becomes another focus of the film's critique of genetic determinism. First, the search for the flight director's murderer reveals the totalitarian possibilities that lie within the employment of genetic technologies in tandem with information and communication technologies. With the relentless repetition of biometric testing, the ways that genetic patterns can be used to police citizens and restrict personal freedoms are underscored and questioned. Vincent's paranoid cleansing both at home and at work reminds us of how the slightest skin flake can betray us in a world dominated by biometrics.

But Vincent's ability to pass becomes a critique of both the technology's deployment and the assumptions that are encoded into them. In this sense, as Stacey has shown, the reliance on informatics to authenticate identity becomes a way to read for the performative nature of constructed identities, especially those of gender and sexuality. In a detailed analysis of Vincent's masquerade and impersonation of Jerome, Stacy shows

> Vincent's genetic disguise makes him the impostor who exposes the more general facade of "authentic" masculinity. It is as much about the repetition of the impossibility of masculinity (as the invincible, autonomous agent of events, as the original and the originator of meaning) as it is about the securing of its authentic form [1862].

However, this form of gender difference might be specified further as both heterosexual and able-bodied. Although Vincent is accepted as Jerome through his canny use of swapping blood and urine, his ability to pass successfully is also linked to the fact his heart and eye defects are *invisible*. Unlike Eugene who is visibly disabled and sits in the hallmark of disability, an ironically old-fashioned wheelchair (Ellis 113), Vincent's disabilities remain unseen and undetected only because he provides the visible signs of an able body. As McRuer points out, compulsory able-bodiedness is revealed in relation to the disabled body in which case it is both Eugene's and Vincent's disabled bodies that reveal the ideological underpinnings of compulsory able-bodiedness and its intersection with white masculinity. Vincent's masculinity remains acceptable precisely to the extent that he is able to pass the various physical fitness regimes that comprise his routines at GATTACA. Should his disabilities be discovered, he will be invalidated as a masculine subject.

Vincent's masculine performances, however, must also be framed within the spectrum of male homosociality that shapes both the space agency GATTACA and the film. As Sedgwick and others have noted, the line between the homosocial and homosexual is one that is actively and often violently policed. In this context, Vincent's ability to pass is unacceptable, a "crime" that cannot be ignored. Following Briggs and Kelber-Kaye's argument that homosexuality is positioned as threat, it is precisely that Vincent, a less-than-perfect masculine subject — an In-valid —*can pass* in the straight world of *GATTACA* that poses the threat to the future. Vincent's real crime is more about his superior performance of the masculine role of astronaut that underscores the lack of visible difference between the homosexual and heterosexual male. Vincent's invisibility is criminal and must be punished in exactly the same way that Tom Hanks' character Andy in the film *Philadelphia* was held to be criminal for being invisible to his lawyer partners in their otherwise straight locker room. Once again the film's ambiguous politics are evident. In its critique of biological determinism, *GATTACA* must perforce suggest that difference in the end does not matter, that the human spirit, for which there is no gene, will not submit to promises of genetic perfection. But, at the same time, Vincent's ability to perform white heterosexual masculinity so flawlessly underscores that, at the core, there is *no difference* between the queer male and the straight one.

Pass 3 —*v.* change (*into, from*) as in from homosexual to heterosexual

GATTACA's preoccupation with passing draws on long lineage of science and science fiction that deals with anxieties about authentic identity and determining what constitutes such identity. With respect to AI discourses, for example, many are familiar with the Turing Test, which gave the parameters that would determining whether/when a machine can "pass" as human. Fewer might be aware that Turing's first tests dealt with how to determine whether a woman could pass as a man. In taking up the third sense of the word "pass," we turn to consider the nature of Vincent's transition from in-valid to valid subject in GATTACA. This early link is allusive since in many ways Vincent's impersonation of Jerome is precisely an attempt to move from an abject feminized position — Stacey notes he occupies the role of 'femme fatale' — to that of normal masculine identity. In short, Vincent can be accepted as a Valid because of the substantial changes he has made to achieve an acceptable physical appearance that allows him to pass as Jerome a straight-acting man.

Because the homosocial production that is Jerome/Vincent stands at the nexus of the homosocial continuum and institutional heterosexuality, his identity must be secured. We come then to the homo heart of the film where Vincent must move from his homo relationship with Eugene to perform Jerome's heterosexual identity in relation to Irene. This central moment of heterosexism is not just to affirm the connections between white masculinity and heterosexuality but also to illustrate precisely how performing a heterosexual act becomes an authenticating action proving heterosexual identity. But here again, Vincent may be construed as simply passing himself off as straight-acting Jerome. Just as one situational act of homosexuality does make one gay, one strategic act of heterosexual sex does not make one straight. In fact, GATTACA's ambiguous ending undercuts any easy assumption that Vincent has "converted" entirely to heterosexuality. After all, Vincent carries a locket into space containing not Irene's hair, but that of Eugene. And it is Eugene who sacrifices his life for Vincent and Eugene who confirms that the heart of their relationship rests in the romantic terms of exchanging a body for another's dreams.

This performance is crucial, for the heterocentric discourses of the film cannot produce a sexually ambiguous hero whose desires might run towards both men (Eugene) and women (Irene). To pass as a man, he must perforce perform sexually and, in so doing, authenticate his masculine identity. Even with his visual disability, he can still miraculously find the woman who will ensure that he passes as Jerome. Unlike Eugene, who barely manages to "get it up" the staircase when required, Vincent overcomes his hidden visual defect and miraculously crosses a busy freeway to join with Irene. The night of sexual pleasure they enjoy of course safely anchors Vincent as securely heterosexual — one night of heterosexual activity being, in institutional heterosexuality, good enough to pass as heterosexual regardless of other desires.

Pass 4 — *v.* proceed; go past

The film's crucial moment occurs in the concluding moments when Vincent awaits final clearance to board the space-bound ship and Eugene prepares to consign himself to the flame , not unlike a widow committing suttee. Revealed as an impostor, Vincent races against time to reach the safety of the launch pad. Much is at stake in this climactic sequence. Ellis excoriates Eugene's decision to cast himself into the fire as a sign of the tragic disabled person for whom there is no hope; others position Eugene as the sad homosexual whose only fate is to die in order to save an unattainable man, while Vincent's success is viewed as representing the triumph of white heterosexual masculinity. These readings are important but they must be held in tension with Vincent's success in leaving behind the world of GATTACA for space. Vincent's successful impersonation and his invisible defects are central to this point since he will continue his impersonation in the heavens above and on earth should he return. At the very least, Vincent's presence on the mission ensures that his disruption of hegemonic white straight masculinity remains active in galactic space. The final moment of Vincent's ascent from Earth is therefore a queer moment, as one might contemplate with exquisite pleasure the spectacle of Vincent going where — according to most SF texts — few queers have gone before.

The caveat to this reading lies in the fact that Vincent's successful departure relies on the doctor's collusion with Vincent's masquerade. It turns out that the flight physician has noticed a fault in Vincent's performance of masculinity: Vincent has been using the wrong hand to urinate. This intimate observation is passed off through the rationale that the doctor identifies with Vincent's struggle since he has an in-valid son, whom he hopes will succeed as has Vincent. The doctor's collaboration with Vincent's ruse underscores how passing requires allies in the dominant group, but also underscores that white masculinity is effectively a performance that is always monitored and accepted by other men. More importantly, though, in a deleted scene, we discover that the doctor is also implicated in the homoerotic exchange of bodily fluids: he drinks Vincent's/Eugene's regular urine samples to ensure they cannot be further tested. Deleted for the purposes of suspense and revelation, this scene creates an even queerer circuit of homosocial knowledge and desire, extending Eugene and Vincent's queer production of Jerome from a duo into a threesome, or even a foursome if we include the doctor's son. The film originally proposes different models of queer kinship, even more radical than what Stacey outlines. Finally, the physician's actions reinforce the point that production of white hetero masculinity is inextricably linked to ability defined through medical knowledge and practices. GATTACA reminds viewers in a severely critical moment (McRuer 96) that ableism is social construct maintained by social practices. Vincent's dis/abled body becomes the homoerotically, queerly produced body that is a reminder that there is no place where difference will not be active. Yes, we're here and queer — and we're going to the moon!

Pass 5 — *v.* move onward

Gay/Straight. Able-bodied/Disabled. Masculine/Feminine. What to make of all these different passings? First, employing a severely critical lens suggests that the multiple ways in which Vincent passes makes it difficult to determine whether the film finally itself passes any litmus test for progressive or reactionary politics. On one hand, *GATTACA* can be read, as it has been here, against the narrative's grain, as a story of queer desire exposing the fault lines of performed identities and a story of queer heroes leaving behind, at last, a suffocating heteronormativity for a more nomadic home among the stars. In one sense this is a fitting end for Vincent, since passing constructs a diasporic identity that is never at home no matter where it is located" (Liera-Schwintenberg 372). On the other hand, Vincent's passing, because relatively unnoticed, has not changed the social structures of *GATTACA*'s projected reality. Other faith-born will do no better because of Vincent and Eugene's struggles and triumphs. Because all traces of their passing have been eliminated, there is no record of their struggle. And so it is with the act of passing itself: for all its transgressive force, the individual who passes still leaves the larger social structures intact, their coercive power only temporarily subverted.

But, there is still something that can be taken from the film. Like other passing bodies, Vincent's body too "passes over and in transit and its transformation is disturbing; it lacks definitive placement and therefore can be misrecognized" (Liera-Schwintenberg 372). In this sense, the fact that Vincent's body can be made to stand for so much means this surplus of significance can be used strategically to imagine a world where heterosexuality might be displaced. The problem of *GATTACA* and other popular texts that attempt to question dominant discourses from within the popular is that they remain mired in the heterocentric discourses that keep science fiction futures on the straight and, alas, narrow. The trick, then, is not to place a text on one side or the other of social change, but rather to find the ambiguous queer spaces that evade such binary thinking.

NOTE

1. For convenience and clarity, "Vincent" refers to Ethan Hawke's character and "Eugene" refers to the name Jude Law takes up when Vincent assumes his identity as Jerome. The latter term, Jerome, is the shared identity.

WORKS CITED

Allen, Garland E. "The Politics of Genetic Determinism: Social and Political Agendas in Genetic Studies of Homosexuality, 1940–1994." In Rosario, 242–270.

Briggs, Laura, and Jodi I. Kelber-Kaye. "There Is No Unauthorized Breeding in Jurassic Park: Gender and the Uses of Genetic." *NWSA Journal* 12.3 (Fall 2000): 92–113.

Ellis, Kathleen. "Reinforcing the Stigma: The Representations of Disability in *GATTACA*." *Australian Screen Education* 31(2002): 111–114.

Dyer, Richard. *The Culture of Queers*. New York: Routledge, 2002.

Franklin, Ursula. *The Real World of Technology*. Rev. ed. Toronto: Anansi, 1999.

GATTACA. Dir. Andrew Niccol. Perf. Ethan Hawke, Jude Law, and Uma Thurman. Sony Pictures, 1997.

George, Susan A. "Not Exactly 'of Woman Born': Procreation and Creation in Recent Science Fiction Films." *Journal of Popular Film and Television*. 24.4 (2001): 177–183.

Hollinger, Veronica. "(Re)reading Queerly: Science Fiction, Feminism and Defamiliarization of Gender." *Science Fiction Studies* 26 (1999): 23–39.

Kirby, David A. "The New Eugenics in Cinema: Genetic Determinism and Gene Therapy in *GATTACA*." *Science Fiction Studies* 27 (2000): 193–215.

Liera-Schwichtenberg, Ramona. "Passing, Or Whiteness on the Edge of Town." *Critical Studies in Media Communication* (September 2000): 371–74.

McRuer, Robert. "Compulsory Able-bodiedness and Queer/Disabled Existence." *Disability Studies: Enabling the Humanities*. Eds. Sharon L. Snyder, Brenda Jo Brueggemann and Rosemary Thompson-Garland. New York: MLA, 2002. 88–99.

Rosario, Vernon A., ed. "Homosexual Bio-Histories: Genetic Nostalgias and the Quest for Paternity" *Science and Homosexualities*. New York: Routledge, 1997. 1–25.

_____. *Science and Homosexualities*. New York: Routledge, 1997.

Squires, Catherine R., and Daniel C. Brouwer. "In/Discernable Bodies: The Politics of Passing in Dominant and Marginal Media." *Critical Studies in Media Communication* 19.3 (September 2002): 283–310.

Stacey, Jackie. "Masculinity, Masquerade, and Genetic Impersonation: *GATTACA's* Queer Visions" *Signs: Journal of Women in Culture and Society* 30.3 (Spring 2005): 1851–1879.

Terry, Jennifer. "The Seductive Power of Science." In Rosario. 271–295.

Tolin, Jonathon. *Twilight of the Golds: A Play in Two Acts*. New York: Samuel French, 1994.

6

The Changing Role of Women in Science Fiction: *Weird Tales*, 1925–1940

Mary Hemmings

Science fiction pulp magazines have long been considered an entertaining pastime that appealed exclusively to male interests. Their covers generally presented adventure, strange machines, bizarre alien creatures and other images designed to attract male readers. Above all, it was the sensational images of women on those covers that created a market for sales. It is difficult to imagine women being involved in the production and consumption of pulps at all, and yet women played an important role as readers, writers, editors and illustrators in the early years of these magazines.[1]

Between the years of 1925–1940, the cultural and social roles of women in society were changed. The interwar years produced flappers, feminist activists, and adventurers such as Amelia Erhardt, (aviator), Dorothea Lange (photographer), and Katherine Hepburn (actress). These women and many others captured the spirit of self-confident accomplishment. By contrast, the 1940s saw a shift, valuing domesticity in preparation for war. Similarly, the history of publishing moved from hard-cover books, giving way to the pulps, then to comic books and paperbacks.

One of the most important and prominent pulp magazines in this period was *Weird Tales*. Its letters-to-the-editors section ("The Aeyrie") provides some understanding of its readers. Contrary to what some researchers claim, its geographical base was broad (Taraba 124). Letters arrived from the United States, Britain, and even from rural towns such as Ponoka, Canada. For the most part, the letters were intelligent and literate. They praised the craftsmanship of the writing, as well as the exciting plots. Each issue contained at least one letter from a woman reader and almost every issue had a story that could be easily identified as having been written by a woman writer. This suggests that women writing for *Weird Tales* in this period did not require male pseudonyms in order to have their articles bought by an influential magazine. But, all considered, it was still the female form on the cover of pulp magazines that attracted sales.

Women as Cover Art Icons

The representation of women in the images of popular culture can be traced to the rise of urban cultural development, and specifically to the rise of consumerism. From the 1890s to the 1920s, the visual images of women were increasingly evident on billboards, posters and book illustrations. Magazines were becoming the currency of popular reading. Textual and cover illustrations became easier and cheaper to produce as high-speed presses could produce photogravure (rather than woodcut illustrations) as well as four-color illustrations for covers (Malnig 37). The iconic "New Woman" for this time was the precursor of the flapper. She was not as exotic as the dancer, Isadora Duncan. She was more Venus than cool Gibson Girl Athena. She was also a working woman, "graceful and smart... clever and judicious, cultured and well-rounded... who could easily grow magnolias... manage the household finances or conduct a tango tea" (Malnig 35).

In the world of science fiction, the iconography has been divided into four neat categories. According to the *Encyclopedia of Science Fiction*, women are objects to be Desired, Feared, Rescued or Destroyed (Clute and Nicholls 1343). *Weird Tales* covers between 1925 and 1940 show that the remnant of the modern, desirable Venus was still existent in the early 1920s. By the late 1920s, in keeping with the new fashion of Orientalism, the ladies became more fashionably "flapper" and in fact somewhat exotic. There are occasional artistic references to themes of Tarzan or King Kong (September 1929). Although the movie *King* Kong was not released until 1933, the jungle motif had been popular since the early century. Rescue and Desire were clearly the dominant motifs.

Woman to be Feared/Destroyed became a more common motif in the

1930s. Occasionally, a figure was depicted that suggested a woman to be reckoned with, or annihilated (October 1933, January 1935). It was not until the later 1940s that the pulps began to feature the Female Alien: an iconographic depiction of what Simone de Beauvoir, in *The Second Sex*, called the Other, in contrast to the normative male voice in culture (Roberts 34).

It is interesting to note that the 1934 Hays Law in the United States, governing morality in the cinema, had no effect on pulp illustrations. In fact, it appears that the covers became racier between 1934 and 1937. Some scholars have dismissed the 1930s as being so entirely sexist and racist that delving into gender politics is not merited (Larbalestier 110). However, once the shock-factor has been acknowledged, the covers show a rather uninhibited cultural expression of values that embraced the exotic side of human experience.

Between 1937 and 1939, women on the covers of *Weird Tales* were becoming more modest, and by 1939 were almost entirely clothed. There are several reasons why this may have happened. First, *Weird Tales* relied less on its most sensational artist, M. Brundage, for its cover art. Second, publishers were faced with growing competition among more pulps. In an attempt to compete in an increasingly specialized market, *Weird Tales* publishers reviewed their policies and decided to return to an original influence: the weird, gothic and strange.

In September 1939, when the cover picture featured Edgar Allan Poe, the price dropped to 15 cents (down from the 1927 price of 25 cents), and frequency dropped to once every two months. The editorial announced a return to the original purpose of the magazine: the publication of truly weird tales. By December 1939, the *Weird Tales* publisher and editor, Farnsworth Wright (ed. 1924–1939), resigned for reasons of poor health. His successor, Dorothy McIlwraith (ed. 1940–1954), continued his editorial shift to "more weird, less science" (Clute and Nicholls 1310).

Throughout the interwar years, the covers reflected current popular cultural trends such as jungle stories, detectives and, by 1940, cowboys. The protagonist on the July 1940 issue featured a "Gone with the Wind" theme shortly after the release of the blockbuster in 1939. The hero bore an uncanny resemblance to Cary Grant. Clearly, editor Dorothy McIlwraith believed he would appeal to women.

Readers were only mildly offended by the near-nudity on the covers of *Weird Tales*. The Aeyrie letters, especially during the mid-1930s, focused on the question of racy covers. Most men liked the art, but they were also concerned that the illustrations should be accurate reflections of featured stories. One male reader from Pennsylvania wrote in the January 1934 issue, "I like the sexy covers, but I will vote against them because they are misleading to those who do not know *Weird Tales*. One must mutilate the magazine before passing it on to his maiden aunt." This suggests that *Weird Tales* was considered good reading, even for spinster gentlewomen. Most readers considered the covers to be a bonus feature of a splendid magazine. Were the illustrations on the inside equally sensational? For the most part, they were not. During the 1930s, the fine ink work of Virgil Finlay dominated the pages, but he did not have the sensational flair of the dominant cover artist, M. Brundage. Whereas the inside illustrations were crafted and technical, the covers were part of the marketing package and meant to attract non-subscribers.

Artists: The Case of M. Brundage (1900–1976)

By far, the most prolific and the most sensational cover art for *Weird Tales* was attributed to M. Brundage. *Weird Tales* readers in 1933 and 1934 wrote to The Aeyrie page, commenting and debating on the artistic merits of the graphics. Controversies raged and ebbed, but the editors declined to specify what the "M" in "M. Brundage" stood for. It was not until February 1935 that the editors began to print the full name: Margaret Brundage.

Brundage was the first woman artist to work in science fiction and the first artist whose work featured nudes (Clute and Nicholls 165). She was a Chicago housewife who worked exclusively in pastel chalk. Brundage was editor and art director of her Chicago high-school paper and attended the Chicago Academy of Fine Art with Walt Disney. Coincidentally, she and Disney also attended the same high school, but Disney never received his diploma. Brundage was married in 1927, divorced by the late 1930s, and had one son. She was hired by the publisher of *Weird Tales*, Farnsworth Wright, to illustrate the magazine *Oriental Tales/Magic Carpet*, and began doing cover art for *Weird Tales* in 1932. She produced 39 consecutive covers for the pulp from June 1933 to November 1936. In total, she produced 66, and received ninety dollars for each.

Personally, she considered the September 1933 issue of *Weird Tales* the most risqué.[2] Asked to describe her methodology, she explained that she would receive the assigned story and would be asked by the editor to submit three sketches of a particular scene. She then produced a pastel on sandy paper twice the size of the cover in the span of one week. She would hand-deliver her work to the magazine's Chicago offices. For her models, Brundage relied on a personal library of clippings, her imagination, an occasional female friend, as well as her "deadbeat" husband for the male hero. Although noted for her abilities with the female form and her use of background and color, Brundage has been criticized for her shortcomings in depicting male heroes and threatening characters (Taraba 126).

Not all covers reflected a story contained within the covers of an issue. The December 1933 issue, for example, depicted a theme of "universality." Asked to render her interpretation of the "universality" of *Weird Tales* stories, Brundage provided a blonde damsel in pink frills, a zodiac, and a Confucian scholar. Despite occasional complaints in The Aeyrie, she was never asked to alter or cover up the (semi) nudes. On one occasion, she was asked by the editor to increase breast size on a female form, but she refused because she believed that this would create unrealistic proportions (Everts). Brundage particularly liked illustrating the works of "Conan" creator, Robert Howard, and was deeply affected by his suicide in June 1936 (Taraba 125).

By 1938, *Weird Tales* was sold and the offices moved from Chicago to New York. Although it seems that Wright was perfectly willing to accept Brundage's work, her pastels smudged in postal transit to New York, and the one-week turnaround was no longer possible due to communication distances. Her cover art was eventually replaced by the work of Virgil Finlay. He had been the primary sketch illustrator for the text of the magazine, and although his work was technically superior to that of Brundage, he lacked her exuberance. Only one other woman artist, Ruth Bellew, was able to sustain a career illustrating pulps. She is noted for her work in the 1940s, producing map back-cover diagrams for Dell's Dashiell Hammett books.

Women Writers and Their Stories

Some of the earliest science fiction written by women includes: Margaret Cavendish, *The Blazing World* (1666); Mary Shelley, *Frankenstein* (1818) and *The Last Man* (1826); Jane Webb Loudon, *The Mummy* (1827); Mary Griffith, *Three Hundred Years Hence* (1836); Mary Bradley Lane, *Mizora: A Prophecy* (1880); Charlotte Perkins Gilman, *Herland* (1915); and Thea von Harbou, *Metropolis* (1926). Harbou had been a German actress and was married to Fritz Lang, whom she divorced in 1933, and who produced the landmark film of *Metropolis*. In 1928, Virginia Woolf wrote *Orlando*. The titular character lives 400 bender-bending years, beginning as a man in the Elizabethan era, ending as a woman at the end of World War I.

One impression that some scholars foster is that there were few engaging or original female protagonists before the 1970s, since Woolf's *Orlando* was creative and interesting but not widely known. *The Encyclopedia of Science Fiction* refers to the popular stereotypes: Virgins, Amazon Queens, Spinster Scientists, Good Wives and Tomboy Kid Sisters (Clute and Nicholls 1310). While these stereotypes did abound, it is also true that male protagonists tended to be equally as flat and stereotypical, since authors were busy churning stories for pennies a page.

One woman wrote to *Weird Tales* commenting on a Seabury Quinn tale ("Washington Story," August 1939). She noted that it was a timely piece of propaganda painting a moral story. The tale was about a very capable woman who had risen in social station from a variety of menial jobs, and was now a socialist pushing a liberal agenda in Washington. The female protagonist did not fit any of Clute's popular stereotype categories, nor was the reader commenting on gender. The issue, in this case, was over political allegiance.

With the rise of the pulps, women continued to write speculative fiction. By the 1920s, the more specific term "science fiction" had been coined by Hugo Gernsback, founder and editor of *Amazing Stories* (who also coined the clumsier "scientifiction"). Gernsback had once written, "As a rule, women do not make good scientifiction writers because their education and general tendencies in scientific matters are usually limited" (qtd. in Donawerth 39). Still, the appropriation of the word "science" did not prevent women writers from writing good fiction through the following decades. Although few women originally wrote SF for pulps such as *Amazing Stories* and *Wonder Stories*, women writers like Bassett Morgan and C.L. Moore still featured prominently in the speculative fiction of *Weird Tales* (Taraba 124). Other noted writers such as Leslie F. Stone began publishing fiction for *Air Wonder Stories*. Stone's other works, "Men with Wings" and "Women with Wings," are seen as prime examples of early satire of the masculine movement of Nazism based on its virile ideology of procreation (Weinbaum 301). Her stories deal with racial themes and are a conscious answer to the social concerns of the regeneration of Europe after WW I. In the two tales, set during the rise of the Weimar republic, a race of women lose their wings when they are subordinated to a race of winged men. Another gender-conscious work of the period was 1935's *Woman Alive*, by Susan Ertz. A British writer, she produced only one science fiction novel about a gender-specific plague that wipes out all women, save for one, by 1985. The ending is disappointing: the heroine becomes the Queen of England and marries the male protagonist.

The following is a rough and partial "catalogue" of names determined to be those of women writers for *Weird Tales* (Jaffery and Cook):

- Meredith Davis — "The Accusing Voice," Mar 1923
- F. Georgia (George? per index) Stroup — "The Horse of Death," Mar 1923
- Myrtle Levy Gaylord — "The Wish," Apr 1923
- Mollie Frank Ellis — "Case No. 27," May 1923
- Helen Rowe Henze — "The Escape," June 1923
- Isabel Walker — "Black Cunijer," July-Aug 1923
- Valma Clark — "The Two Men Who Murdered Each Other," July-Aug 1923
- Nadia Lavrova — "The Talisman," Sept 1923
- Mary Elizabeth Counselman — "The Black Stone Statue," Dec 1937; "Parasite Mansion," Jan 1945; "The Lens," Nov 1947; "A Death Crown for Mr. Hapworthy," May 1948; "The Bonan of Baladewa," Jan 1949; "The Shot-Tower Ghost," Sept 1949; "The Green Window," Nov 1949; "The Tree's Wife," Mar 1950; "Something Old," Nov 1950; "Rapport," Sept 1951; "Ani-Yunwiga" (poem), Fall 1990
- Ellis, Sophie Wenzel — "The Dwellers in the House," June 1933
- Heald, Hazel — "The Horror in the Museum," July 1933 (with H.P. Lovecraft); "Winged Death," Mar 1934 (with H.P. Lovecraft); "Out of the Eons," Apr 1935 (with H.P. Lovecraft); "The Horror in the Burying-Ground," May 1937 (with H.P. Lovecraft)
- Edith Lichty Stewart — "The Sixth Tree," Feb 1934
- Florence Crow(e) — "The Nightmare Road," Mar 1934
- Greye La Spina — "The Tortoise-Shell Cat," Nov 1924; "The Remorse of Professor Panebianco," Jan 1925; "Fettered (Part 1)," July 1926; "Fettered (Part 2)," Aug 1926; "Fettered (Conclusion)," Sept 1926; "A Suitor from the Shades," June 1927; "The Portal to Power (Part 1)," Oct 1930; "The Portal to Power (Part 2)," Nov 1930; "The Portal to Power (Part 3)," Dec 1930; "The Portal to Power (Concl.)," Jan 1931; "The Devil's Pool," June 1932; "The Sinister Painting," Sept 1934; "The Rat Master," Mar 1942; "The Great Pan is Here," Nov 1943; "The Antimacassar," May 1949; "Old Mr. Wiley," Mar 1951

It has often been noted that women writers effectively abandoned science fiction writing in the 1950s and 1960s only to re-emerge as a significant force in the 1970s (Laz 56). This may have been a reaction to Gernsback's pronouncement that women did not know enough about the "science" of good "scientifiction." What is clear, particularly up until the 1940s, is that women were very capable of writing the "literature of cognitive estrangement" (Laz 56). By taking the familiar status quo, and twisting it, creating "what if" scenarios, women pulp writers continued to contribute to a rich and diverse genre.

Readers

The Aeyrie letters-to-the-editor section of *Weird Tales* during the years 1925–1940 illustrates not only the geographical appeal of this magazine, but also the wide readership and diversity of opinion. Letters from women readers appeared in almost every issue. In the February 1926 issue, Mrs. Lila Le Clair of Templeton, Massachusetts gushed "every page was a thriller, and such chills of delighted horror ... give us more blood-curdling ghost stories, and keep the magazine as it is, for it surely is crackerjack."

Greye La Spina, a *Weird Tales* writer herself, wrote to say that the December 1925 issue was the best, and that Seabury Quinn's story was "corking" because the author had managed to make the monster seem logical. And Sylvia Bennett of Detroit complained in the Oct 1933 issue about Robert E. Howard's stories: "I am becoming weary of his continuous butchery and slaughter."

Conclusion

In 1995, one science fiction researcher concluded that "Women have not been important as characters in science fiction. Women have not been important as fans of science fiction. Women have not been important as writers of science fiction" (Badami 6). This premise is extreme, even if "science" was appropriated as an exclusively masculine interest by Gernsback in the 1920s. Rather, the period 1925 to 1940 reflected a time of transition. It was a time when pulp magazines became products of mass consumption, and when women and their roles in society became visually prominent. It was a time when women demonstrably continued as successful writers of speculative fiction and as active participants in publishing.

NOTES

1. The contents pages and covers of *Weird Tales* are freely available through the online resources of the Miskatonic University Department of Library Science. Miskatonic is a web site devoted to speculative fiction. <http://yankeeclassic.com/miska tonic>.

2. The Bob Gibson Collection of Speculative Fiction, at the University of Calgary, does not have this issue. Nor does it have either the Canadian or American cover of the September 1935 issue depicting variations in national tastes in women. The Bob Gibson Collection does have the Canadian November 1935 edition and cover. The heroine's frontal nudity is discreetly covered by an advertisement announcing a "Magazine of the Bizarre and the Unusual" for 25¢.

WORKS CITED

Badami, Mary Kenny. "A Feminist Critique of Science Fiction." *Extrapolation* 38.1 (1995): 6–19.

Burleson, Donald R. "On Mary Elizabeth Counselman's 'Twister.'" *Studies in Weird Fiction* 15 (1994): 16–18.

Clute, John, and Peter Nicholls. *The Encyclopedia of Science Fiction*. London: Orbit, 1999.

Contento, William G. *Index to Science Fiction Anthologies and Collections, Combined Edition*. 29 October 2005. 13 June 2006. <http://users.evl.net/~homeville/isfac/0start.htm#TOC>.

Donawerth, Jane. "Teaching Science Fiction by Women." *The English Journal* 79.3 (1990): 39–46.

Everts, R. Alain. "Margaret Brundage: An Interview." *Weird Tales* website. 29 April 2006. <http://members.aol.com/weirdtales/brundage.htm>.

A Guide to Feminist Science Fiction Resources in Print and on the Net: Bibliographies and Indexes. Feminist Science Fiction, Fantasy and Utopia. 13 June 2006. <http://www.feministsf.org/femsf/crit/whipple/rg.bib.html>.

Jaffery, Sheldon R., and Fred Cook. *The Collector's Index to Weird Tales*. Bowling Green, Ohio: Bowling Green University Press, 1985.

Larbalestier, Justine. *The Battle of the Sexes in Science Fiction*. Middletown, CT: Wesleyan University Press, 2002.

Laz, Cheryl. "Science Fiction and Introductory Sociology: The 'Handmaid' in the Classroom." *Teaching Sociology* 21.1 (1996): 54–63.

Malnig, Lulie. "Athena Meets Venus: Visions of Women in Social Dance in the Teens and Early 1920s." *Dance Research Journal* 31.2 (1999): 34–62.

Roberts, Robin. "The Female Alien: Pulp Science Fiction's Legacy to Feminists." *Journal of Popular Culture* 21.2 (1987): 33–52.

Taraba, Frederic B. "The Weird Tales of Margaret Brundage." *Step-by-Step Graphics* 11.5 (1995): 118–29.

Weinbaum, Batya. "Leslie F. Stone's "Men with Wings' and Women with Wings': A Woman's View of War Between the Wars." *Extrapolation* 39.4 (1998): 299–313.

7

Storytelling and Folktales:
A Graphic Exploration
Gail de Vos

There is an emergent awareness of the strong correlation between the art of storytelling and the visual technique of comic book format. This is particularly apparent in the reworkings of traditional folktales in various graphic formats, and also the depiction of actual storytelling events in comic books and graphic novels. The focus of this paper is a brief appraisal of that correlation as represented in three contemporary titles of science fiction comic books: "Hob's Leviathan" from Neil Gaiman's *Sandman* series, the recent story arc of "Echo's Story" from David Mack's *Daredevil*, and "The Corpse," a Hellboy tale by Mike Mignola.[1]

One crucial aspect of storytelling is its use of the audience to help develop visual detail, to fulfill and co-create the story. Direct interaction between teller and audience is an essential element of the storytelling experience. One of the powers of oral storytelling is that storytelling audiences do not passively receive a story from a teller, as a viewer receives and records the content of a television program or motion picture, but actively create their own images based on the performer's telling and the audience's own experiences and beliefs. Thus every story is an individual experience. Oral storytelling is, by its nature, personal, interpretive, and uniquely human: it passes on the essence of who we are and is an intrinsic and basic form of human communication.

Both the told tale and the comic book depend on dialogue and tone of voice, body language and gesture, and timing for an effective experience for the audience. Both of these storytelling forms require the audience to actively participate in the understanding of the story. Comic books use panels and the turning of pages to add pauses and to elicit drama much in the same way as a storyteller uses pacing and silence: to arouse interest and intensify emotional responses to the story. The listening audience must decode the words and silences of the teller, the body language and the voice, to make its own images of the characters, stage and action come alive. The comic-book reading audience must speculate on what happens in the gutters, as well as read the visual cues to interpret the story and "hear" the dialogue according to the prompts. In both, the experience and background of the reader/listener not only enriches the story but also individualizes it.

In comics, the story is told visually but employs the oral storyteller's toolkit of sound, gesture/body language, timing and mythic stereotypes or archetypes. In comics, the sound is revealed by how the words are presented in sound balloons for the "actor" to say out loud (or to him or herself). Clues in the font and the shape of the sound balloons indicate the pitch, volume, and rate of speech of the dialogue. Further clues to the sound as well as the character traits embodied by the characters are illustrated by the facial expressions and non-verbal body cues. Timing, an essential ingredient of oral storytelling embodied by the effective use of the pause, is exemplified in comics by the number of panels on each page, the shape and layout of the panels on the individual pages, and the actual turning of the page to continue the reading. The use of stereotypes, in both oral storytelling and in the comic book format, assists in the immediate transmission of information about the characters or setting without having to furnish a great amount of detail. Everyone knows what a beautiful princess looks and acts like — right?

Sandman: "Hob's Leviathan"

For the purpose of this essay, we will focus attention on the young storyteller, Jim. His storytelling event begins with a simple request: "Call me Jim." In the panel, the storyteller's face is highlighted, with a strong focus on his eyes. Jim, as most effective storytellers must do, establishes the setting of his tale to make it relevant to his listening audience. This setting is established in three narrative boxes in one panel where the panel's illustration is that of the inn where the storytelling is taking place, not of the story location. The storyteller is still in the process of getting the audience interested in the listening of the tale. When the reader turns the page, she finds Jim still conversing with audience, establishing a connection to *his* tale, *his* setting and the truth of *his* story: "It's true as ever I'm sitting here."

The telling of an oral tale is usually immediately proceeded by an opening: a brief encounter between the teller and the audience that takes the audience out of the real world and into the world of the story. It is an important element of a storytelling occasion, and this is what is being illustrated here. Jim is getting his audience's focus out of the inn and into the setting of his tale.

The reader sees four regular panels topped by a close-up of the teller's eyes. The eyes seem focused inwardly as Jim moves back to his past. The setting of tale has now been established and the main character has been introduced (the storyteller him/herself). The story deliberately does not have any mention of gender in either the words or the illustrations although a strong hint is given when Jim says he "dressed in old clothes I'd begged and borrowed from friends." He has already let us know his mother is not wealthy; old clothes should have been readily available for him on his adventure.

The turning of the page initiates the telling of the body of the story, Jim's voyage on the *Sea Witch*. The reader follows the story of his experiences on ship until page ten, when he introduces an embedded tale told by the stowaway found on board. This tale begins with a traditional beginning "Once there was a king..." and the reader is first shown a close-up of the teller and a finger pointing to the audience of two.

The embedded tale is told over three pages, all organized with the same four-panel pattern, framed as a flashback. Each page has a different animal at its center — an elephant, snake and tiger — reflecting the setting, atmosphere and tone of each page. The reader turns the page, out of the embedded tale and into the moment of Jim's story once again. Jim tells of how the conversation among his three main characters resumes, to assess the truthfulness of the embedded story and one of its themes: the unfaithfulness of women. Here, once again, Jim's reaction to his own characters' discussion is a giveaway to the listener/reader. The embedded story is not touched upon again, but the reader is now in possession of some vital pieces of information gathered by understanding the silences, the interaction of the characters and the symbolism depicted in the illustrations.

Jim's story about his adventures continues on for another ten pages until the final turn of the page and we once again look upon the face of the storyteller. He ends his story by repeating a remark made by his mentor in the story, Hob. Hob talks about the fact that they may tell stories about what has happened but "no one'll believe either one of us." Jim looks at his audience, back in the present once again, and restating the truth of the tale, completes the circle of the story with the same phrase as he began his telling: "You can call me Jim."

The shape of "Hob's Leviathan" corresponds to the story structure of an oral tale. The storyteller and the story told within the story use many of the techniques of oral storytelling already discussed. There is an emphasis on the face and eyes of the teller of both tales told in this story. Storytelling is theater of the face, something the illustrator understood very well in this example. The final comment of the story, echoing the opening of Jim's tale, completes the circle of the opening and closing of an oral tale.

Daredevil: Echo's Story

Our next example also focuses on the storyteller, but not on the telling of the tale as in the above instance. This recent story arc, presented in five issues of the regular *Daredevil* comic book series, has been either panned as boring or praised by readers as extremely innovative. As in our other examples, there are many layers to Echo's story. One of the most obvious is the intentional irony in the naming of the character. The original, mythical, Echo loved the sound of her own voice, which is what led to her particular punishment by Hera.

David Mack's paintings and page arrangements are conducive to this type of introspection by a character who is telling herself (and the reading audience) her personal story. Unlike Jim, who relates his experience in linear fashion with an embedded story, Echo gathers in memories, experiences and emotions to discover something about herself through her own story. It is however, someone else's story and the telling of it that places everything in perspective for her as a person. Stories are powerful but the listener can only take what is available to them at that particular time of the listening — based on their experiences, understanding and needs. Echo has known this story before — but it doesn't have power until she heeds it again, when she is ready to "hear."

In the first issue of the five-issue story, Echo is talking about her father and his experiences storytelling with her as a deaf child. She introduces the reader to her father, his (and her) Native heritage and his relationship with her and one of the elders on the rez, the shaman/storyteller. In the third installment, Echo returns to the Rez to talk to the shaman/storyteller. He is familiar with her artistic work and tells her she has become a storyteller just as he had once told her she would be. She needs further reassurance and so goes on a vision quest. During her vision quest, Echo sees numerous animals, but it is a meeting with Wolverine that coagulates her thoughts and stories. Wolverine, from *X-Men* fame, eventually sits down to discuss the vision quest with her. When asked what she has seen, she tells him of "two dogs fighting." It reminds her of something, but she cannot remember what. Wolverine thoughtfully responds: "The chief told me a story called 'Two dogs fighting.'" He then tells her that the tale helped him a great deal. She asks him to tell her the story.

The final issue begins with Wolverine's telling of the tale and the importance of it to his life, and concludes with Echo presenting her own understanding of story, which emphasizes modern heroes and updated mythic tropes, and the perpetual re-writing of mythology in the acts of everyday life. Throughout the story arc, creator David Mack is paying homage and recognition to the power of story, the necessity of understanding just what story is, and the importance of the telling regardless of medium.

Hellboy: "The Corpse"

Unlike the two examples already discussed, Mike Mignola's *Hellboy* incorporates a traditional folktale into its narrative universe. While there are numerous examples of the reworking of folktales in comic book format, Hellboy is particularly interesting for several reasons, not the least being the recent movie and accompanying hype. Mignola has continuous references to folklore motifs and tales throughout the entire series, and these references and reworkings embrace folklore from all parts of the globe. "The Corpse" is an almost flawless reworking of the traditional Irish tale, "Teig O'Kane."

The splash page contains an excerpt from the poem "The Fairies" by William Alligham, placing the subsequent story in context. Upon turning the page, the reader is introduced to the crisis of a changeling invading the household of a family in Ireland. This changeling presents the reason for

Hellboy to appear in the story. The rather weak traditional protagonist will not do for a hero of a *Hellboy* tale!

Mignola aptly demonstrates knowledge of the folklore of the changeling: the throwing of the changeling into the fire, the threat of iron, and the immediate change in character and appearance when discovered. Hellboy's mission is to recover the child that the changeling replaced from the land of the Faery folk. Mignola continues to utilize folklore motifs such as the crossroads at midnight, three wee men and a corpse tree. While the changeling no longer figures in the text, he continual appears in the illustrations to remind us that he is not about to accept defeat graciously.

It is not until the seventh page of this story that we actually move into the traditional tale. Mignola sets the scene, providing a reason for the need to bury the corpse (it was never offered in the traditional tale) and giving the corpse the same name and traits as the main character in the traditional tale. With a turn of the page, Hellboy, and the reader, are entirely immersed in the Irish tale, and other than the appearance of the changeling in the illustrations, the story now mirrors the story structure of the traditional tale. There are, however, several divergent elements in Hellboy's journey through the traditional tale, perhaps to bulk up the story, but also to build suspense and foster fear that the necessary burial of the corpse will not take place in time. In the traditional tale, the main character experiences the fear. Here, however, we have Hellboy, a character who is not afraid of walking about with a corpse hanging onto him. So the fear must be externalized: the tension arises from the possibility of failure to accomplish the deed in time and, thus, failure to rescue the child from the wee folk.

Hellboy faces monsters and witches, and must deal with missing body parts (all folklore motifs). Needless to say, he buries the corpse with moments to spare, ending the traditional tale. He then moves out of the traditional tale, and back to his modern world with the rescue of a child. This rescue, symbolized by Hellboy's journey out of the dark and into the daylight, acts as a closing for the story. It completes the circle created by the opening of the story: the crisis of the changeling is no more.

All three of these examples explore the power of story, storytelling and traditional motifs and tales. They use story, personal and traditional, to further the understanding of a specific character and the connection of that character to his or her society and background. More importantly, story is used to connect the character to the audience who, in both the oral telling and the reading of the comic book format, is receiving the tale actively and individually. There is a strong correlation between the ritual of oral storytelling and that of reading graphic novel, whether the stories are personal and particular or drawn from the world of folklore, or — in some cases — both at once.

NOTE

1. This tale has been republished as an individual comic book and is available, at the time of writing, online at <http://www.playboy.com/darkhorse/the_corpse/index.html>.

WORKS CITED

Gaiman, Neil, Michael Zulli, and Dick Giordano. "Hob's Leviathan." *The Sandman: World's End*. New York: D.C. Comics, 1994.
Mack, David. "Echo — Vision Quest." *Daredevil Vol. 8*. New York: Marvel, 2004.
McCoy, Paul Brian. Review of *Daredevil # 54*. *Line of Fire Reviews*. 28 June 2006. <http://www.silverbulletcomicbooks.com/reviews/106975819640203. print.htm>.
Mignola, Mike. "The Corpse." *Hellboy: The Chained Coffin and Others*. Milwaukee: Dark Horse Comics, 1998.

8

The Graphic Novel as New Testament: On Narrative Progress, Cultural Change, and the Heroic Story

Richard Harrison

Start with the obvious: the graphic novel represents progress in the art of the North American heroic comic book. Question the obvious: what is meant by "progress in the art"? Keep going: what is meant by "progress" at all?

Try to answer: one necessary element of progress is increased possibility. The graphic novel expands the sequential artist's universe in terms of subject matter, length of treatment, range of language and situation. It reaches beyond its ancestral comic-book description (and hence restriction) as "a story for children" to create where pure-text literature has been creating relatively freely for a long time.

The readership has expanded, and so has its patience. Authors and artists of 10 to 20-page mainstream or underground comics, or single-strip or panel satires have been able to explore 100-page narratives. The graphic novel possesses the luxury of what might be called "literary time." The readership is willing to savor the pause, the part in the story where the author looks around, and, through a character's eyes, says, "This is the world, piece by piece."

But evil also increases possibility. More happens, it is said, in war than in peace when the ordinary rules are suspended and all sorts of crimes fall open to nations and common folk alike. So there has to be a defensible notion of good contained within a defensible notion of progress. If the graphic novel is progress for comics, it has to be so because it achieves a good not achieved within the history of the form in which is has so far been practiced. This is not to say that there is or must be a morally good element in every story, but that in marking a *progressive* shift in the *form* of story-telling itself, the graphic novel offers us a case study of the way in which the judgment that an art form has progressed is structured along moral lines.

What is fascinating — and what makes this investigation more complex — is that while religious, political and philosophical leaders in the West make explicit laws and arguments based on interpretations of the Bible, the Old and New Testaments themselves do not express most of their moral code explicitly or philosophically. Rather, the Testaments use a multitude of stories drawn together under a larger narrative. As a whole, the Bible sets out both a moral code and the form in which that moral code is to be communicated — the story. In doing so, it follows both earlier traditions (in both related and unrelated cultures) and predicts later practice.

It does so because the moral *code* within the Bible itself— if we take that code as a set of commands about what is and is not to done for the good of all — is incomplete, and admittedly so. No one who only knew the 10 Commandments and the "Golden Rule" could be said to understand the whole of biblical morality: the over-arcing narrative and individual stories within it — of David, Abraham and Isaac, Moses, Christ, the Apostles — fill in the gaps where there are no moral injunctions expressed either as rules or law. The story does more than just tell its readers what or what not to do. Through the aesthetic experience of the story, the reader is open to the reality where moral decisions are made. It is one thing to say "do this" — or to know that "this is what should be done" — and quite another to engage with the lived-in world, determine which code truly applies, look both into oneself and into the eyes of the other and find the right action that morality demands and with which one can live. In the way in which the aesthetic experience of any art object refers not only to the questions of its beauty, but to its ability to engage the reader in the next best thing to having the bodily experience itself, the story that conveys a moral *is* the aesthetic experience of that morality.

That notion of the incompleteness of the code-book is not restricted to the Bible — or a criticism of it. It is to the credit of the wisdom of the Bible-makers that the Book is not reduced to consistency or the pretense of an exhaustive code. While many have attempted to create such exhaustive lists — indeed it might be said that the ambition at the heart of any beginning moral code is a complete and self-consistent list of moral rules and principles — as well as their proof— in the end, such lists collapse, and stories emerge. This explains why Plato's *Republic* turns away from nine books' worth of demonstration of the superiority of good over evil, and, after banning those poets who lead people astray, is content to end itself with myth. Or why Marx, in *Theses on Feuerbach*, attacks materialism (though the attack weighs against all philosophy) on the grounds that "the thing, reality, sensuousness, is conceived only in the form of the object of contemplation, but not as sensuous human activity, praxis, not subjectively" (qtd. in Rosen).

Morality, then, is only truly communicated through those things that bring to life in the mind the sensuousness of lived experience. For the Bible — as for so many key moral texts and bodies of myth — morality is a form of story, and story a form of morality. Moral development is not restricted to intellectual or intuitive capacities alone; it is to be found in and through the sensibility cultivated by art. Yet art is not static; even as it guides and changes the lives of those it reaches, it is changed by its creators. Though the Bible is represented as The Word of an eternal spirit, the narrative of the Bible changes in its storytelling form as its own moral argument evolves. The tension between the God of the Old Testament and the God of the New is often used to criticize the Bible for its inconsistency. This paper, though, argues that that very change is what allows the Bible both to represent moral life and to be part of social change. The short version of this paper's point, then, is that the shift from Old Testament to New is the *pattern* of progress in the Western World — in story-telling, if not in other aspects of our lives — and that pattern is re-created in the shift from comic book to graphic novel.

Begin with the Old Testament: Superman, while not the first of his kind, or even always the most popular, is the paradigmatic superhero with "powers and abilities far beyond those of mortal men" — and mortal machines as well. Perhaps paradoxically, Superman's dominance of the machine asserts the continued promise of the dominance of the human being, of human flesh, over whatever technology can devise. Superman's powers arise from the mingling of the specialness of his birth and adopted planets, combined with the accidents that place him in the hands of those good folks from Middle America who shape his character and purpose. Superman is not a hero because of his powers, but because he dedicates those powers to the good. Pretty well all superhero origin stories follow this path — with the accidents that create and shape them, as in the story of Job, often putting them through their own and personal hells. But redemption of the character is gained, even after a fall, like Samson's, in the rededication of the hero to his essential good nature.

From the 1930s on, superheroes, like the long-lived (Noah), super-strong (Samson), or intellectually and strategically gifted (David) heroes of the Old Testament *physically* fulfilled their audience's wishes and needs — whether those wishes and needs are thought of in psychological or political terms, or, as feminist arguments have now made clear, as an inseparable mixture of the two. All such characters demonstrate the equation found in most ancient storytelling — not that might makes right, but that the righteous will be made the mighty. Even when Plato unpacks this equation in *The Republic*, it is shown that evil, no matter how powerful in the world it might seem, ultimately falls to the good because evil is *self*-destructive. Evil powers within individuals, like thieves fighting over loot, will inevitably work against them and cause their undoing. Only good motives are capable of producing unity of action and purpose; hence the good will endure; good, lacking the weaknesses of evil, is inevitably the mightier of the two. Back in the legend, only Herakles' goodness, mightily tested, puts his superhuman powers in harmony with his happiness, with his social role as hero — the protector of others — and with the good graces and will of the gods.

The stories of such superheroic figures satisfy our deep need to see justice done before the eyes of transgressing characters and readers alike. The tradition of superhuman characters is a rich metaphorical vocabulary in both aural and visual terms through which the reader can escape the normal and often wounded world and return to it comforted, and sometimes, cloaked in our own version of Superman's cape, emboldened. No wonder we love such figures and the stories that bring them to us.

So why move from them? One obvious answer is that such stories fail, to coin a phrase, the "test of exteriority"— there is neither Superman nor Hercules, nor anyone like them in the real world. But that failure, notably, is only obvious to *us*, and only for the characters we saw someone make up; it is for *us* that a world where Hercules exists is impossible, and for us that Hercules' only form of return is through movies or comic books. We are committed to a faith in a realism grounded in reason and the proper use of the senses. For the ancients — as Eliade tells us in *The Myth of Eternal Return*—and for those living today who, as Charles Montgomery writes in *The Last Heathen*, remain true to the way of thinking consistent with the oral traditions of the past, Herculeses of all kinds are observed and encountered. Stories of them are true because *they are* real.

Yet those cultures are not ours; neither can we return to them. However much superheroic stories serve their functions for us, though, we know that they are fictions to which, by and large, only children offer up their belief and subsequent emotional engagement. We are weaned from these stories as we grow and realize that no Superman comes to save us from the terrors of grown-up life or the fall of the towers. In many senses, too, no matter how escapist or distant from the real world their stories are, our superheroes suffer from our world. Since the turn of the century, most of the characters in both Marvel and DC comics have become decidedly *less* able to change the course of events in their own worlds, and ply their trades under the shadow of threats, most recently, terrorist ones, which they can battle but not defeat.

But while social change or trauma can lead to the rise or decline in the particular types of stories that a people tells, it is the problem of the super-powers themselves that offers the *interior* reason for the shift from Old Testament to New, comic book to graphic novel, a change that, in turn, at least in the biblical context, contributes to social change itself.

The problem — and ultimate failure — of superhuman heroes is that their powers must be *constrained* by their goodness. This means that structurally, power is opposed to good. Power is temptation, power is the easy transition from desire to fact, power is what Satan lays down between Jesus and His God in the wilderness, and reaching lustfully for power (using power to build power) is what the gods punish when they strike Bellerophon from the back of Pegasus and stones from the backs of stones in the Tower of Babel. If power made us saintly, or immune from the consequences of our actions, Peter Parker would never have to learn that with great power comes great responsibility: as much as power might let a character do good work, the first good work must be against power.

The New Testament changes the Bible. Godly power is replaced by Christly powerlessness. The story of the powerless becomes the story of those closest to the good, even as they are beset by the power of others. The Jesus myth begins as many heroic myths do — a special birth, a display of youthful and inexplicable superhuman powers — but it is exactly at the point when The Savior, hero of heroes (in whose body lies the defeat of all the evil powers around him), is stripped of his powers and fallen that the heroic story of the New Testament renounces its parents and precedents.

Yet in that renunciation, the superhero becomes one of us — not a metaphorical representation of something in us or some part of us, but us, whole, in our mortal and helpless state before death and time and the evils that others do. In the story of the Son of Man (the epithet by which Jesus is known most of the time He is mentioned in the New Testament), the very powers that separate the hero from the good are put aside. In that putting aside of power, the Christ story puts aside, if only for a moment, the distinction that the old heroic stories make between the audience and the subject of the tale.

A novel imagines a world in which its characters undergo the changes in their lives. The novel's world, like ours, is closed, its characters trapped, as we are, between beginning and end. Superheroes do not do well there. When they go there, in one sense they die. Or if not die, bring at least one of the endless narratives of their immortal lives to a close. In *Kingdom Come*, Alex Ross — the painter who gave us versions of superheroes whose costumes do *not* look as if they are painted on — brings the DC Universe to an end completely consistent with the logic of power: superheroes in conflict with their own offspring (the super-powered results of their own existence) while the rest of the world looks on and trusts that its machines (the bomb) will make things right. It is a conflict that can only be resolved by Captain Marvel, the sole figure in the group who is both superhero and child, god and human.

Once it puts aside the superheroic, and all the distance between the superheroic and us, the graphic novel takes up the cause of the weak and the helpless. It understands and tackles the world as *adults* know it, the world full of injustice and ugliness, bad ends and bad endings. Yet still it uses the visual and textual vocabulary of the superheroic to divine ("divine" with all its possible meanings), the lives of characters who could be us. Gone is the necessity for costume and super-powers, though such things, like Christ's small miracles, still appear if the story demands them. As stories, the graphic novel stands to the comic book as the New Testament does to the Old. Each, graphic novel and New Testament, contains fragments of the stories that preceded it, but for each those fragments are fables — stories that do not have to be understood as true to be profound and meaningful. And each, graphic novel and New Testament, becomes what we might call the fiction of real life — a story acknowledged believed by some to represent the truth, and even by those who do not believe as the story of what *might have been*.

And yes, on a literary level, in terms of the art form itself, this is the kind of change we want to call expansive and progressive. By their leotards, the superheroes have been pulled into a form that demands they confront the world that created them as fantasies and is no longer satisfied with the purely fantastic. Conversely, the vocabulary of a form that, like television and film harnesses the vivid color and words-on-the-fly feeling of a child's dream, has been used to speak of the Holocaust, of fundamentalist repression in Iran, of the siege of Sarajevo, and of the downtroddenness of American urban loss.

But I would be remiss if I did not sound one sad and personal note, for every progressive step leaves something behind, something that seems nostalgic to want at the time, but may be the sense of the loss of something good. Mourning the loss of the pen to the computer is not just mourning a writing implement; it is mourning the old-style intimacy between hand and letter. The graphic novel's emphasis on main characters that are not visually or politically different from the surrounding cast or readership, and the graphic novel's popularity, have created a kind of Graphic Novel Effect as the comic-for-kids has aspired to become a serialized Graphic Novel. Just as an example, at random I picked up the two last issues of a three-part *Iron Man* series called *The Best Defense* (2004). In those two issues, pictures of Tony Stark outnumber pictures of Iron Man approximately three to one. In the story, Tony Stark, it seems, is going to give up his Iron Man identity to serve as Secretary of Defense to George W. Bush (one of the few other characters in the story who appears in panels on his own). Thus the Iron Man technology is coming to the US military as a whole in its fight, of course, against burnoose-clad terrorists (who still, it should be noted, jump out in front of US military personnel and shout "Die, American!" before they fire). Compare that ratio to Captain America's "retirement" story from *Tales of Suspense,* number 95 (1967) in which the ratio of pictures of Steve Rogers to those of Captain America in a story deliberately focusing on the man within the hero is only about one-and-a-half to one. In the accompanying Iron Man story in that book, a more usual "hero vs. villain" battle piece, pictures of the character as hero and pictures of the character in his secret, civilian identity are roughly equal.

In the most recent issue of the *Avengers,* Henry Pym (the size-changing superhero who began as Ant Man, became Giant Man, then Goliath, then Yellowjacket, then just Dr. Pym and now seems to be whatever name suits his size) not only never appears in costume, but is both nude and the size of The Sands Hotel for five panels spread over three pages of story — and why not? He becomes a giant; his Dockers do not. In this issue, Janet van Dyne appears in her Wasp costume compared to appearing in street clothes — or naked — in the previously seen one to three ratio. Henry Pym is only in costume for one of the 57 pictures of the character in the book. This issue opens with a scene of Henry and Janet enjoying a night of super-powered sex in Vegas. I am happy for them. I am glad to see sexual love portrayed positively, but on one level I note that the scene requires — or has to assume — a very sexually well-educated audience in order to be understood. And since the old fables require a darkness that equals the light, the comic moves to a scene in which the supervillain, Whirlwind, who has stalked Janet since the seventies, dresses up a prostitute as the Wasp, pummels, then murders her in order to pump himself up for the real battle ahead. I have not yet got an answer to what I find disturbing in this consequence to the increased sophistication in the form: perhaps at this point I can only note that just as the New Testament, once believed, justifies the claim that the Old, once enough, has become an *incomplete* portrait of the faith, so the Graphic Novel tests the faith of those like Jack Kirby and Julius Schwartz who told their stories within more innocent confines, and those who, like me, read them and are fulfilled.

But the graphic novel exists because its creators are committed to their art's ability to tell any story that needs to be told. It is flourishing now because just as the audience for oral, super-human stories of gods and God and humankind were ready for the democratization of power through the New Testament story, so the readership of the super-heroic comic universe understood the limitation of the superheroic story and looked to find something closer to God and themselves within a form that had always given them both morality and a great story strikingly told at once.

WORKS CITED

Eliade, Mercea. *Cosmos and History: The Myth of Eternal Return.* Trans. Willard R. Trask. New York: Harper, 1959.

Johns, Geoff, and Steve Sadowski, "Whirlwinds." *The Avengers* 3.71. New York: Marvel, November 2003.

Lee, Stan, and Gene Colan. "The Invincible Iron Man: If a Man Be Stone." *Tales of Suspense* 1.95. New York: Marvel, November 1967.

Lee, Stan, and Jack Kirby. "Captain America: A Time to Die — A Time to Live." *Tales of Suspense* 1.95. New York: Marvel, November 1967.

Miller, John Jackson, and Jorge Lucas. "Logistics." *The Invincible Iron Man: The Best Defense, Part 2.* 3.74. New York: Marvel, January 2004.

Miller, John Jackson, and Jorge Lucas. "Technology." *The Invincible Iron Man: The Best Defense, Part 3.* 3.75. New York: Marvel, February 2004.

Montgomery, Charles. *The Last Heathen: Encounters with Ghosts and Ancestors in Melanesia.* Vancouver: Douglas and MacIntyre, 2004.

Plato. *Republic.* Trans. G.M.A. Grube. Indianapolis: Hackett. 1986.

Rosen, Michael. "Marx, Karl." *Routledge Encyclopedia of Philosophy.* Ed. E. Craig. London: Routledge. 18 May 2006. <http://www.rep.routledge.com/article/DC051 SECT5>.

Waid, Mark, and Alex Ross, with Todd Klein. *Kingdom Come.* New York: DC Comics, 1997.

9

Science Fiction, Religion, and Social Change

Steven Engler

Science fiction and social change are integrally connected. The central role of scientific and technological developments, with their many potential blessings and curses, makes this obvious. This essay explores a subtler link between SF and social change. It suggests that this link rests on the fact that SF is itself fundamentally religious.

Of course, all this depends on how we define our terms. In defining "religion," it is important not to ask, "What have typical religions always looked like?" This would be misleading, if only because the place of religion in the modern world has changed (as works of SF often note). It would be ridiculous to suggest that SF looks like, for example, Christianity or Hinduism. It is not ridiculous to define religion in terms of the *functions* it has traditionally performed in societies around the world. A focus on what religion does, not on what it looks like, is more useful for comparing certain things (like Methodist or Roman Catholic Christianity) to other things (like fundamentalisms, Marxism, or professional sports). We can ask if these things do what religions do, for individuals and for societies. In this light, we can consider the possibility that SF, as a literary and media genre, *acts like* religion in certain very specific ways. In some ways, it tells a similar sort of story: about what it means to be a human being; about human limitations (e.g., ignorance, suffering, disease, and death); and about ways to transcend those limits.

Looking at Religion

In general, religion links individuals to that which transcends them; but the meanings of both "individual" and "transcendence" have changed over the last few hundred years. Science today plays an important role in linking individuals to a new sort of beyond. SF gives us a front-row seat for this new variation on that old-time theme. Focusing on points where scientific and religious themes converge or overlap reveals common concerns. Looked at in this light, SF is characterized by a distinctly modern sense of "religion": it explores links between short-term individual agency and long-term social and cosmic order.[1]

Religion generally appears in SF in the form of a specific religion, usually Christianity. Common motifs include *doctrinal themes* (e.g., Creation, Fall, salvation, redemption, prophecy, Apocalypse, Millennial utopia), *sacred times and rituals* (e.g., holidays, prayers, blessings, commemorations, offerings, marriages, funerals, conversion, initiation), *sacred spaces and artifacts* (e.g., temples, churches, shrines, relics, crosses, religious clothing), and *institutional forms* (e.g., priesthood, papacy, church hierarchy, charismatic leadership, sectarian and utopian communities, monastic groups). Unfortunately for those concerned with religion in its global context, this means that the religion in SF is almost exclusively Christianity or something modeled on it.

The academic discipline of Religious Studies suggests a different approach, one that focuses on religion in general, not on religions in particular. This approach asks what religions have in common, i.e., what justifies our applying the one label, "religion," to so many different things? A religious view of religion generally holds that one religion is true and all others false. A religious studies view looks for common features among religions, without asserting the truth or falsehood of any set of beliefs. For example, some religious studies scholars hold that all religions offer different views on the same sacred reality. Others argue that all religions are attempts to reassure ourselves in the face of existential anxieties, or that all religions reflect evolved human cognitive characteristics, or that all religions are false ideologies that prop up capitalist systems, or that all religions are a disguised means by which people worship society itself.

The most important thing to note here is that talk about "religion" does not necessarily try to capture the essence of what people experience as their religion. These religious studies approaches attempt to describe aspects of religion, selected perspectives that help us make some sense of what religion does for individuals and societies. Although some would claim that there is one correct theory of religion, it makes more sense to limit our claims to partial understanding. After all, even after all our theorizing about religion, it remains a lively possibility that one of the many religions (or sub-religions) of the world might be True, and that religious faith, not religious studies, might offer the only path to that Truth. However, even granted this possibility, there remains a role for those who try to ask questions about what religion *does* in the world, what its *functions* are, and whether other aspects of human cultures and societies perform similar functions. This essay takes such an approach.

In discussing relations between SF and religion, it is useful to emphasize social functions of religion. According to one view of this sort, "religion," in part, refers to beliefs, practices, and institutions that mediate between individual human activity and long-term social and cosmic order. This claim is neither the truth of religion nor the whole of it. Nor does it necessarily fit with people's common understanding of the term. (After all, Christians will tend to see religion in whatever resembles Christianity, and many language and cultures have no word or concept for religion as a separate sphere of life at all.) But this approach casts valuable light on relations between SF and religion, even if that light is partial.

The focus here is limited, then, to one of the key functions of religion. One of the things that religion has traditionally done is persuade human beings that our actions in our lifetimes, whether ethical or self-interested, contribute to (or undermine) an order that outlasts us. In medieval Europe, for example, God was the guarantor of this order, and human activity was directed and constrained by Christianity. However, in much of the modern world, beliefs like individualism, practices like market exchange, and institutions like the global economic system perform the same function of linking short-term agency and long-term order. This approach to thinking about religion seems especially relevant given a set of prominent themes in SF. Of course, no single feature captures all of the genre's complexities, but SF very often deals with the impacts — intended or unintended, ethical or unethical, utopian or apocalyptic — of technique and technologies, seen as extensions of human agency. To say that SF is religious, in this sense, is merely to point out that SF performs in our society one of the many functions that religions have traditionally performed in the past.

Seeing Beyond Black-and-White

A useful first step toward a broader understanding of religion's place in SF is to look at relations between science and religion more generally. Over the last century and a half, this relation has been commonly, though misleadingly, portrayed as one of contrast and conflict (Peterson). In a black-and-white view, religion and science are often portrayed as opposed in a wide variety of ways. For example, while science in its knowledge mode is often perceived as rational, material, literal and objective, religion in its knowledge mode is often seen as irrational, spiritual, metaphorical and subjective; while science is often understood as descriptive, impersonal, innovative, egalitarian, modern, and future-oriented, religion is often construed as ethical, personal, authoritative, traditional, conservative, and past-oriented.

Views of religion in SF sometimes reflect the assumptions of this limited, black-and-white contrast, in which religion is the Other of science. Above all, "Religion is repeatedly depicted as dangerous, diverting humans (and aliens) from the path of reason and true enlightenment" (Mendlesohn 269). Examples from SF works illustrate a variety of these sorts of stark contrasts between mutually conflicting worldviews:

• Religion is Irrational: "Why did she believe in [the afterlife]? She was a scientist, a rationalist, a logical thinker. But, of course, her religious indoctrination had occurred long before she'd been trained in biology" (Sawyer 277).

• Religion is Concerned with the Immaterial: B'Elanna Torres: "Do you believe in an afterlife?" Chakotay: "I accept that there are things in the universe that can't be scanned with a tricorder." ... B'Elanna Torres: "My whole life I've immersed myself in science and schematics, but what if it's time to start looking beyond that?" ("Barge" Star Trek).

• Religion is Dysfunctional: "'This Snow Crash thing — is it a virus, a drug, or a religion?' Juanita shrugs. 'What's the difference?'" (Stephenson 200).

• Religion is Escape: "The Church of the Trust ... merely offered another form of escape from the realities of life; more socially acceptable than smuggling or drug addiction, but just as ritualized and habit-forming. Neither alternative offered real change...." (Hinz 260).

• Religion is Untrue: "Who needs the ritual of religion when we have the far superior ritual of science to replace it? Religion is a reasonable substitute for knowledge. But there is no longer any need for substitutes....

Science offers a sounder basis on which to formulate systems of thought and ethics" (Moorcock 114).

- Religion Tries to Explain What Science Cannot: "Man is so built that he cannot imagine his own death. This leads to endless invention of religions. ... Science hasn't solved [the resulting questions] and who am I to sneer at religion for trying?" (Heinlein *Stranger* 337).

Beyond this black-and-white contrast between religion and science fiction is a complex picture, in which science and religion can reverse roles. Examples of this more nuanced view can be found even alongside the black-and-white view, in works by these same authors. Sometimes, religion in SF looks like science. For example, religion is portrayed as the source and medium of a virus, the "Babel/infocalypse" of Neal Stephenson's *Snow Crash*; but this has the effect of scientizing religion, of reducing it to ways of thinking and causal relations. Religion also looks like science in a number of works, especially where it takes the form of transcendent forces that are treated instrumentally as spiritual technologies, e.g., magic in Robert A. Heinlein's *Magic, Inc.* or psionic powers in Julian May's four-volume *Saga of the Exiles.*

Sometimes, on the other hand, science in SF looks like religion. Science is sometimes portrayed as so far advanced that it seems like magic, as in Arthur C. Clarke's *Childhood's End*, where Clarke illustrates his well-known and oft-repeated dictum that "any sufficiently advanced technology is indistinguishable from magic." In other cases, future humans use technologies beyond their comprehension to act like gods, as in Roger Zelazny's *Lord of Light*. In a sort of limit case, humanity moves out into the galaxy to find that science and religion converge on ultimate transcendence: e.g., the Prime Monitor in Gentry Lee and Arthur C. Clarke's *Rama* series; and the "applied theology" that deals with Powers in the Transcend beyond the Beyond in Vernor Vinge's *A Fire upon the Deep*. In these and other works, scientific knowledge reveals transcendence. Other examples illustrate these sorts of convergence between religion and science:

- Scientific Knowledge is a Transcendent End in Itself: "He was among the high-status Labs, the temples of Hardscience. Beside him was the ever-lighted alcove holding the sacred tape of Mission Requirements in its helium seal.... Into these Laboratories flowed all the data ... fit to be fed finally into the holy of holies, the Main Computer" (Tiptree 454).
- Science and Technology Offer Life After Death: "Only a rare mind can continue after losing its body.... Rimbaut sleeps now in Eternity Hall ...

like so many others, waiting for some advance of technology to bring his consciousness, memories, and emotions together again" (Barnes 12) .

• Science and Technology Recast the End-Times as Material Progress: "Be my guest! I'll sell you the ... [digitally stored minds and cloned bodies] of the dead and the [evolved post-human] demons who could raise them. Go ahead! Have another crack at immanentizing the eschaton [i.e., realizing the end of the world]!" (MacLeod 241).

This convergence between science and religion in SF leads us beyond superficial contrasts, beyond black-and-white views as science as rational and religion as irrational, etc. It raises the question of what science and religion have in common. Two further parallels suggest that the issues of social order and change are central to the commonality. In the first place, religion and science are often portrayed as ambivalent in terms of their relationship to ethical and social values. In *A Door into Ocean* and *Daughter of Elysium*, by the Quaker biologist Joan Slonczewski, the beliefs and practices of the raft-dwelling Sharers are the ethical conscience that science lacks; yet the Sharers' power to impose their values rests on their own scientific knowledge: their science of life trumps the Elysians' more materialistic science.

In the second place, religion and science are often portrayed as ambivalent in terms of their relationship to social change. On the one hand, in Walter M. Miller, Jr.'s *A Canticle for Leibowitz*, for example, religion is a conservative institution that preserves social stasis, and science is a force of sudden, cataclysmic change. Similarly, in other works, religion is an impediment to scientific progress: e.g., in Kingsley Amis' alternative-history, *The Alteration*, and in Christopher Hinz's *Liege-Killer*. However, other works portray religion as a more ambivalent agent of change. The world of Frank Herbert's *Dune* series is framed by two religious wars: the anti-technological Butlerian jihad that results in social stasis and the religious jihad fueled by Paul Muad'Dib's prophetic leadership that results in social discontinuity. George Lucas' *Star Wars* series also illustrates both sides, as the Jedi-ascetics use both material technologies and the transcendent Force to support social stability under the Republic but to foment revolution under the Empire.

These similarities or areas of overlap between science and religion can be interpreted in several ways. In part, SF and religion both lead us to think beyond current realities: as Brian Aldiss notes, "Religion is an integral part of the SF vision. Directly we look to the future or to mankind in the mass, we have a pararational situation on our hands" (qtd. in Ryan 11). More specifically, both SF and religion express expectations for alternative worlds and futures:

> SF establishes ... a fantasy world which literally transgresses the boundaries of everyday existence..., constructing a world of different structures of meaning, based on the future or an alternative environment.... [This] exploration of the possible and the imagined automatically bring[s] SF closer to religious spheres of meaning, which likewise thematise and define another world" [Mörth 89].

This raises the question of how such alternatives are brought about: how do we get from here to there?

Reading SF Religiously

This question, in turn, leads to relations between agency and order, casting light on portrayals of religious agency in SF: "often ... in science fiction, little distinction is made between the concept of God as he would have to be defined to be worthy of the name, and an architect, who may perform any number of secondary tasks in a cosmological model" (Zebrowski 13). Technical agency in SF takes on religious characteristics (keeping in mind that "religious" refers here not to the essence of religion but to one of its key functions).

When science and religion in SF run on parallel tracks, it tends to be because each links the actions of individuals to the maintenance or alteration of long-term social structures and institutions. The convergence of science and religion in SF links technique and technology to social order and change, either directly or by addressing society's material conditions. This raises another important point: the flip side of social change is social stability. Neither of these states should be taken for granted; neither is natural; both require intense human effort to bring about.

The theme of relations between agency and order is a defining characteristic not just of SF but of modernity: it is a big part of what makes the modern world "modern." To see this we need to let go of the common misperception that religion has been dying out with the increasing prominence of science over the last century. Many writers on religion suggest that secularization — the erosion and marginalization of religion in the modern world — reflects not the weakening of religion but its diffusion throughout society. From this perspective, religion is not dead; it now props up society indirectly from within, rather than directly from above.

One way to see this point is to compare a classic religious connection between short-term agency and long-term order to a modern scientized version of this same connection. Every society has a story to explain the relationship between the limited actions that individuals can perform during their short and fragile lives and the creation and maintenance of long-term social and cosmic structures (Bloch). One story is that gods do most of the work and humans contribute by orienting their lives to the gods. The "modern" story is that most of the universe is furniture, and the rest takes shape as humans each do their own thing, with the cumulative impact of their actions guided by science, technology, bureaucracy, and the invisible hand of economic markets. This second story is a story of optimism that human activity is the engine of progress, the source of social order and change, and this view plays the role that religion has always played: linking agency to order, expressing faith that our lives make sense against the structures that transcend them. This latter view of religion highlights precisely those aspects of SF in which religion and science converge, and this view relates SF to broader social and intellectual tendencies in the modern world.

If we follow writers who look at religion in this way, then many aspects of SF are inherently religious; that is, they link agency to order. (Again, this is not all there is to say about religion. This just isolates one of its traditional functions, and notes that SF is one of the places where we find a similar function performed today.) This link between agency and order is found in the themes set out above: where religion is brought under the umbrella of science as a form of technology; where human society progresses along the path of science to achieve transcendence; where the extended agency made possible by science and technology both reflects and shapes basic social and ecological values; or where activity under the banners of both science and religion plays a fundamental role in social order and change.

This link also appears in SF's common modes of address. Works in the genre tend to presume a certain sort of reader with interests in these themes (e.g., the impact of human action, especially as extended by new technologies, and the changing faces of social and cosmic order) and with background knowledge appropriate to following this assisted leap from local action to global impact. Prominent among the many responses that the texts expect from readers is the wonder of contemplating dramatic new connections, for better or worse, between individual human actions and the social, cultural, environmental, and cosmic structures that frame our lives.

To sum up, if we define "religion" in terms of similarity to the things we are familiar with that go by that name (e.g., Christianity or Buddhism), then SF often *contains* religion. But SF's appeal to this sense of "religion" is often out of date. Religion has changed in the modern world. It has become diffused and now links agency and order in many spheres of society, not just in the sphere traditionally called religion. If, on the other hand, we see religion in terms of the functions it has performed in many societies, then SF is, in this limited sense, itself religious: it is fundamentally concerned with this same linkage between human action and social and cosmic order. Depending on what one reads, SF both affirms and denies the possibility of social change; it sees such change as both good and bad. Either way, it places central emphasis on the effects that individual human agency — mediated by science and technology — can have on long-term social structures and institutions. In other words, for the same reasons that traditional "religions" are playing reduced roles in the modern, scientific and technological world, SF has stepped in to help perform one of the key roles that has traditionally been assigned to religion.

NOTE

1. "Agency" refers to the nature, conditions and limitations of human action. "Agency" makes more sense than "action" in this context, given SF's focus on the possibilities of human activity and the ways that technology can extend them.

WORKS CITED

Amis, Kingsley. 1976. *The Alteration*. London: Triad/Panther, 1978.
Barnes, John. 1992. *A Million Open Doors*. New York: Tor, 1993.
Bloch, Maurice. *Prey into Hunter: The Politics of Religious Experience*. Cambridge: Cambridge University Press, 1992.
Clarke, Arthur C. *Childhood's End*. 1953. New York: Ballantine, 1974.
_____. "Technology and the Future." *Report on Planet Three and Other Speculations*. 1967. New York: Signet, 1973.
Heinlein, Robert A. *Stranger in a Strange Land*. 1961. New York: Berkley, 1968.
Heinlein, Robert A. *Waldo & Magic, Inc.* 1940. New York: New American Library, 1970.
Herbert, Frank. *Dune*. 1965. New York: Berkley, 1980.
Hinz, Christopher. *Liege-Killer*. New York: Tor, 1987.
Lee, Gentry [and Arthur C. Clarke]. *Rama Revealed: The Ultimate Encounter*. New York: Bantam, 1994.
MacLeod, Ken. *The Stone Canal*. New York: Tor, 1996.

May, Julian. *The Saga of the Exiles.* 4 vols. [*The Many-Coloured Land, The Golden Torc, The Non-born King, The Adversary*] London: Pan, 1982–84.

Mendlesohn, Farah. "Religion and Science Fiction." *The Cambridge Companion to Science Fiction.* Eds. Edward James and Farah Mendlesohn. Cambridge: Cambridge University Press, 2003. 264–75.

Miller, Jr., Walter M. *A Canticle for Leibowitz.* Philadelphia and New York: J.B. Lippincott, 1959.

Moorcock, Michael. "Behold the Man." *The New Awareness: Religion through Science Fiction.* 1972. Eds. Patricia Warrick and Martin H. Greenberg. New York: Delacorte Press, 1975. 47–121.

Mörth, Ingo. "Elements of Religious Meaning in Science Fiction Literature." *Social Compass* 34.1 (1987): 87–108.

Peterson, Gregory R. "Going Public: Science-and-Religion at a Crossroads." *Zygon* 35.1 (2000): 13–24.

Ryan, Alan. Introduction. *Perpetual Light.* Ed. Alan Ryan. New York: Warner, 1982. 11–13.

Sawyer, Robert J. *Hominids.* New York: Tor, 2003.

Slonczewski, Joan. *Daughter of Elysium.* New York: Avon, 1993.

_____. *Door into Ocean.* New York: Avon, 1986.

"Barge of the Dead." *Star Trek Voyager.* Episode No. 223. Teleplay by Bryan Fuller. Story by Ron Moore and Bryan Fuller. 6 October 1999.

Stephenson, Neal. *Snow Crash.* New York: Bantam, 1993.

Tiptree Jr., James [Alice Sheldon]. "And I Have Come Upon This Place by Lost Ways." *The New Awareness: Religion through Science Fiction.* 1972. Eds. Patricia Warrick and Martin H. Greenberg. New York: Delacorte, 1975. 447–77.

Vinge, Vernor. *A Fire upon the Deep.* New York: Tor, 1992.

Zebrowski, George, "Whatever Gods There Be: Space-Time and Deity in Science Fiction." *Strange Gods.* Ed. Roger Elwood. New York: Pocket, 1974. 9–18.

Zelazny, Roger. *Lord of Light.* 1967. New York: Avon, 1976.

10

Science and Science Fiction
Todd C. Nickle

How does "real world" science influence science fiction? Certainly, extrapolating storylines into the future involves a certain amount of conjecture as to new developments that impact upon the human condition. SF writer Robert J. Sawyer once noted that there is something special about the genre of SF that allows exploration not possible through other forms or settings of stories. But Sawyer also mused that — due to the exponentially accelerated pace of technological advancement — SF might soon be useful only a social commentary. Ray Kurzweil's book, *The Singularity Is Near*, investigates the impact of technology on biology. It begins with a survey that supports the idea that the increasing pace of technological change will cause a "technological singularity," which is defined as a rate of technological change that is so rapid that humanity will be completely transformed (7). The singularity can be displayed as a graph where the rate of change approaches infinity. Can it be true that a singularity from scientific progress will restrict the validity of the kinds of scenarios worth exploring through SF? Extrapolating future events from past experience suggests this is the case. But we must remember the multitude of past events that have been ignored, particularly technological dead-ends or redirections: picking and choosing technological milestones does not make for robust prediction.

The ever-increasing progress of science does show up as a steady acceleration of the pace of discoveries. Depending on how one measures it, the curve of progress heads towards a vertical asymptote — a condition which essentially ends the ability to predict new technologies and their use. If Kurzweil is correct, is it true that the anticipation of new scientific discoveries through SF will be devalued because of the integration of so many cheap and affordable technologies? Will we see Vernor Vinge's technological singularity around 2020? Will we be able to change our DNA? Will we someday alter physics?

Consider the history of the field of DNA: if one were to plot the pace of progress, one would find an approximation of the Vingean Singularity. Bright, curious minds such as those of Pauling, Watson, Crick, and a host of other biologists and chemists were drawn to the concept of a chemical establishing form, function, flesh, bone, and even personality. To them, the end-point of knowing the chemical structure of DNA might represent a point very close to some kind of technological asymptote. Indeed, the mere structure of DNA suggests how it is used by the cell. The structure also hints at methods for how it is made, which is of particular interest because of the high fidelity with which this must occur, lest mutations render the information useless. Spontaneous self-assembly and reliable records of information both can contribute to technological advances.

From determining the structure of DNA, though, science has moved to new questions, such as how other biological machinery interprets DNA. Experiments have propelled us along the technological progress curve and we now view microscopic particles such as ribosomes as similar to the robots found on an assembly line making cars in Detroit. We are now exploring the concept of nanotechnology, and therefore have created a new discipline for scientists to explore. This shift in scientific direction means we have to make choices. Do we pursue nanotechnology? What about the remaining questions about the genetic code? Either of these questions provides fodder for science to take on radically new challenges, with each pushing the asymptote further into the future. New understanding reveals new limitations, which hold back cries from the scientific community of "Eureka! Our work is done." We cannot pursue both exhaustive understanding of the genetic code and the construction of molecular machines simultaneously due to limited resources, including both financial and intellectual capital, which must be carefully allocated to the task.

Consider the genetic code for the moment, and think of the technological implications and solutions the discovery implied. What did the scientists who determined DNA structure envision as the singularity of interpreting genetic information? They knew that the most sophisticated molecule in living cells is that of protein, and that DNA has the role of dictating protein assembly. The "big story" was then thought to be the exact mechanism by which DNA encodes protein information. Once this mechanism was worked out, and the so-called "codon table" was determined so that protein construction was understood, popular press essentially reported that the work of geneticists was done, and that the rest would be mere details.

However, any molecular biologist will say that, as in most scientific endeavors, every new answer spawns more questions. Each question pushes that singularity further into the future. Recently, a phenomenon known as RNA interference is modifying our understanding of genetics substantially, and is outdating traditional views of how the genetic code is used by cells. It was thought that the secret of how DNA dictates form and function could be unlocked by using a top-down approach, looking at the entire DNA sequence that makes up the human genome.

When first conceived, the utility of knowing the human genome was mostly speculation. Pioneers in this area were using manual techniques to determine the order of nucleotides — the As, Gs, Ts, and Cs from which DNA is made. Ordering tens of millions of these four "letters" is tedious. It was thought that the drudgery of this work could be picked up by a mindless machine. Automation of the techniques was thought to be beyond the near reaches of engineering. However, convergence of biochemical techniques, robotics, and computer-processor speed resulted in output of 1000 nucleotides per second. In fact, the singularity of instantaneous information dissemination worldwide was being approached: these data were streamed out live through the Internet. That we could perform these feats and use them in this fashion would have been very hard to predict, even by imaginative SF enthusiasts.

The human genome project has given us a parts list of what it takes to make one person. The most complete human genome sequence available to scientists is that of the president of a private sequencing facility: Craig Venter of Celera Genomics. Perhaps it is because we are approaching a DNA sequencing singularity — that is, the convergence of computing power, robotics, and biological background — that it was Dr. Venter's own dog, Shadow, who claimed primacy over the most complete canine genome sequence available to scientists. The selection of Shadow is a deep well of controversy — there is no particular genetic distinction of this poodle that would merit such scrutiny of his DNA. Perhaps in this instance, SF would indeed have its best opportunity as an agent of social commentary. Having a genomic sequence has now spawned the new disciplines of "bioinformatics," the analysis of so-called "interactomes," and ethicists have seen their range of study topics expand substantially. The approach towards one conceived singularity has fragmented into directions leading to separate potential singularities, if not a repositioning of the next milestone further into the future.

The movie *GATTACA* is a masterful example of how modern society might be influenced if we were able to read and analyze a person's genetic makeup with high accuracy, if we were such a technological singularity. In fact, geneticists in the film are able to apply corrections to the genetic code when a person is in an early enough stage of development. Changing the DNA in all of the trillions of cells in a full-grown individual will probably be forever beyond our capacity, although we might soon see the practice of "gene therapy" being as useful to people with a variety of genetic diseases, as insulin is valuable to diabetics. Maybe some day, treatments will be created that make the "afflicted" and "normal" indistinguishable, but the cost in money and effort will likely cause us to settle for "good enough." The friction created by decisions over the cost of improved treatments gives SF speculators hot sociological dilemmas to consider.

Now, again consider the nanotechnology field that Genetics has helped inform. Is the engineering singularity — the ability to create any kind of machine at any kind of scale — one that will alleviate the "problem" of being diagnosed with "bad DNA"? Should "bad" DNA be "corrected"? Assume that nanomachines could be created, with the help of rapid technological advances, to fix genetic problems. How would we power such an army of molecular surgeons? Michael Crichton's book, *Prey*, posits an army of nanomachines that function together. The novel uses artistic license so that each soldier in that army coordinates and "learns" using only incident radiation as its power source. But the laws of thermodynamics are inviolate. Each soldier in that army would require energy to perform work, to move to the locations where it needed to be deployed. The army would need to be directed not as a collection of individuals, but as a coordinated unit. It might take the energy equivalent to powering a small town to organize billions of units in this manner.

Since each molecular machine would be powered, the numbers needed for trillions of corrections, not to mention the coordination to ensure work is not repeated, would be phenomenal. This cost would need to be paid, and energy is not cheap. We are running out of the cheapest forms of energy, and even as we bring down the cost of alternative forms, our demand increases. Hydrogen fuel sources are a poor second choice to petroleum, but the media pretends that hydrogen will eventually produce a solution. We will see a "hydrogen economy" at some point, but only due to necessity, not preference. We have a much longer path to freedom from petroleum than the general public realizes.

What of mastering and then controlling the laws of physics? Quantum physics and String Theory provide a theoretical framework that might allow us to understand our universe better. We all experience gravity and yet we really do not know anything about it. Einstein's analogy of a "rubber sheet" serving as "the cosmic fabric" is a neat tool for visualizing heavenly bodies, but it serves only as a way to predict *how* they react and tells us nothing of *why*. We have observed subatomic particles called "tachyons" that travel faster than light (a finding which turns contemporary physics on its head). Other particles seem to stop in time, while others seemingly move *backward* in time. It is unlikely we will soon — if ever — hitch a vehicle and sidestep the restraints imposed upon us by our physical world. Should we be able to do so, the cost in energy will likely put a halt to our plans. Carbon dioxide and water are low-energy products of the combustion engine. They result from freeing the energy locked up in high-energy reactants such as oxygen and hydrocarbons. We will never use water and CO_2 to power our cars. Instead, we will search for and find some other high-energy molecules to combust until we run out of them. There is no reason to think the laws of physics will change or that we will side-step them sufficiently to provide unlimited, cheap energy.

Humankind long ago reached the moon using the computing power equivalent of a Commodore VIC-20. This kind of computing power can now be worn on the wrist, and can be given away to children in fast-food promotions. Though the computing was state-of-the-art at the time, we can now build far more complex systems for a trivial amount of capital. Why, then, have we not ventured to other worlds since? We are clearly at a technological level that makes moon travel possible. So why do we not travel to the moon? It is a matter of diminishing returns: we *could* afford the energy to boost the spacecraft, but we choose not to. Even if a country decided to take on the task, it would have to convince its taxpayers to pay for recruitment, testing, design, manufacture, and countless other expenses required to put footsteps outside of Earth. This convincing would, again, require an investment of money and power, making the venture that much more difficult. Techno-resistance due to diminishing returns will forever defer any realization of a technological singularity.

Asimov's short story "The Martian Way" is similar to Heinlein's *The Moon is a Harsh Mistress,* because both deal with how groups handle looming and life-threatening resource shortages. Although technology in the two novels is so advanced that interplanetary travel is commonplace, the simple scarcity of water has the fullest impact on human life. It is likely that no matter how technologically advanced we become, solutions that merely invoke the "next generation of toys" will not suddenly save the day. We are still ruled by the laws of physics, which include a conservation of mass and energy.

Formal studies that map technological progress as being a logarithmic progression are interesting, but not a valid tool for prediction. It is true that we can use a variety of methods to plot accomplishments, but all are, at best, "postdictions." We are ordering, then plotting, what has already been accomplished. Truly, the pace at which new gadgets emerge is staggering, but we are *still* dealing with dead batteries. Untold prototypes molder on shelves because the power sources outweigh the machines' utility. How many new avenues remain unexplored because of obstacles that remain unsolved? There is no denying new abilities are constantly being invoked through technological advances, but we are still chasing our tails looking for a way to revamp our transit system. It is possible that in twenty-five years, North Americans will live their entire lives without ever having exceeded sixty miles per hour on freeways, simply because solar and hydrogen power cannot meet these challenges. We will have better uses for petroleum power than to waste it on cars. People will have a great quality of life, but social priorities will shift: people will have pinker lungs and will revel in marathons and hiking as methods of entertainment. The point is that we will not breech the laws of thermodynamics: it is *society* that will have to adapt to technology. Our demands must accommodate what we can afford. We will select what is available, and we will improve our selections based on the availability of our resources. The unexplored potentialities that would be available to us if there were unlimited, lightweight power will never be enjoyed, and will never be plotted on a graph. There will be no singularity.

Progress marches on in numerous technological fields, but not to one particular intersection. For a growing tree or coral, destinations for the tips of the new branches to reach extend outward. Some tips may meet and interact, forming exciting patterns. Like a crystal polymerizing on a microscope slide, directions of scientific investigation can fork into separate lines. These may meet and create unexpected and exquisite formations — new, unexpected disciplines. For reasons of energy cost alone, a technological singularity that precludes SF as a showcase for new innovations and predictions, that confines SF to the role of social commentary, is unlikely.

WORKS CITED

Asimov, Isaac. "The Martian Way." *Isaac Asimov Presents the Great SF Stories #14.* 1952. Ed. Isaac Asimov and Martin Greenberg. New York: Daw, 1986. 243–88.

Crichton, Michael. *Prey.* New York: HarperCollins, 2002.

GATTACA. Dir. Andrew Niccol. Perf. Ethan Hawke, Jude Law, and Uma Thurman. DVD. Sony Pictures, 1997.

Heinlein, Robert. *The Moon Is a Harsh Mistress.* New York: Tor, 1966.

Kurzweil, Ray. *The Singularity Is Near: When Humans Transcend Biology.* New York: Viking, 2005.

Sawyer, Robert J. "Reflections on Science Fiction and Social Change." Plenary Address at FutureVisions 6.0: SF and Social Change. Mount Royal College, Calgary, Canada. February 2004.

Vinge, Vernor. "The Coming Technological Singularity." *Acceleration Studies Foundation.* 1993. 1 June 2006. <http://accelerating.org/articles/comingtechsingular ity.html>.

11

Olaf Stapledon's
Americanized Planet
Robert Boschman

In the more than seven decades since Olaf Stapledon's *Last and First Men* (1930) initially appeared, he has been rightly credited as a fascinating and influential master of the deep future narrative. *LAFM* looks two thousand million years into the future of humanity. Its narrator is one of the "last men" or eighteenth version of the "extremely variable" (284) hominid family, of which we readers are the primitive first. Speaking to us from the endgame of humanity on the planet Neptune, Stapledon's detached philosophical narrator recounts the evolution of the human organism through many distinct mutations, mutations that include, finally, the ability to communicate backward through time from the distant future.

Since 1930, readers of Stapledon have appreciated his cosmic narrative in which the protagonist is humanity itself. We have been entranced by his convincing imaginative projections — like his flying men and women living on Venus. And as Doris Lessing comments in the prologue to her Stapledonian *Canopus in Argos* series, "I do think there is something very wrong with an attitude that puts a 'serious' novel on one shelf and, let's say, *Last and First Men* on another" (9). Writers such as Lessing, Brian Aldiss, J.P. Priestly, Arnold Bennett, and C.S. Lewis have indeed taken *LAFM* very seriously, with one caveat: they and others (reviewers, critics, and some readers) dismiss his portrait of the near future, our time, as having a "period charm" (Aldiss 9). This view needs redressing. The tendency to chuckle at, for example, the narrator's description of a western culture religiously obsessed with flying "aeroplanes" misses the larger point regarding mindless consumption of resources, which Stapledon sees as part of the cause of the first men and women's demise. Brian Aldiss points out that Stapledon is not writing prophecy, and he is right: but even in 1962, some thirty years after the publication of *LAFM*, he is equally wrong not to recognize Stapledon's accuracy as a cultural critic. As is the case with Stapledon's predecessor, Jonathan Swift, the truth (and at least half the fun) in *LAFM* is found not so much in the minutiae as in the crucial overall direction that Stapledon sees humanity taking.

A readjusted critical perspective of *LAFM* would therefore take into account the following: what Stapledon calls "an Americanized Planet," with Europe's "common fear of American economic imperialism" (31); the gradual undermining of Russian communism (37); the violent tension between cosmopolitan and nationalist forces; the search for, and eventual depletion of coal, oil, and gas reserves; the juvenile individualism of American culture exported globally; the development and use of WMDs, including nerve gas, biotoxins, smart weapons, and nuclear devices; the growth on the world stage of something like the UN and something like the EEC; the sometimes violent opposition to the spread of American consumer products worldwide; the environmental crisis; and, finally, the impact of American Christian fundamentalism on attitudes to work, wealth, and sex.

Stapledon's 1930 assessment of the role America might play in the future of the world is, of course, shaped by the Great War, the stock market crash of 1929, a nascent League of Nations and growing European fascism. A lecturer in philosophy at Liverpool University, he joined the British Interplanetary Society along with G.B. Shaw, and shares with Shaw a socialist leaning. The influence of Shaw, H.G. Wells, Bertrand Russell, and Aldous Huxley on Stapledon's view of America cannot be minimized. *LAFM's* fourth chapter, "An Americanized Planet," describes what the world might look like given a few centuries of continual and overwhelming American influence. Early in the novel, his narrator describes the consequences for Europe as "America sank further and further into Americanism" (45). Europe, we are told, "chafe[s] under the saddle of American finance" (45), and there is "constant friction" between the more powerful states, such as Germany and France, and America. Here is the Neptonian narrator's decisive description of the U.S. and its citizenry:

Vast wealth and industry, and also brilliant invention, were concentrated upon puerile ends. In particular the whole of American life was organized around the cult of the powerful individual, that phantom ideal which Europe herself had only begun to outgrow in her last phase. Those Americans who wholly failed to realize this ideal, who remained at the bottom of the social ladder, either consoled themselves with hopes for the future, or stole symbolical satisfaction by identifying themselves with some popular star, or gloated upon their American citizenship, and applauded the arrogant foreign policy of their government [45].

LAFM sees the ultimate and irreversible destruction of Europe stemming from America's too-powerful adolescence. Not wanting war, the Europeans are finally not given a choice, and in one of those misunderstandings that leads to brutality, America "[floods] Europe with the latest and deadliest of gases, till all the peoples were poisoned in their cities like rats in holes" (52). Canada, we read, "sided with the United States" (53). Stapledon's detached narrator is strident in his indictment of the U.S.: "One who looks back across the aeons to this remote people can see their fate already woven of their circumstance and their disposition, and can appreciate the grim jest that these, who seemed to themselves gifted to rejuvenate the planet, should have plunged it, inevitably, through spiritual desolation into senility and age-long night" (43).

Atomic power, it should be noted, plays a part in this destruction. Like Mary Shelley, Stapledon sees technological knowledge in the hands of the unprepared as a great threat to humanity. In *LAFM*, atomic knowledge, once discovered, cannot be erased, try as Europe might to do just that. This is not melodramatic anti-Americanism: the Europeans also blunder with what they know. Stapledon portrays human error in the stark terms of the satirist as he describes the group of scientists who try to decide what to do with the discovery of nuclear power before the Americans find out. Even the suicide of the young scientist who knows the most cannot prevent the inevitable use of nuclear weapons, plunging Europe and the U.S. into a catastrophic war.

Through his remote narrator, Stapledon makes acute comments on Europe's mistakes borne partly of fear and resentment of America. The French are "so obsessed with the idea of 'France' as to be wholly incapable of generosity in international affairs" (33). The English are "most ready to betray their visions in the name of common sense" (32). Given to romanticism, Germany would "assert its virility now and again by ludicrous acts of brutality" (34). The Russians, despite their revolution, are gradually co-opted by American big business and eventually come to blows with

Germany. All of this brings about the formation of "a European Confederacy, in which all the nations of Europe, save Russia, surrendered their sovereignty to a common authority and actually pooled their armaments. Ostensibly the motive of this act was peace; but America interpreted it as directed against herself, and withdrew from the League of Nations.... All the peoples of Europe had long watched with horror the financial conquest of Russia by the United States, and they dreaded that they also must presently succumb to the same tyrant" (39). It is telling that from the vantage point of the late 1920s, Stapledon imagines "a second-rate German author" arguing "that the cosmos was a dualism in which a heroic and obviously Nordic spirit ruled by divine right over an un-self-disciplined, yet servile and obviously Slavonic spirit" (39), thus propelling Europe into war with Russia backed by America. Also interesting is the description of and prognosis for the League of Nations, which Stapledon sees as having "preserved itself by an extreme caution, amounting almost to servility to the 'great powers'" (55).

There are other League of Nations issues that might sound familiar: the league cannot prevent large wars but seems adept at dealing with smaller ones; the scourge of tribalism or nationalism never goes away; the influence of Americanism, even on China, which so dominates the League that it actually splits it, grows increasingly insidious, until the Chinese refer to Americans as the "tape-worms of the planet" (67). There is, from the Asian perspective, an "earnest hate of that strange blend of the commercial traveler, the missionary, and the barbarian conqueror, which was the American abroad" (57). America claims to "have outgrown nationalism, and to stand for political and cultural world unity. But she conceived this unity under American organization; and by culture she meant Americanism" (57). The average Chinese individual uses "American cutlery, shoes, gramophones, domestic labour-saving devices, ... his vocabulary was permeated with American slang, his newspapers and radio were American in manner, though anti-American in politics. He saw daily on his domestic television screen every phase of American private life and every American public event" (57).

On religion, sex, the environment, science and technology, Stapledon's omniscient but human narrator recounts the consequences of Americanism. American religion is "a belated and degenerate mode of Christianity, ... a kind of inverted puritan faith" (58). Eventually, what readers encounter is an American president who stumbles sexually, creates great scandal, but still manages to sell his unethical conduct to the public: "The lovely form of the [President's lover] (decently clad) was transmitted by television to every receiver in the world. Her face, blended of Asia and the West, became a most potent symbol of human unity. Every man on the planet became in imagination her lover. Every woman identified herself with this supreme woman" (76). In time, with the emergence of a one-state world dominated by American culture, an aeronautic religion emerges in which individuals must get to a certain level of acrobatic flying in order to get a license to have sex: "though legal maturity, the Wing-Winning, might occur as early as the age of fifteen, sometimes it was not attained till forty. If at that age the individual still failed in the test, he or she was forbidden sexual intercourse and information for ever" (91). The narrator calls this an "extravagant sexual taboo," mitigated in Asia by the quibble that sex knowledge imparted in a language other than American English is not wrong.

However, the rampant flying of aeroplanes depletes the planet's petroleum reserves even while human intelligence and technological know-how begin to wane. The acuity of Stapledon's long-term prognosis for the planet under Americanism is not in the details, such as *en masse* piloting of aeroplanes, but rather in the much more important trends, such as resource exhaustion for frivolous activities, the unethical use of scientific knowledge, global urbanization, and the disappearance of wilderness. Replace the aeroplane with the automobile and Stapledon's prescience becomes clear, even in the connections that can be made between human sexuality and the operation of powerful machinery. Combine that further with the fact that he projects a downturn in American technological prowess, and current readers recognize that civil collapse becomes, in the longer term, inevitable.

Finally, and most disturbingly for readers today, Stapledon envisions the use of biological WMDs during a long cultural decline — the microbes produce a pulmonary and nervous affliction called "the American Madness" (96) — as producing a global catastrophe: "Only in the most naturally fertile areas of the world could the diseased remnant of a population now scrape a living from the soil. Elsewhere, utter desolation. With easy strides the jungle came back into its own" (97). From this point in the text, approximately one-third of the way into *LAFM*, the story of the first humans gives way to a new one, as a form of hyper-intelligent hominid slowly emerges, the second of eighteen in Stapledon's wildly imaginative narrative. And it is here that readers since 1930 have become understandably enthusiastic about this novel. Still, Olaf Stapledon's stance as an early-twentieth-century cultural critic with accurate insights about what we in our own time could see under American capitalism invites a serious re-evaluation nearly a century later.

WORKS CITED

Aldiss, Brian. General Editor's Foreword. In Stapledon.
Lessing, Doris. "Some Remarks." *Re: Colonised Planet 5, Shikasta*. London: Panther, 1979.
Stapledon, Olaf. *Last and First Men: A Story of the Near and Far Future*. 1930. Ed. Brian Aldiss. London: Penguin, 1963.

12

Nalo Hopkinson's Colonial and Dystopic Worlds in *Midnight Robber*

Ruby S. Ramraj

In a recent article in *Quill & Quire*, Donna Bailey Nurse mentions an observation by Nalo Hopkinson, the Canadian science-fiction/fantasy writer, which touches on the central concerns of many science fiction writers. She observes that science fiction is primarily "a literature in which humans are traditionally white, and aliens, by definition are the other" (14). Further, Hopkinson — not being part of the white majority in Canada (she is in fact a black writer born in the Caribbean but living and writing in Canada since 1975) — finds it disquieting to be living in a country she says "systematically tells me I'm not good enough"(14). In an attempt to put herself in the mainstream of the society and affirm her own worth, she takes pains in her writing to make "black women's *otherness* normal" (14). This is why she has been attracted to the genre of science fiction and fantasy: here is a genre that allows her to construct possible worlds in which she can redress the problems of this world. As she puts it, "science fiction offers models for change. This is immensely hopeful" (14). With this in mind, it comes as no surprise to see her ground her texts in a Caribbean setting and use the demotic language of the Caribbean to portray females — black and white — who fight oppression of all kinds (colonialism, racism, sexism, and patriarchy, among others). In her portrayals of these women in her texts, she shows that despite the harshness of their lives, they are resilient and do not merely survive, but are able to find some measure of joy and solace in both spirituality and sexuality. Her highly acclaimed science fiction novel, *Midnight Robber*, is a prime example. In this work, she depicts a technologically advanced planet called Toussaint (a word that echoes the slave rebellion led by Toussaint L'Ouverture), which has been colonized by Caribbean people; it is a place where everyone seems to be happy and content. But juxtaposed with this world is the nightmarish dystopia of New Half Way Tree (the name identified with the brutality of slavery in Jamaica, a former British colony), a mirror planet where the inhabitants, mainly outcasts and criminals, eke out a miserable existence. Thrust into this dystopic world, the protagonist Tan-Tan battles violence, oppression, and even incest, but in the end she is able to assert herself as a saviour (the Robber Queen) of the disenfranchised people of this place, finally earning the respect of the villagers and the love of Melonhead, her childhood friend and protector.

What sets the dystopic world of *Midnight Robber* apart from dystopias created by other science fiction writers (such as Huxley, Asimov, Ellison, Russ, Sawyer, and others) is the fresh and unique setting of her futuristic Caribbean worlds. Not only does Hopkinson people these worlds with oppressed women, children, criminals and despots, but she also employs the myths of the Caribbean in her use of the douens[1] (pronounced "dwens") as the antithesis of the tall people (the term she uses for the humans), and by comparison shows that the douens, seen as the Other in this text, are indeed the more normal, caring family unit.

Another effective technique Hopkinson uses to impart a Caribbean texture to *Midnight Robber,* to enhance the narrative, and to authenticate the setting is her employment of well-known West Indian folk songs to further the narrative or to explain certain events. Tan-Tan's father sings a familiar sailor song:

> Captain, captain put me ashore
> I don't want to go anymore
> Itanami gwine drownded me,
> Itanami gwine burst me belly,
> Itanami is too much for me [74].

In referring to this folk song, he is linking the journey he and Tan-Tan have just made with voyages of the Caribbean sailors of old who had to cross the rapids of mighty rivers like the Essequibo in order to traverse the

Guyanese terrain. Hopkinson explains, "Itanami was river rapids. People in ships would go through it like we going through dimension veils. Itanami break up plenty vessels" (74) before people could get from one side of the river to the other, or, in the case of Tan-Tan and her father, from one world (Toussaint) to the other (New Half Way Tree). Other references to the slaves, and later the indentured laborers crossing "the Kalpani, the Black Water on Earth to go and work their fingers to the bone as indentured labourers in the Caribbean" (49), strongly bring to mind the oppressive colonial legacy of slavery and indenture in the Caribbean. Hopkinson's passing references to "Jankanoo season" (year's end festivals in Jamaica), and "red sorrel drink" and "black cake" (18) also give the text a unique Caribbean ambiance. In an effort to blend the traditions of the past with the technological advances of a futuristic world she has created, she intermingles effortlessly references to AIs and "web connections" with legendary myths of the Robber Queen and douens to depict a Caribbean world that embraces both technology and superstition.

Hopkinson's explorations of the history of the Caribbean people are given a postcolonial emphasis when she examines the imperial-colonial hegemonic divide, paralleling it sometimes with patriarchal domination. She appears to share the view of such postcolonial writers/theorists as Sara Suleri, who has stated that the "category of postcolonialism must be read both as a free-floating metaphor for cultural embattlement and as an almost obsolete signifier for the historicity of race" (274). In both *Midnight Robber* and her latest sociohistorical/fantasy novel *The Salt Roads*, Hopkinson links the negative aspects of the ever-expanding power of technology with imperialism and demagogues (both black and white), showing how such power compounds the individual's feelings of helplessness and inferiority. The location of these two works predominantly in fictive places in the Caribbean, where the little person struggles against insurmountable odds, encourages us to read the novels as postcolonial/dystopic texts.[2]

In her explorations of what it means to be marginalized or oppressed, Hopkinson, in *Midnight Robber* (and more specifically in *The Salt Roads*), investigates the "complicity of a large part of Western culture ... in the attitudes and values underpinning the process of expansion overseas" (Moore-Gilbert 8), given from the perspective of the now ex-colonials. She details in *The Salt Roads* the complicity of the Europeans, especially of the French in Haiti, who degraded and brutalized their fellow humans mainly because of their ethnicity and color. Whatever sexual relationships exist between master and slave is exploitative. White males found slave women exotic and subjected them to their sexual whims. Given their harsh life on the plantation, many of the slave women counter-exploited their masters' sexual infatuation with them, and using their sex appeal to enhance their status in the slave society, and to eventually obtain freedom for themselves and their hybrid children. As Homi Bhabha has shown, the colonized were capable of temporizing with, and countering in their own limited way, imperial domination. Hopkinson clearly meditates on the challenges of the oppressed, showing the complexity of the situations the slaves found themselves in and that fact that there were no easy ways then for them to change the system.

In her attempt to get not merely the time and place of her novels right, but to capture as well the speaking voice of the Caribbean people in the past (in *The Salt Roads*) and in the future (in *Midnight Robber*), Hopkinson employs the demotic language of the Caribbean, variously termed "creole" or "patois." This language hybridizes English and French words to produce a distinct (generally understandable) Caribbean English. From the very beginning of *Midnight Robber*, we see Hopkinson's deft use of the Caribbean language in authenticating the Caribbean society, and in creating the subtle texture of the place and people:

> Oho. Like it starting, oui. Don't be frightened, sweetness; is for the best. I go be with you the whole time. Trust me and let me distract you little bit with one anasi story. It had a woman, you see, a strong hard-back woman... She name Tan-Tan; and New Half-Way Tree was she planet [1].

The Salt Roads begins with a sly and somewhat raunchy comment on the condition of hybridity on the slave plantation which she describes in earthy Caribbean tones:

> It went in white, but it will come out a mulatto in a few months' time, yes. I was right; the oven of Georgine's belly was swelling up nice with the white man's loaf it was cooking to brown. I cackled at my own joke like the old woman I was becoming [1].

Readers familiar with Caribbean dialect would not have to turn to such glossaries and dictionaries as *The Dictionary of Caribbean English* by Richard Allsopp to grasp the meaning of such fairly accessible words like "anasi," or "mulatto." However, they may need them for words Hopkinson takes from Caribbean demotic of the past, such as "bassourdie" (crazy) or "buckra" (white). These unfamiliar words evoke authenticating nuances, which impart realism to Hopkinson's futuristic dystopic worlds.

In *The Poetics of Science Fiction* (2000), Peter Stockwell[3] introduces the word "architext" to describe "any science fictional narrative which configures a fully worked-out, rich world" (204) that interests the reader "not so much in the narrative progression, but in the lyrical description of the environments" (204). In its recreation of colonial worlds — Toussaint and New Half-Way Tree — *Midnight Robber* can be seen as an "architext." Toussaint is a technologically advanced planet where people have their own "eshus" (bodyguards) and their own "AIs"[4] (artificially intelligent servants) and where most people like the protagonist Tan-Tan (whose father is a mayor) live luxurious, carefree lives pampered by human and mechanical servants. At first, the planet seems to be utopia, a place where people live privileged lives, moving from games, to parties, to carnival. But the "illusion" that this is utopia quickly vanishes when we read that this world is "seeded by nanomites" (10) that make up "one enormous data-gathering system that exchanged information constantly through the Grande Nanotech Sentient Interface: Granny Nansi's Web" (10). We begin to realize that not only are the inhabitants of this planet under constant scrutiny, but they are also in the power of a technology far greater than themselves. Here humans are the servants of advanced technology, however. The pedicab runners, ironically descendants of the "programmer clan" (52), baulk at advancing technology and are dismissed as "Blasted luddites" (52), but they are reminiscent of the Medievalists in Isaac Asimov's *The Caves of Steel* who wish to return to the simple world of the past. The surveillance of the characters by AIs and eshus in *Midnight Robber* recalls George Orwell's *1984* with Big Brother watching, and Robert Sawyer's quantum computer JASON — in his science fiction novel *Golden Fleece*— who sees and hears everything the crew of the space ship *Argo* say and do and eventually uses this information against them; or of the Canadian science fiction and fantasy writer Robert Charles Wilson who in *Darwinia* describes "noospheres" that store memories of all generations — memories that are misused to create a parallel universe. Hopkinson's texts would appear to be suggesting that oppressive societies, whether in the Caribbean or elsewhere, have such totalitarian hallmarks.

The justification for oppressive measures imposed on people in many societies is that they have a civilizing effect. Hopkinson resists such seductive reasoning. In *Midnight Robber*, although she is conscious of the beauty of Toussaint, she is aware of its darker totalitarian side. New Half-Way Tree, its binary opposite, is unmitigatedly an "ugly place" (76), rendered frighteningly as a nightmarish, dark place. It is this repulsive planet to which Tan-Tan and her father are exiled: "New Half-Way Tree, the mirror planet to Toussaint ... [is a place where] the mongoose still run wild, the diable bush still got poison thorns ... the jumbie bird still stalk through the bush" (2). It is a place of dense forest, mud, slime, and make-shift huts, "where the air was too cold, and it had a funny smell, like old bones" (76), a place where the douens of Caribbean folklore wander and make their homes. Ironically, it is the douens and not the "tall people," the condemned humans, who show compassion to Tan-Tan and her father when they are exiled to this place. They face constant obstacles and dangers from these tall people (the criminals) of New Half-Way Tree, whose violent behavior and selfishness are reminiscent of that of the planters and "buckras," the imperial masters during the time of slavery depicted in *The Salt Roads*. Tan-Tan and her father wander through make-shift villages and towns with names like "Duppy Dead Town," "Corbeau," and "Begorrat," names that connote death and corruption so evident in these run-down places, names whose Caribbean origins conjure up the colonial Caribbean world. The nightmarish, ghastly places so vividly described remind us that Tan-Tan does indeed live "in hell" and needs to be redeemed.

Hopkinson's depiction of the exiles living in New Half Way Tree recalls another group of colonial victims, the British criminals exiled to New South Wales in Charles Dickens's *Great Expectations*, but unlike the rehabilitated Magwitch, Antonio, Tan-Tan's father never learns generosity or kindness; he associates himself not with the victims but with their exploiters; his behavior deteriorates and he is seen as an unrepentant, domineering man who belongs to this place to which the dregs of society are condemned. He is as much a brutal imperialist as a brutal patriarch. Tan-Tan's worst experience comes not at the hand of the resident criminals of New Half Way Tree, but at her father's hands, when he rapes her at nine, and repeats this abuse until she is fourteen (137–40). Hopkinson does not spare us details of her suffering, underscoring her father's brutality. Tan-Tan suffers personal anguish and guilt; with no friend to confide in, she endures the disgrace of a pregnancy and has an abortion. This tragic situation is not alleviated until she inadvertently murders her father in her struggle to free herself from his unwanted advances. There is relief and a sense of poetic justice when, on her sixteenth birthday, she uses the dagger given to her as a gift (for self-protection) to stab and kill her father when he attacks her again (169). Perhaps Hopkinson is suggesting that there is recourse for such victims. Hopkinson uses the death of Antonio as a kind of purification rite for Tan-Tan: now that she is free from him, she is able to rejoin her childhood friend Melonhead, whose selfless love for her and her son (the product of incest) provides the "healing balm" (326) in Tan-Tan's life.[5] The conclusion of *Midnight Robber* is not dark and dismal; it shows that even in the worst societies, people can eventually obtain freedom, and can regain their humanity and dignity.

In both *Midnight Robber* and *The Salt Roads*, Hopkinson presents the experience of the victims of power not generically but in individual ways, making us aware of the personal pain of the victims. In dealing with subjects such as incest, sexual abuse, and violence that take place in the dystopic world of *Midnight Robber*, Hopkinson sheds light not only on the guilt and shame the victims of such abuse feel, but also on the aversion of the douens who represent the ordinary people of Toussaint. Chichibud, her douen protector, reassures her: "AI could read the signs for myself. I know he attack you" (169). Even the criminals of New Half-Way Tree, after hearing the story of her ordeal with Antonio, show their approval of Tan-Tan's action with an emotional outburst, but also in a tangible way: "The crowd erupted in cheers. Carnival pounds and pennies rained on Tan-Tan's head" (326). In describing this reaction, Hopkinson is censuring the violent behavior of men in power like Antonio who inflict physical and psychological damage on women and children, but she is critical also of women such as Ione, Tan-Tan's mother, and Janisette, her step-mother, who are shown to be equally promiscuous and irresponsible. She emphasizes that dominance, whatever the form, is intolerable and dehumanizing as it undermines the stability of the individual, the home, and the society. In taking such a strong position against dominance and abuse, Hopkinson hopes that her work will be a vehicle for effecting some change in the actual values and norms of the societies of today.

Like many contemporary writers of science fiction, Hopkinson sees the writer's role in society as a valuable one. In *Midnight Robber* she demonstrates that powerful forces can be defeated and changes can occur if there is a will for change. In many talks and addresses, Robert Sawyer makes a similar observation when he suggests that science fiction writers should be more than just commentators on their social world; they need to become the vehicles of change. Clearly, such science fiction writers can become the ethical conscience of our society, reminding us of our social and moral responsibilities. Peter Stockwell, in assessing the works of science fiction writers, has noted that "most dystopias are extrapolations of aspects of the present, and thus serve as political statements against certain ideologies, or as warnings about trends that need to be averted" (211). Nalo Hopkinson's novels caution us that such warnings need to be heeded if we are to construct a world that is truly gender blind, color blind, and accommodating of all beings — human, non-human, and cyborg — who will inevitably be part of the human community of the future.

NOTES

1. In Caribbean folklore, the douens are "children who'd died before they had their naming ceremonies [and] came back from the dead as jumbies with their heads on backwards" (*Midnight Robber* 93). Generally considered fearful, the douens in this text are actually the embodiment of the good and the kind; it is the "tall people" in this text, the humans, who are wicked and oppressive.

2. The appropriation and colonization of other places is a central myth in most science fiction and fantasy texts; so, clearly, the works of writers from Isaac Asimov to modern science fiction writers like David Brin, Octavia Butler, Ursula Le Guin, and Nalo Hopkinson are part of the postcolonial science fiction genre.

3. Stockwell sees this genre as "the true literature of the present" (9) and outlines how neologisms are incorporated into descriptions of new worlds created by science fiction writers into striking images and metaphors that appeal to global readers.

4. Hopkinson uses West African mythology here. She explains that "Aishu" is the African deity that wants to go everywhere and see everything (Nurse 14). Her use of the terms "AI" (commonly used in science fiction to refer to "artificial intelligence") and "eshu" (meaning servant) in *Midnight Robber* play on the name of the god.

5. Robert Sawyer in *Golden Fleece* has a human protagonist Aaron Rossman who is the product of incest as well; both authors suggest that children should not be punished for the mistakes of their parents.

WORKS CITED

Allsopp, Richard. *Dictionary of Caribbean English Usage*. Oxford: Oxford University Press, 1996.
Bhabha, Homi. *The Location of Culture*. London: Routledge, 1994.
Hopkinson, Nalo. *Midnight Robber*. New York: Warner, 2000.
_____. *The Salt Roads*. New York: Warner, 2003.
Moore-Gilbert, Bart. *Postcolonial Theory: Contexts, Practices, and Policies*. London: Verso, 1997.
Nurse, Donna Bailey. "Brown Girl in the Ring: How a Caribbean-born Writer Reinvented a Genre." *Quill & Quire*. (November 2003): 14–15.
Sawyer, Robert. *Golden Fleece*. New York: Tor, 1990.
Stockwell, Peter. *The Poetics of Science Fiction*. Harlow: Longman, 2000.
Suleri, Sara. "A Woman Skin Deep: Feminism and the Postcolonial Condition." *The Post-Colonial Studies Reader*. Eds. Bill Ashcroft, Gareth Griffiths, and Helen Tiffin. London: Routledge, 1995. 273–80.
Wilson, Robert Charles. *Darwinia*. New York: Tor, 1998.

13

"Wartime Inventions with Peaceful Intentions": Television and the Media Cyborg in C.L. Moore's *No Woman Born*

Linda Howell

Writing on the ethics of television spectatorship in the late twentieth century, Avital Ronell alludes to Nietzsche: "The death of God has left us with a lot of appliances" (281). Referring to technology's displacement and privatization of public trauma in general, she attributes a special ideological function to television as a result of its mass emergence after World War Two: "[I]t is not so much the beginning of something new, but instead, the residue of an unassimilable history" (280). Long anticipated in science fiction, its commercial development slowed by the war, and its advent figuring prominently in the retooling of America's war economy, television had a lively prehistory in the public imagination long before the war was officially over and television sets were mass-manufactured. Its idealization as a potential agent of peacetime conversion is captured in DuMont Corporation's 1943 slogan, "Wartime Inventions with Peaceful Intentions" (Tichi 13). Yet as Ronell and others indicate, television is unable to fulfil its utopian promise because it remains "haunted" by traumatic memory, a collective, public memory which can be neither fully integrated nor adequately communicated (287) via the secularized, consumer-oriented medium that television was to become. Positioning its viewers as helpless survivors and witnesses of "excessive force," television instead repeatedly points to this unassimilable memory in images of "wasted, condemned bodies that crumble" (282).

Published in the December 1944 issue of *Astounding Stories*, C.L. Moore's *No Woman Born* is a science fiction novella that takes as its premise a wasted and crumbling body — and quite specifically, a human, female body once tremendously enhanced by the medium of global broadcast television. Even before she is burned beyond recognition in a theater fire and subsequently equipped with a cybernetic body, "airscreen" performer Deirdre is a media cyborg — that is, a combination of organism and machine that functions by virtue of its representation as image (both visual and acoustic), its transmission over distance and its reception by the human organism. By premising the narrative on a backstory of larger-than-life female beauty destroyed, Moore evokes the trauma of wartime destruction in a way that might have particularly resonated with readers separated by wartime duties from the opposite sex. For like Deirdre's audience "outside the bounds of civilization," men in World War Two military service were largely segregated from women, yet tenuously connected to them by virtue of such media images as Rosie the Riveter — represented most memorably in the poster image of the patriotic, muscled women in Westinghouse coveralls proclaiming "We Can Do It" — or Betty Grable in pinup form, or the curvaceous, scantily clad girls painted on the fuselage of bomber planes, or indeed, the "bombshells" themselves. Drawing largely on the already-established phenomenon of movie fandom, Moore foresees television's preoccupation with trauma and its mass production of what Avital Ronell calls "corpses that need not be mourned" (281).

Equipped with a sophisticated cybernetic body in much the same way as World War Two amputees were equipped with myoelectric prostheses in the 1940s. Deirdre is indeed Moore's equivalent of a corpse that need not be mourned. She has struggled for over a year to adapt her surviving human brain to her mechanical body, the brilliant invention of scientist Maltzer and a dedicated team of artists, sculptors, technicians and designers. But in contrast with Maltzer's fears that he has re-created Frankenstein's monster, and in equal contrast with her agent John Harris's inability to "think of her as other than dead" (237), this television diva rebuilds her career by emulating the cybernetic consciousness forged between men and machines as a means of survival in the military. Conditioned by her career as a television singer and dancer, Deirdre becomes so successful in simulating her former voice and body movement that her unlifelike appearance becomes a benefit rather than an obstacle to rebuilding her career. When she invents an ostensibly "new" form of dance in her television comeback, Deirdre gains unparalleled success with her mass audience: women adopt her metallic robe as the latest in fashion, while men welcome her, as Harris does, in grateful recognition of an apparent "return" of the old Deirdre. As she explains to Harris, "motion is the other basis of recognition, after physical likeness" (247) In other words, we might say, if it walks like a duck and talks like a duck, it doesn't have to look like a duck.

More specifically, Deirdre's newfound powers of mass cultural appeal through imitative motion rely on a basic principle of human sensory perception that C.L. Moore fashions to her own ends in *No Woman Born*. As the technologies of film and television demonstrate, and as Moore's omniscient narrator remarks when Harris first encounters Deirdre in cyborg form, "the human brain is often too complicated a mechanism to function perfectly" (242). This imperfect functioning of the organism, namely its reliance on memory to fill in perceptual gaps, is the principle of "persistence of vision" enabling humans to invest projected film images with continuity and transmitted television images with an almost instantaneous coherence. By contrast, in the comparatively slow medium of writing, it takes Moore's omniscient narrator a full page to relate the imperfect process by which Harris's brain struggles to make sense of what he sees when first encountering Deirdre after her long recovery. First seen as "an arrangement of brooms and buckets" that Harris remembers mistaking for a human figure, Deirdre's cyborg body impels Harris' brain to shift backwards in memory to "the old Deirdre" before the fire: "This is Deirdre! She hasn't changed at all!" the brain tells Harris. Succeeded by the "worst" perception of Deirdre as "machinery heaped in a flowered chair" (242), Harris's brain then probes the traumatic memory of "the old Deirdre's" death. "It was like walking from a dream of someone beloved and lost, and facing anew, after that heartbreaking reassurance of sleep, the inflexible fact that nothing can bring the lost to life again" (242). Only when she moves and speaks, animating the machinery with her own brain, can Harris begin to make sense of cyborg Deirdre as an "illusion [that] steadied and became factual, real" (242).

This early episode in *No Woman Born* serves several narrative functions that enhance the interpretation of Deirdre's postwar significance as an appliance that, like television, functions by interrupting and diverting mournful memory. First, it corrects an unfortunate misperception on the part of some critics that Harris is either the story's narrator or a Jamesian central consciousness mediating the reader's perception of Deirdre. The former interpretation — Harris as narrator — supports Jane Donawerth's reading of *No Woman Born* from the stance of performance theory. As a television performer, Donawerth argues, Deirdre is conditioned to manipulate masculine perceptions of "women as sex objects, machinery for arousing and satisfying men's desires" (62). While Deirdre is thus empowered to "assert ... her autonomy by showing that she can act her sex role, that she can put it on and take it off" (63), ultimately she amounts to the cyborg equivalent of a "Plastic Woman," meaning one who uses "the artifice of makeup, costume, and stylized movement to become an idealized sex object" (61). Citing Harris's power as narrator to manipulate point of view and Malzer's definition of her as a "freak," Donawerth concludes that "the power of establishing a norm for what constitutes the human, the power to see women as defective, even when serving men, is still in the hands (or the eyes) of men" (63). Yet as suggested both by consistent references to Harris in the third person and by the narrator's ability to probe the workings of his brain, Donawerth builds her interpretation of Deirdre as "Plastic Woman" on critical blindness to the omniscient narrator who often blends with Harris's perceptions, yet also distances itself from Harris's interpretation of "the new Deirdre." Struggling throughout the story with eyes, ears and muscles that refuse to do what Harris consciously wills them to do, Harris is more accurately the "central consciousness" through which the story is narrated. To endow him with narrative control over Deirdre's story is to miss the irony of the observation that the human brain is "too complicated a mechanism to function perfectly" (242.) The standard of "perfection" by which this brain is measured is clearly that of a machine.

More specifically, as suggested by the luxuriant time taken in describing Harris's shifting memories back to a point of almost irrecoverable trauma, Moore's omniscient narrator is reminiscent of another medium and another appliance functioning as instrumental means to the promotion of "wartime inventions with peaceful intentions." The technology of the typewriter is arguably enabled more women to pay the rent on Virginia Woolf's "room of her own" than television ever did. As Paul Donawerth points out, Moore's autobiographical essay, "Footnote to 'Shambleau' ... and Others" attributes her own writerly origins to a typing exercise that combined with random memories of sophomore English to become the short story "Shambleau." Thus appropriating the machinery of her boring bank job to launch her career as science fiction writer, Moore's tale of an identity metamorphizing through the typewriter illustrates Donna Haraway's definition of cyborg writing as the revision of origin stories to fashion alternative subjects. Like the writers of slash fiction studied by Constance Penley, often clerical workers who appropriate workplace technologies to publish homoerotic versions of *Star Trek*, Moore fashions her writerly origins in the technocultural practice of poaching — diverting the institutionally-sanctioned means of production to unforeseen ends. In Donawerth's assessment, "she tells a tale of appropriation rather than marginalization, one which figures her power as central, authorial, productive; she counters one originary narrative with another, defining herself (and her story) for herself (383–84).

Nevertheless, by defining the interests of feminist science fiction as "making a science that does not exclude women, creating an identity for women as alien, and finding a voice in a male world" (xviii), Donawerth commits it to a separatist script for playing out sexual difference. Her definition denies the heterosocial uses of white womanhood as seal of approval on the war machine. Instead the motif of the machine-woman represents "the social role of women serving men" (178). Deirdre's pleasure in Harris's gaze upon her — a pleasure which might conceivably be warranted after one has spent a year in therapy — does not register in *Frankenstein's Daughters*. Coupled with erroneous attribution of the narrator's role to Harris, reliance on a "separate spheres" model of feminist cultural politics sketched in Gothic tones ill-serves the Jamesian subtleties of Moore's narrative technique.

But the critique of the "Plastic Woman" motif in Donawerth is perhaps better voiced by Moore herself, whose second masculine point of view is that of the Gothic scientist Viktor Frankenstein who fears the autonomy of his invention. Viewed jealously by Harris as a rival who has enjoyed "a closer intimacy" with Deirdre "than any two humans can ever have shared before," Maltzer is a wreck of a human being after spending a year with Deirdre in "a sort of unimaginable marriage" (239). Like Victor Frankenstein, with whom he compares himself, Maltzer has reinvented Deirdre's body in the spirit of a scientist's public duty: "I meant what I did ... to be for everyone who meets with accidents that might have ruined them" (275). As in the tale's pretext of a body ravaged by fire and in Harris's first contact with cyborg Deirdre, Maltzer's hopes of rehabilitation subtly speaks to memories of war. Yet his fear that he has created a "freak" forecloses on the utopian promise of rehabilitating prosthetics, while his nervous condition after a year of "unimaginable marriage" demonstrates that while

Harris has been too long away from Deirdre to see her clearly, Maltzer has been too long with her.

Narrated in the third person yet mediated largely through the central consciousness of Deirdre's agent John Harris, the story thus frames Deirdre within the fluid narrative convention of free indirect discourse. As a "framed" woman, Deirdre figures the ethical problem of media spectatorship in content and form: the historical trauma of World War Two returns in the ethical problem of media spectatorship, her disappearance from the screen deeply mourned by her agent John Harris, whose central consciousness mediates the reader's perspective. Like a wartime amputee, however, she persists in learning control of the prosthetic body supplied by scientist Malzer and his team of designers, as well as the prosthetically-enhanced television career that results from her determined control of her shiny new body. Engaging the ethical problem of mass cultural control over large audiences, *No Woman Born* also engages the political unconscious of a nation traumatized by war and anxious for peace.

Published in 1944, the story addresses a traditionally masculine audience of "hard" science fiction readers at a pivotal point in the war effort. By then, writes Donald Albrecht,

> with victory almost in sight, the country focussed on peacetime conversion. Congress passed the G.I. Bill of Rights to ease the return to civilian life. The dream house would be central to postwar material comfort. [...] The publication of Wendell Wilkie's 1943 best-selling book, *One World*, anticipated a postwar climate of expansive internationalism [Albrecht xx].

Within the combined efforts of government, media and industry to effect that postwar climate, two ultimately successful strategies were the widespread installation of the television in American households and the dissemination of a postwar ideology of nuclear family "togetherness." Characterized by promises of unparalleled domestic entertainment, a "reward for years of forbearance" (Macdonald 7) and a "window on the world" (Spigel 9), television was more than another appliance in the panoply of electrified consumer goods promised to the nuclear housewife. A technology held in abeyance by the war effort, it promised to reunite the divided families of the nation around what Cecilia Tichi calls "the electronic hearth" (passim), and to bring the world into the American home. Similarly, as Maureen Honey has argued, the ostensible "return" of women employed in wartime industry to their prewar roles as housewives promised to stabilize gender roles disrupted by the demands of wartime to deploy existing labor reserves.

In fact, as Maureen Honey shows, the "return" of women to the household at war's end was more evidently their return to lower-paying jobs in clerical, sales and service positions which they had occupied before the war (24.) In sustaining the myth of Rosie the Riveter, the U.S. Office of War Information relied on film, radio, print media and the advertising industry to change public perceptions of working women and to recruit women into the labor force. Yet assumptions on the part of this propaganda machine that women did not need to work, except when called on by their country to great feats of self-sacrifice, meant that the feminist potential of this propaganda campaign went unrealized:

> The identification of working women with the country and its representatives ... blurred the distinctions between nontraditional and female occupations while it masked the benefits women received from moving into male spheres. As defenders of liberty, women were cast into a selfless role that conflicted with the concept of female self-actualization through new work opportunities [Honey 215–16].

Although campaigns to recruit women into military and industrial jobs continued as late as spring 1944, the rationale that "women would be easier to displace when veterans returned" (Honey 39) illustrates the limitations of Rosie the Riveter as an image of *temporary* feminine sacrifice. Unlike the ultimate the sacrifice of the soldier's life, this feminized sacrifice could eventually be "rewarded" by the application of industrial power-knowledge to a revised domestic sphere.

Although it is unlikely that *No Woman Born* could be considered an active element of the government's propaganda campaign, evidence exists that science fiction pulp magazines, of which *Astounding Stories* would have been a foremost example, were among its targets. Honey documents suggestions by the Magazine Bureau of the Office of War Information that "An Amazonian economy might trace its inception to this war-enforced change in our mores" (i.e. the acceptance of women as workers) (48). However, A.E. Van Vogt's 1943 story "The Storm" individualizes the Amazonian economy in the figure of an aristocratic fighting woman who tricks her lover into seducing her. Murray Linster's 1944 story, "First Contact" projects the utopian aspirations of "peacetime intentions" through interplanetary bonds established by the swapping of dirty jokes. And Clifford Simak's 1944 "Desertion" replaces an unsatisfactory working relationship between a man and a woman with the utopian mind-melding of a man and his dog. As indicators of science fiction's participation in the social construction of Rosie the Riveter, these stories posit solutions to "Man's" aggressive impulses by dismantling rather than sustaining feminized structures of social authority.

No Woman Born's opening description of Deirdre as former television star posits a similar dismantling. As previously noted, her human body, destroyed by a theater fire, is a civilizing body of feminine influence consigned to the nostalgic space of an irrecoverable past. Partially framed within the consciousness of John Harris, Deirdre is simultaneously disseminated and monumentalized by her passage through organic death into a media(ted) afterlife. In Harris's inability "to think of her as other than dead," she becomes a symbol of Harris's Pygmalienating desire to assimilate historical trauma from a humanist perspective. Hence, for Harris, cyborg Deirdre's accurate simulation of the "lost" human Deirdre defines her value.

The Pygmalienating aspects of Harris's nostalgia for "the magic of the lost Deirdre" are also evident in his citation of the Irish legend of another Deirdre, a woman whose beauty foments war between the Irish people and their king. Harris's citation of the Irish legend assigns the "lost" Deirdre to a mythical place of mourning where "there are no words" — but the pattern of "no" and "not" in these lines sympathetically invokes a drumbeat of protest as language decays into a collective silence of men. Such a shared state of "no words" works on the suspension of verbal language to evoke both the memory of collective trauma and the desire to master it. In this passage from James Stephens, rhythm patterns meaning where words fail. The citation of the Deirdre legend momentarily masters Harris's grieving memories of the "lost Deirdre" as he musters his courage to meet her in her new form. Moore's time-leaping premise in which television is always already a feminized global phenomenon, and the heroine is always already "dead" and "lost," prepares her readers for adventures in posthumanity.

What kind of change in the utopian view of television might a science fiction writer of the war years imagine? What *more* could Moore want than a technology of visualization that, as suggested above, not only foregrounds feminine artistry, but unites both "civilized" and "non-civilized" worlds? Celia Tichi's description of the Allen B. DuMont Corporation's advertising campaign, inaugurated in 1943, suggests that at issue for Moore was the continuing militarization of American consciousness:

> Television, said DuMont in 1943, would mean the peacetime application of technology currently militarily successful against German torpedoes and the Japanese navy. "Wartime Inventions with Peaceful Intentions," proclaimed DuMont of its oscilloscope, cathode tube, and cyclograph.... And the company familiarized the televisual process in ... figures of electrons moving in "squads"

under the direction of "sergeants..".. [T]elevision was figured as a more powerful Deadeye Dick shooting his cathode ray bullets with "incredible rapidity" [13].

The anticipation of television's military applications was a tradition in men's magazines, Lynn Spigel tells us, since the 1930s (110). Although DuMont also relied on a number of non-military metaphors which were to become commonplace in the industry after the war, its slogan of "wartime inventions with peaceful intentions" captures a brief moment of appeal to a masculine audience in terms which ironically reinstall the trauma of war on the domestic front. The latent promise of television in DuMont's "wartime inventions" campaign is "peaceful intentions" by rewarding the returning soldier with clips of his performance in the line of duty — an immodest proposal at best. By contrast, Moore's premise of the fire-ravaged body of a television star magnifies the human sacrifice obscured by this re-medial treatment.

Yet even DuMont Corporation's happy containment of global strife within the television set pales in comparison to the idealism of Federal Communications Commission Chairman Paul Porter. Speaking in 1945, Porter hails television as a primary agent of peacetime conversion:

> Television's illuminating light will go far, we hope, to drive out the ghosts that haunt the dark corners of our minds — ignorance, bigotry, and fear. It will be able to inform, educate, and entertain an entire nation with a magical speed and vividness.... It can be democracy's handmaiden by bringing the whole picture of our political, social, economic and cultural life to the eyes as well as the ears [MacDonald 41].

Porter's gendering of television as "democracy's handmaiden" echoes Harris's memory of Deirdre as a TV performer whose reach extends to both "civilized" and "uncivilized" lands. Illustrating a remarkably resilient vocabulary of technological advance as the light and magic of feminizing influence, his words would not be unfamiliar to Henry Adams.

The contrast between Porter's view of television as "democracy's handmaiden" and DuMont Corporation's "Deadeye Dick" captures a gendered moment of contestation between government and industry for the definition of the public good. As Fred J. MacDonald writes, industry was ultimately successful in articulating this good as one of commercial entertainment for a homogenized nation rather than representation of local, regional and minority interests. He points to FCC decisions in 1944 and 1945 to limit the number of broadcast channels as one source of this homogeneity:

> For most Americans this would mean creation of one nation under television, network television. TV would be for broad, indiscriminate tastes. As had been

the case with commercial radio, less popular interests such as educational TV, minority entertainment, and even locally oriented programming would be stunted by a few networks able to assemble large numbers of viewers and deliver them regularly to advertisers [38].

Like Rosie the Riveter, close ties between government and industry forged during the war years limited television's emancipatory potential.

Although Deirdre is an entertainer and not an industrial worker, her allusion to war and to men's dependency on the female machine resists Harris's aestheticizing perceptions of her as a quasi-Shakespearean "creature in armour": "Only a knight from another world, or a knight of Oberon's court, might have shared that delicate likeness" (245). These perceptions contain the cyborg within a framework of cultural allusions that blurs the distinctions between science fiction and fantasy, largely as a result of Moore's subtle understanding of fantasy's inherently ambiguous functioning, as both a literary genre and a psychological phenomenon. For example, the scene in which Harris first meets Deirdre after her rehabilitation illustrates a formal wavering between incredulity and belief that Tzvetan Todorov hails as the hallmark of fantasy. The fantasy of Deirdre unchanged quickly disintegrates into a vision of "machinery heaped in a flowered chair" as Harris reflects on "the inflexible fact that nothing can bring the lost back to life again." And in turn, this reflex shifts point of view into the present tense: "illusion steadied and became factual, real. It was Deirdre" (242). Rejecting a (psychological) fantasy of full presence, Harris brings (literary) fantasy into science fiction by passing as social science.

This act of passing can also be said to replicate the process of fine-tuning a television set — adjusting the brain's picture and sound by screening out unwanted signals. A technology that, like film, depends on the relative slowness of human perception to produce its effects of realism, television also depends on human visual memory to fill in the blanks of its pixillated forms. Although Moore herself was not to become a television and film writer for several more years, her description of the human viewing the cyborg emphasizes the influence of memory on perception and the corresponding unreliability of vision as a marker of the real. As Moore's narrator tells her readers, "the human brain is often too complicated a mechanism to function perfectly" (242). Thus likening Harris, the human, to an unreliable machine, Moore extends the network of cyborg relations in the text to include both subject and object of a resolutely nostalgic masculine gaze.

Harris's shifting perceptions of Deirdre as a thing of the past contrast with her own pragmatic observations on her new body. Whereas "he had known her too well in the flesh to see her objectively now, even in metal" (252), she knows her body as a wonderful machine manipulated by electromagnetic currents from her brain. Years of training as a dancer enhance her ability to mimic human appearance, as well as her delighted appreciation of her machine-body. Like her voice, produced by "mentally play[ing] on the keyboard of [her] ... sound-unit" (249), Deirdre's body is a technological wonder which nevertheless depends on her disciplined, ever-learning mind to simulate humanity.

By contrast, Harris's likening of the new Deirdre to various works of art discounts the value of her own artistic labor. He muses instead on "the secret collaboration of artists, sculptors, designers, scientists and the genius of Maltzer" (239). He is thankful that "they had not tried to make a wax image of the lost Deirdre" and that the mask of her featureless face "was symbol enough for the woman within" (243). The manager appreciates the artistry of her metal skull and the "robe of very fine metal mesh" clothing a body made up of flexible metal rings. Contrasting Deirdre's golden, sinuous body with the "great, lurching robot forms" (241) of earlier science fiction, Harris's aesthetic appreciation of Deirdre's appearance nevertheless tends to frame her as a static image rather than the image in motion that she was even before her cybernetic enhancements.

In the same way that Harris relies on vision to assess Deirdre's rehabilitation, he perceives his rival Maltzer largely on the basis of the scientist's appearance: "He was a thin, wire-taut man with all the bone and sinew showing plainly beneath the dark skin of his face. Thinner, now, than he had been a year ago..." (239). Defined in part by the "distorting lenses" that he wears, Maltzer's perception of Deirdre is influenced less by Harris's aesthetic distance and more by the past year of "strange, cold passionless intimacy" with Deirdre as she adapted to her cyberbody (239.) Maltzer's Frankenstein-like fear is that in losing the senses of touch, taste and smell, Deirdre's sensually-based humanity is subject to "drainage" into the machine. But his great nervousness, in contrast with Deirdre's confidence, strongly suggests osmosis rather than drainage: a slow leak of her shock and trauma into the scientist in exchange for what Harris remembers as his once imperturbable confidence. The "unimaginable marriage" between Maltzer and Deirdre, with its swap of their personality traits, echoes Deirdre's understanding of the relation between her mind and body as that of a soldier dependent on its war-machine. At the same time, it echoes a similar exchange between Harris and Deirdre: while he is closely scrutinizing her, he periodically feels "from behind the mask a searching of his face" (251).

From a twenty-first century feminist perspective, it is perhaps easier to see the number of ways in which Maltzer's solicitous fears for Deirdre embody a one-sided view of the relations between humans and machines. Like Harris's sense of Deirdre as "lost" and "dead," Maltzer's assumptions about Deirdre's frailty indicate the chauvinistic limits of his ability to understand what he has made. Worried that she can no longer "compete" in television performance because "she hasn't any sex. She isn't female anymore" (258), Maltzer organizes his perceptions of Deirdre according to a heterosexual model of desire in which competition among women for male attention animates an essential femininity. Here is Donawerth's "Plastic Woman" — a female "type" — offered through the unreliable point of view of a scientist drinking to steady his nerves and admitting that he is "no longer fit to handle a hammer and saw" (258). Predicting disaster in Deirdre's television comeback, Maltzer's assumption of "sex competition" as the motivation of Deirdre's "type" participates in a discourse of Social Darwinism fraught with anxieties about the racial and sexual dehumanization of women. While Maltzer's drinking indicates that Deirdre's loss of the need for "primitive" sensual stimulation is his ironic gain, the narrator's attribution of sexual jealousy to Harris rather than Deirdre similarly indicates that "sex competition" is not a quintessentially feminine trait. Through ironic contrasts between the words and behaviors of her male characters, Moore produces a narrative space of lack — an aporia of masculine perception that mimics the linguistic aporia produced in the citation of the Deirdre legend, as well as the inevitable aporia of visual perception produced in the strictly textual description of Deirdre's body.

Moore builds on these various absences in the text by thematizing them in subtle contradictions between the men themselves. While Harris sees that "Maltzer seemed to be drawing nearer Deirdre in her fleshlessness with every passing week," Maltzer undermines the authority of this perception by indicting the sense of sight as "the last to come" and therefore "a cold, intellectual thing compared with the other senses" (259). The two men disagree on Deirdre's ability to make a viable television comeback, with Maltzer calling Harris a fool and Harris telling him to "Shut up" (261). The subtle web of aggression between the men and their shared displacement of concern for Deirdre thus combines the perspectives of Pygmalion and Frankenstein in a doubly mediated perspective blurred by nostalgia and fear.

Moore enlarges these contradictions by staging a contest for historical meaning defined by the two perspectives in a television variety show — the "vaude" in which Deirdre is scheduled to appear. As Lynn Spigel notes, early television often relied on theatrical conventions such as the proscenium set, curtains, exits and entrances, and a studio audience to produce an "ideology of liveness": the sense of the spectator as being installed "on the scene" (24). Enhanced by mise-en-abime structures (the stage within the stage) and alternations between real-time and edited time, the early use of stage conventions familiarized audiences with television by drawing parallels between old and new representational modes. Like Harris's nostalgic view of Deirdre as essentially unchanged, the "ideology of liveness" thus relies on cultural memory for its power. In *No Woman Born*, however, Moore contrasts stage conventions with the mobility of the television camera to demonstrate the nostalgic limits of this cultural memory.

Deirdre's performance is preceded by an array of spectacles that highlight television as an agent of nostalgia and anachronism: "On the television screen Mary of Scotland climbed the scaffold to her doom, the gown of traditional scarlet clinging warmly to supple young curves... (260). Foreshadowing Deirdre's doom, the anachronistic Mary of Scotland also comments retroactively on Maltzer's limited view of Deirdre's capacities and the limitations of television itself as a medium of historical revision. Moore's point may be that television lacks historical accuracy, but Maltzer "seeing another woman" (260) indicates that sight is not, as he has described it, "a cold, intellectual thing" (259). From Maltzer's point of view, Mary of Scotland's "supple young curves" define the femininity which Deirdre lacks; from Harris's point of view, they define his desire for "the lost Deirdre." From the faintly machinic perspective provided by Moore's omniscient narrator however, the "vaude" scene expands on the theme of the limitations of human perception. By demonstrating television's limited power to contain the flux of history in theatrical form, Moore projects the limitations of the written word ("playwrights") onto the visual medium. The "vaude" thus redefines the aporia of Maltzer and Harris's conflicting perceptions as a larger gap between human senses and technology's extension of these senses.

Moore's entire, detailed description of the variety show in which Deirdre is scheduled to appear highlights the limitations of television as a medium for representing the human and the historical. Indeed, it reads like a microcosm of history itself stuck in the linear motions of fast-forward and reverse. From the "great golden curtains" which sweep over Queen

Mary, "all sorrow and frustration wiped away once more as cleanly as the passing centuries," the show leaps to a "line of tiny dancers ... with the precision of little mechanical dolls too small and perfect to be real" (261). Reminiscent of the 1920's era of mass ornament, these "performing dolls" maintain their "perfect rhythm" even when seen from the grotesquely distorting perspective of a rapid pan and an aerial shot. An "invisible audience" applauds, and more performances — of a dance with torches and "the new singing ballet form of dance" in "gorgeous pseudo-period costumes" (261) continue to emphasize television as a medium vainly searching for a form of representation which reconciles the sweep of the camera eye with the limits of the human form. The "invisible audience" of these performances thus parallels the dehumanization of the "dancing dolls."

Deirdre sublimely fulfills and exceeds the historical lack inscribed by these toys. Watching intently, Maltzer and Harris sense an anticipation on the part of the studio audience "as if time had run backward here and knowledge of a great surprise had already broken upon them" (262). The temporal complexities of this clause, in which a surprise is always already known, combine past and future into a present which is both empty and filled with sublime promise: "The world might have looked like this on the first morning of creation, before heaven and earth took form in the mind of God" (262). But this allusion to a Genesis that might have been falls short of Deirdre's dance. Initially camouflaged as one in a row of golden columns, Deirdre emerges from neither heaven nor earth, nor from the wings of the stage, but rather from the stage set itself. *No Woman Born*, but rather replicated from theatrical props, set against "dim synthetic stars," Deirdre narrates an inhuman development from object to manikin to robot, encompassing Harris's perception of her as a medieval "creature in armour," yet also moving beyond that moment, insisting on its power as that of a fluid, inhumanly graceful machine. As Harris observes, "it was humanity that seemed, by contrast, jointed and mechanical now" (264). Deirdre's fulfillment of the televisual medium is illustrated by her command over both the camera and the studio audience: "The screen did not swoop to a close-up on her. Her enigma remained inviolate, and the television watchers saw her no more clearly than the audience in the theatre"(263). What Spigel calls the "ideology of liveness" thus works in *No Woman Born* by first matching human and technical perception, then gradually exceeding this match by layering sound on vision: Deirdre's practice in modulating her "sound-unit," like her years of bodily discipline, allow her to replicate and redefine the song which she had once made famous. Parodying "The

Yellow Rose of Texas" by having Deirdre sing "The Yellow Rose of Eden," Moore also subtly parodies television's ideology of liveness by exposing its dependence on technology's manipulations of human perception, emotion and collective memory.

In contrast with the formerly "invisible audience," Deirdre's audience is drawn together in a responsive, tumultuous roar of appreciation interrupting her song. Deirdre's invention of an entirely new dance form, her control over the audience, the stage set and the camera, and her "irrelevant" similarity to Valentino inscribe a history of cyborg development from object to subject by denaturalizing the Biblical story of Genesis and the theatrical conventions of the politely attentive, yet invisible audience. Her earlier statement to Harris — that the human ego "instill[s] its own force on inanimate objects" (249) is hence realized from a doubled point of view: while Deirdre as artist exerts her will over her machine-body, her audience also exerts a collective will on her. As the cyborg assumes gender and humanity before the audience's eyes, she illustrates that women, like cyborgs and matinee idols, are made not born. But as shown when her audience begins "applauding themselves as much as her," this "media cyborg" illustrates Donna Haraway's point that it is not technology per se, but rather a historical convergence of technologies *as perceived by a human community* that provides opportunities for contestation and redefinition. The persuasive power wielded by Deirdre over a mass audience expands the significance of the earlier scene in which Harris's perception is fine-tuned by his memories. Here, it is a larger cultural memory, enhanced by stage conventions, which Deirdre draws upon to articulate an alternative technocultural history.

But Deirdre's television comeback, as triumphant as it is, is only the beginning of her development as a cyborg. Insofar as it fulfills and exceeds Harris's hopes for her continuing popularity, her performance as a mobile object of the human gaze begs the question of what she will do with the renewed and expanded consensus of belief indicated by the roar of applause which shakes both the theater and the television set. After her public triumph, Deirdre refuses further bookings and takes time off at her farm in Jersey. "I've got a lot to think about," she tells Harris (271). Harris and Maltzer believe that she wants to think about her growing distance from humanity, and Maltzer hopes that she will consequently retire from public appearance. However, Deirdre's successful television comeback, her joyful confidence, and her landed wealth suggest that she might rather spend the time reconsidering her investments in humanity.

Jealous of Maltzer, yet inclined to believe the words of the scientist, Harris at first retreats from an immanent showdown between the inventor and the cyborg: "This was a matter between Deirdre and her creator, the culmination, perhaps, of that year's long intimacy so like marriage that this final trial for supremacy was a need he recognized" (269). One of the great delights of rereading *No Woman Born* is catching such aggressive assumptions woven into a discourse of solicitous male concern for Deirdre's future. In contrast with Harris's view of Maltzer as Deirdre's creator, she has already insisted that "I don't belong to him. In a way he's just been my doctor through a long illness..." (259). Yet Harris's insistence on seeing their relationship as marriage-like subtly reinforces Maltzer's sense of responsibility for the cyborg's future. Indeed, the recognition of a need for a "trial for supremacy" establishes a homosocial bond of aggression between the two men.

Meeting Maltzer and Deirdre again after two weeks, Harris is struck by his increasing decrepitude and her "veil of— detachment —" (273). He believes himself able to see Deirdre "as he supposed her audiences would" — an entirely new creature rather than a resurrection of the lost Deirdre (178). This recognition severs Deirdre's previous dependence on him as the manager of her career. Harris and Maltzer drift together into Maltzer's "terrible fear": "They're going to hate you, after a while, because you are still beautiful, and they're going to persecute you because you are different — and helpless" (275). Although couched in a paternalism that speaks to later efforts to install Rosie the Riveter in the postwar dream home, Maltzer's apprehension of a mob audience mentality also resonates with public anxieties about the effects of mass media on American social life, perhaps especially in terms of war propaganda and the threat of brainwashing. As Spigel notes, the widespread installation of TV on the postwar domestic scene followed years of public contestation, where the new medium was thought to both strengthen and threaten the traditional family (9). Moore's narrative context of a showdown between two partners in an "unimaginable marriage" illustrates this threat of disruption, while the use of the Frankenstein metaphor suggests cultural memory at work in attempts to gauge the effects of the new medium by drawing on literary and cinematic versions of the Gothic tale. Spigel further suggests that the early emphasis on "wartime inventions with peaceful intentions" may have contributed to this Frankenstein imagery: TV's miniaturization "created doubts about its ability to enter the home" (48).

Moore's point in demonstrating the limits of Maltzer's point of view is that Deirdre's greatest threat does not lie in an impending estrangement from the human, but rather in a redefinition of the objects and spaces that humans inhabit. The narrator's description of Deirdre's televised dance at the vaude suggests such a power of redefinition: "she seemed almost to project that completed pattern to her audience so that they saw her everywhere at once" (264). Deirdre's fading and returning rhythms mimic operations of camouflage as well as the flickering visual remainders that promote persistence of vision. As the dancer fills space with her "looping rhythms," she also weaves herself into that space, melding with her environment, and telling a story of strategic disappearance through protective mimicry.

The cultural origins of this defensive manoeuvre are shown in Harris's reaction to the "trick" which she plays upon the men in order to readjust their short-term memories:

> Harris choked, and his mind went blank for one moment of blind denial. He had not sat here watching a robot smoke and accepting it as normal. He could not! And yet he had. That had been the final note of conviction that swayed his hypnotized mind into accepting her humanity [183].

Influenced, as Donawerth notes, by the vamps of 1930s films, Deirdre recites a film trope in which the sharing of a cigarette symbolizes sexual intimacy (62). Donawerth argues that this act brings the men "to the brink of questioning whether all women are merely enacting desire, whether the heterosexuality which they depend upon as natural is really performance" (62). But this cinematic allusion also historicizes the vamp, situating her in the same space of anachronism as Mary of Scotland, with her "supple curves," the human dancing dolls of the "vaude," and the "knight of Oberon's court" first perceived by Harris. Easily adopted and discarded, these historical fragments are now cyborg toys and cyborg tools.

In her "showdown" with Maltzer, Deirdre ultimately demonstrates powers that far exceed her hypnotic effects onstage or her adaptability to male desire. Rescuing the guilt-ridden scientist from a suicidal leap, she demonstrates a newly-discovered ability to master the fourth dimension: "In the same instant she stood drooping by the mirror she was simultaneously at Maltzer's side. Her motion negated time and destroyed space.... Deirdre blazed in one continuous flash of golden motion across the room" (282). Rescuing Maltzer from suicide, she reverses the gendered roles of healer and victim that had framed their year-long "unimaginable marriage."

And Maltzer's conclusion, that perhaps he really is Frankenstein, sadly denies Deirdre's gentle repositioning of the doctor as patient and the husband as child. Maltzer remains in the Frankenstein Continuum, divorced from his "unimaginable marriage" but not from the conclusions of his ex-wife:

> You were afraid I had lost feeling and scent and taste.... Hearing and sight would not be enough, you think? But why do you think sight is the last of the senses? It may be the latest, Maltzer — Harris — *but why do you think it's the last?* [285. Emphasis in original].

As in her control of space and time, Deirdre appears to have entered a new sensory dimension. But the semantic generosity of the narrator is evident here in the possibility that the sixth sense to which she refers may be in fact a human one as it encounters Deirdre's superhuman powers.

Unlike the vampish performance with the cigarette, Deirdre's demonstration of her technologically-enhanced senses and abilities speaks again to the technocultural context of "wartime inventions with peaceful intentions." Echoing the earlier moment of audience recognition impelled by her voice, she threatens to disintegrate the room with "a sound that shook every atom upon its neighbour with a terrible, disrupting force" (284). The coded allusion to atomic power is not so prescient as one might think, since many sf writers imagined the bomb before Hiroshima. Here, the allusion to atomic power brings her technocultural powers of performative persuasion into the realm of global politics and the sheer application of force as a last resort — indeed the same spectre of "excessive force" that Ronell claims as haunting contemporary television. As Deirdre says to Maltzer, she is not subhuman, not Frankenstein's monster, but rather superhuman. At the same time, she realizes that she will grow, learn and die; her mortality suggests a limit to her cybernetic growth.

Exactly whether Deirdre will turn out to have "peaceful intentions" rather than warlike ones is a point deliberately left open by Moore. There are enough demonic allusions in her description, enough indications of global ambition in her sense that "there's so much still untried" (288), and enough hints of metal in her voice at story's end that it is quite possible to read *No Woman Born* as following the Frankenstein story towards an apocalyptic ending in which the exercise of women's power makes no difference in the human history of improved killing machines. But Deirdre's efficient tenderness in dealing with Maltzer belies this conclusion. Instead of fulfilling Maltzer's original aim to serve "everyone who meets with accidents that might have ruined them" (275), Deirdre shows that her aims are larger — to prevent such accidents.

No Woman Born uses such techniques as the contradictory layerings of masculine points of view, the mythic historicizing of film and television, and the subtle extension of a World War II ideology of technologically-enhanced feminine strength, to posit an open-ended future for the cyborg and her human associates. Predicated on the fascinations of mass visual pleasure and its revisionary effects on human memory, this future is also predicated on a lone superwoman's determination to overcome the limitations imposed on her by the assumption that her femininity is genetically hard-wired into her brain. Her insistence that "my brain's human, and no human brain could leave such possibilities untried" is therefore readable as a feminist — or proto-feminist — assertion of women's human right to participate in the technocultural shaping of world history (187).

Nonetheless, this revisionary "media cyborg" is limited in one very important way (aside from her brain's mortality and the limitations of her white power.) Finally admitting, in the midst of wonder at her newfound abilities, that her greatest fear is loneliness, she wishes that there could be others like her (287). Meanwhile, her acknowledgement that she has set a fashion in women's clothing (285) indicates that such others will not come from the scientist's laboratory, but rather from women's identifications with a combination of strength, beauty and compassion that might begin with "Plastic Woman" but does not end there.

WORKS CITED

Albrecht, Donald, ed. *World War II and the American Dream: How Wartime Building Changed a Nation*. Washington and Cambridge: National Building Museum and MIT Press, 1995.

Barrows, Craig, and Diana Barrows. "*The Left Hand of Darkness*: Feminism for Men." *Mosaic* 20.1 (Winter 1987): 83–96.

Bredehoft, Thomas A. "Origin Stories: Feminist Science Fiction and C.L. Moore's 'Shambleau.'" Science Fiction Studies 24 (1997): 369–86.

Clareson, Thomas D., ed. *Voices for the Future: Essays on Major Science Fiction Writers*. Vol. I. Bowling Green, Ohio: Bowling Green University Popular Press, 1976.

Fackler, Herbert V. *That Tragic Queen: The Deirdre Legend in Anglo-Irish Literature*. Salzburg: Institut Fur Englische Sprache und Literatur, 1978.

Gamble, Sarah. "'Shambleau ... and Others': The Role of the Female in the Fiction of C.L. Moore." *Where No Man Has Gone Before: Women and Science Fiction*. Ed. Lucie Armitt. London: Routledge, 1991. 29–49.

Grosz, Elizabeth. *Volatile Bodies: Toward a Corporeal Feminism*. Bloomington: Indiana University Press, 1994.

Gunn, James. "Henry Kuttner, C.L. Moore, Lewis Padgett et al." *Voices for the Future: Essays on Major Science Fiction Writers*. Vol. 1. Ed. Thomas D. Clareson. Bowling Green: Bowling Green University Popular Press, 1976. 185–15.

Harper, Mary Catherine. "Incurably Alien Other: A Case for Feminist Cyborg Writers." *Science Fiction Studies* 22.3 (November 1995): 399–420.

Harrison, Harry, and Brian Aldiss. *The Astounding Analog Reader*. Vol. 1. New York: Doubleday, 1972.

Honey, Maureen. *Creating Rosie the Riveter: Class, Gender and Propaganda During the World War*. Amherst: University of Massachusetts Press, 1984.

Linster, Murray. "First Contact." Harrison and Aldiss, *The Astounding Analog Reader*, 401–430.

Meek, Allen. "Benjamin, the Televisual and The 'Fascistic Subject.'" Online 15 September 1998. <www.latrobe.edu.au/screeningthepast/firsrelease/fir998/Amfr4e. htm> 3 September 2002.

MacDonald, Fred J. *One Nation Under Television: The Rise and Decline of Network TV*. New York: Pantheon, 1990.

Matthews, Patricia. "C.L. Moore's Classic Science Fiction." *The Feminine Eye: Science Fiction and the Women Who Write It*. Ed. Tom Staicar. New York: Ungar, 1982.

Moore, C.L. *No Woman Born. The Best of C.L. Moore*. Ed. Lester Del Rey. New York: Ballantine, 1975. 236–288.

_____. "Shambleau." *The Best of C.L. Moore*. Ed. Lester Del Rey. New York: Ballantine, 1975. 1–32.

Roberts, Robin. *A New Species: Gender and Science in Science Fiction*. Chicago: University of Illinois Press, 1993.

Ronell, Avital. *The Telephone Book: Technology, Schizophrenia, Electric Speech*. London: University of Nebraska Press, 1989.

_____. "Video/Television/Rodney King: Twelve Steps Beyond the Pleasure Principle." In *Culture on the Brink: Ideologies of Technology*, eds. Gretchen Bender and Timothy Druckrey. Seattle: Bay Press, 1994. 277–303.

Rosinsky, Natalie M. "C.L. Moore's 'Shambleau': Woman as Alien or Alienated Woman?" *Selected Proceedings of the 1978 Science Fiction Research Association National Conference*. Ed. Thomas J. Remington. Cedar Falls: University of Northern Iowa, 1979. 68–74.

Rutsky, R.L. *High Techné: Art and Technology from the Machine Aesthetic to the Posthuman*. Minneapolis: University of Minnesota Press, 1999.

Simak, Clifford. "City." Harrison and Aldiss, *The Astounding Analog Reader*, 377–400.

Sontag, Susan. "Fascinating Fascism." *Under the Sign of Saturn*. New York: Farrar, Strauss, Giroux, 1980. 73–105.

Spigel, Lynn. *Make Room for TV: Television and the Family Ideal in Postwar America*. Chicago: University of Chicago Press, 1992.

Stephens, James. *Deirdre*. New York: Macmillan, 1923.

Tichi, Cecilia. *Electronic Hearth: Creating an American Television Culture*. New York: Oxford University Press, 1991.

Warner, Marina. *Monuments and Maidens: The Allegory of the Female Form*. London: Weidenfeld and Nicolson, 1985.

Wolmark, Jenny. *Aliens and Others: Science Fiction, Feminism and Postmodernism*. New York: Harvester Wheatsheaf, 1993.

_____. "Cyberpunk, Cyborgs, and Feminist Science Fiction." *Feminist Contributions to the Literary Canon: Setting Standards of Taste.* Ed. Susanne Fendler. Lewiston, New York: Edwin Mellen, 1997.

14

The Fantasy of Gender/Sex: Angela Carter and Mythmaking

Darlene M. Juschka

This essay explores an intersection with three of Angela Carter's texts, the non-fictional *The Sadeian Woman* (1979), and two of her early novels, the dystopic *Heroes and Villains* (1969) and her post-surrealist text *The Infernal Desire Machines of Dr. Hoffman* (1972) (referred to henceforth as *Dr. Hoffman*) in order to speak of gender ideology and the category of subjectivity as developed within a Euro-western and masculinist oriented ontological frame. It will argue that Carter's politicizing of subjectivity (in regard to gender in particular) makes apparent how subjectivity in Euro-western ontology is only possible at the cost of another: to be a subject in the world means the objectification of another in the process of establishing a subjectivity of self.

Founding/Grounding Narratives: Power and Myth

Myth, according to Roland Barthes, is a mode of signification (making signs) and therefore a semiological system ("Myth Today" 109–11). As a semiological system, myth communicates and makes meaningful what might be called cultural, social, and human truths. Myth functions as the often unanalyzed "truths" of our social bodies. From the perspective of the scholar, myth is that which defines and locates the work of being human within a given social and historical milieu and for that reason the exploration of these truths proves a fruitful endeavor for scholars of myth. Critically engaging myth is not a process of demythologization wherein myth is excised from the "truth" of human narratives as Rudolph Bultmann would have had it. The binary structure of myth, its logic, is a powerful and pervasive force for shaping and limiting social bodies and consequently myth is never jettisoned. One can expose a binary of a myth, but very quickly something similar takes its place. Rather than rejecting myth or attempting to exorcize it from human signing systems, it is far more productive to understand its processes in order to better grasp the formation and operation of human systems of belief. Studying myth, then, operates a little like psychoanalysis: revealing a neurosis is not the cure; rather it is a means for understanding.

Following Claude Lévi-Strauss (*Myth and Meaning*, "Structural Study of Myth," and *Mythologiques*), this essay works from the premise that the structural logic of myth is binary opposition. Binary opposition is a dualistic signing system that subsequently can allow for valuation when deployed within a social body, often one that is stratified and boundary oriented. Beginning with an opposition or dualism, one often understood to be natural and normative, binaries operate as interconnected dyads. Root binaries, or foundational binaries, may be initially neutral, but subsequent binaries, relationally linked to the root binary, can and often do introduce value.[1] Root binaries vary in relation to social and historical location. In the Euro-west some long term root binaries are female/male, out/in, and down/up.

Each of the above binaries can be understood to function within a particular dimension or social environment so that the female/male binary dyad operates in the bios, out/in in the social, and down/up in the metaphysical. Root binaries can be neutral in that there is no initial value placed upon them and their only operative is to give meaning to the other half of the binary: a meaning based on opposition or difference. Secondary binaries, tertiary binaries and so forth introduce a valuative component so that, for example, female/male is related to weak/strong, cold/hot, moist/dry in Aristotelian epistemology; out/in is related to nature/culture, margin/center, other/same during euro-western colonization, while down/up is related to immanent/ transcendent, evil/ good, diabolic/angelic in Catholic Christianity in the Middle Ages. Further to these associations, the development of the elements in the binary relationship is conditioned by the social/cultural location. Therefore female/male (root binary), is given valuation by its association with cold/hot and moist /dry within the Athenian cultural milieu of the Classical period (500–325 BCE), which was then grafted onto Euro-western systems (or medieval Islamic systems) in the adoption of Aristotelian logic.[2]

 Binary dyads (e.g., female/male) share metaphorical (along the vertical axis) and metonymical (along the horizontal axis) relations within the logic of binarism. Accordingly, in the metaphorical relationship one binary dyad is able to invoke another binary dyad. For example, within the Euro-western Enlightenment epistemology the female half of the binary dyad of female/male can invoke, often implicitly, but equally explicitly, weak (strong), and irrational (rational). In the metonymical relationship one half of the binary, for example, rational, evokes its partner, for example, irrational. The following diagram demonstrates this rhetorical function:

Metaphorical Relationships ↕		Metonymical Relationships ↔		
Female	Male	Female	↔	Male
↕	↕			
Weak	Strong	Weak	↔	Strong
↕	↕			
Irrational	Rational	Irrational	↔	Rational

Binarism is the engine or the power of myth.[3] Mythic narratives are structured via the use of a signing system (semiotic system), the logic of which is binarism. This is why mythic narratives continue to be powerful and why when signs fade or carry discursive value no longer in current social systems they are replaced by new signs. We have not left myth behind as a moment in the development of "civilization," rather, mythic narratives continue to operate within our social systems giving full meaning to these systems.

The Mythic Ground of Gender and *the Sadeian Woman*

 The textual strategies introduced by Carter allow for the demythologizing of gender ideology. To demythologize gender ideology is to reveal or bring to consciousness the binarism that continues to fuel the ways in which we understand gender. To first uncover the logic of binarism, noting that the root binary is the male/female, and then to underscore the linguisticality of binarism allows for the socialization and historicization of binaries and, subsequently, gender ideology (gender/sex). Yet this does not fully reveal just what is at stake in gender ideology. Two other aspects are made apparent in Carter's *The Sadeian Woman.*

First, gender ideology includes sex as a mythologized discourse. The foundational quality of myth — its apparent rootedness in nature — means that the social, historical, and political discourse of gender *and* sex is elided and instead the already abstracted and mythified concept of "desire" is interpolated into the text of gender/sex: "s/he is the object of my desire, and I am the subject that perpetuates that desire." Desire (Eros[4]) is seen to have no social, historical or political dimensions. It simply is. But desire is not an "is": it is not a thing (an arrow) that strikes (or pierces) an individual to propel her/him toward some action. Rather, desire is lack; it is an absence. As lack or absence — e.g., lack of a lover, status, wealth, and so forth — it is socially, historically and politically defined. When Angela Carter grounds desire in the social and all its accoutrements, she ensures that desire is revealed as politicized speech.

Second, Carter's introduction and development of the Marquis de Sade's politicizing of sex, found in her text *The Sadeian Woman,* reveals what is at stake in gender ideology: power. Although this would seem evident, evident it is not. "I am a man" or "I am a woman" seem not to be political statements that mark power. But by introducing the pornographic discourse, the innocence of such statements is stripped away and the social power that is concealed is exposed to the light of day. With this in sight, then, female and male subjectivity can be rendered.

Female Subjectivity and *Heroes and Villains*

The world proposed in *Heroes and Villains* is a world stratified into the haves and have-nots. Its dystopic vision does not break with the past, the past is carried into the present and although a new history is produced, the mythic ground that secures history is exposed. The en-valuated (to give value) root binaries of female/male and out/in[5] continue to establish the politics of civilization. Marianne, the protagonist of the text, is inside the walls of these new communities, a daughter of a professor. But as she is female and belongs to the group she cannot represent the group. She can be that by which identity is mediated, the body through which the phallus is passed (Rubin), but within the confines of the villages of the professors, no female subjectivity can be claimed. Marianne, upon the death of her father, cuts her hair, and begins her journey, joining a band of barbarians.

The escape from the old and the entrapment in the new of the barbarian band continues to pose a problem for Marianne's development of a female subjectivity. Although she can lay claim to a new status, outsider-outsider, or female outsider, the power dynamics of the barbarian society demand that she be emplaced within the group. Within this group, the female continues to be that which mediates the phallus rather than that which can represent the phallus. In the text, Marianne, in her bid for subjectivity, begins a process of moving from the passive to the active, but in so doing she imperils male subjectivity: as her subjectivity develops the objectivity of Jewel, her male antagonist, increases exponentially.

The process of developing her subjectivity requires that Marianne become a phallic female: not the object of the gaze but the objectifying gazer. Marianne must stand outside the world and affect the attitude of boredom or alienation in order that she can rationally assess it. She must reject sentimentality for it obscures the political nature of all relations, and she must logically assess sexuality for, as Carter has argued in *The Sadeian Woman,* "we take to bed with us every aspect of the cultural impedimenta of our social class, our parents' lives, our bank balances ... all the bits and pieces of our unique existence" (9). For female subjectivity to be realized in masculine hegemony, Marianne must grasp the scepter (phallus) and rule with an iron hand.

The female subjectivity evinced in the figure of Marianne in Carter's *Heroes and Villains* is a complex mesh between the manifestations of Marianne's own desires and the desire of those others for whom she is Other. The female is but a commodity of exchange in both the professor and the barbarian communities: she is used in order to pass the phallus from one male to the other. But in each social location Marianne resists, incorporates, alters, or rejects the expectations fostered upon her, and assesses her own expectations, produced within and by her varying social locations. In this endeavor she critically engages her own notion of self and the notion of self held by those around her. Marianne recognizes Jewel, her metaphorical male twin and rapist, as the "furious invention of [her] virgin nights," and after Jewel's death, when the others threaten to leave her behind, she rejects this narrative, claims the barbarians as her own, and her role within the community as the "tiger lady" who will "rule them with a rod of iron"

(150). Marianne, unlike Justine found in Sade's text, is the agent of her own story, and like Juliette, lays claim to her own desires: she revels in her own lack. However, Marianne rejects the myth of female subjectivity as commodity, as the virgin and the whore (Justine and Juliette), and instead creates a new mythic role, the tiger lady. She will bring the order from her old world of the professors to the chaos of the new world of the barbarians (Gamble 79), and meld sameness and otherness. This melding of otherness and sameness to produce something new, whatever that new may be, undercuts the traditional utopian discourse.

The interplay between the characters of the novel evincing the desire for each to fix the Other as Object reveals their own lack, and establishes a world of shifting subjectivities and objectivities. Carter eradicates the mythic two-dimensionality of the idealized androcentric world and interposes a feminist view that complicates the situation. The complexities interposed resemble more the intricate aspects of humans bonding: Carter develops the social and political aspects of human relationships. However, within the shifts that represent the complexities of human relations, there is one role that Carter has Marianne resist: the role of female. Instead Marianne takes the desires of the community and melds and shapes them to her own. Marianne, as the feminist hero of the novel, does not remove herself from the social domain, but actively works within the social domain in order to envision a new world that consists of the past and the present.

Carter, in her text *Heroes and Villains* (one should note the binary dyad in the title), attempts to neutralize binarism and to come to terms with such binaries as object/subject; other/same; villain/hero; female/male by first reversing the positive and negative poles (e.g., Jewel is object, Marianne is subject; Jewel is passion, Marianne is reason) and, second, by introducing a dialectic in order to synthesize the binaries, e.g. Tiger Lady. Her point is to examine female subjectivity, but as there is no such thing in a patriarchal social body, Carter must attempt to mold one using androcentric myths of the female, and apply to these feminist tools of engagement. One such tool is reversal so that, for example, the tattooed Jewel stands as Other to Marianne's Same (Marianne as "female" in patriarchal myths means she is undifferentiated from all women, and therefore can subversively draw upon this undifferentiation in order to claim the category of Same, which can then subsequently stand as the normative).

Another tool Carter engages is to dialectically encounter binaries in order to neutralize the values through their combination toward producing a synthesis, for example virgin/whore to Tiger Lady or phallic female.

However, the synthesis achieved in the dialectical operation is not a solution to the problem of binarism as valuation continues to operate so that thesis remains positive, and antithesis remains negative within the synthesis. In gender terms, then, male/men/masculine continues to carry a positive valuation and female/women/feminine the negative. It would appear that the metonymical function (wherein one half of the binary evokes the other, e.g., "cold" brings with it "hot" its binary partner) that evokes the metaphorical linkages of valuation (secondary, tertiary and so forth relationships are implicitly aroused, e.g., linked to female in the Euro-west are emotion, irrationality, evil, etc.) is too firmly entrenched.

In a novel written three years later, Carter continues her attempt to undercut binarism, this time in her text *The Infernal Desire Machines of Doctor Hoffman*. Here she rejects reversal and the Hegelian dialectic as a possible answer to the feminist dilemma of binarism in patriarchal relations and attempts to work this problem out by drawing upon poststructuralism wherein subjectivity itself is called into question.

Male Subjectivity and *The Infernal Desire Machine of Dr. Hoffman*

The post-surrealist text of *Dr. Hoffman* is a different cultural play introduced by Carter. Binaries continue to figure, but rather than entrench binaries in the bios and social as one finds in *Heroes and Villains*, Carter fully engages the semiological signing system through which binarism makes meaning. Symbols as signs are not meaningful in and of themselves; rather they are the *bricolage* of culture invested with meaning. In order to fully understand Carter's play with symbols as signs, Salvador Dali's interaction with and estrangement from the surrealist group of André Breton is evocative. Dali challenged the notion of essence in a symbol, its truth, and underscores the sign, its meaning function within a social body (LaFountain 96). By recognizing the signing function of binarism, binary opposites are unfixed (their oppositional qualities are called into question), and as signs their polysemy is underscored (their multiple meaning) and located linguistically (words have no essence). Root binaries such as female/male, out/in or down/up mean within linguistic systems and hold no inherent meaning: they sign meaning and do not point to innate meaning within the world. The post-surrealist landscape encourages an examination of surfaces for meaning rather than the assumption that real meaning lies beneath the surface.

Carter's text *The Infernal Desire Machine of Dr. Hoffman*, set in South America, envisions a landscape locked between fantasy and reality with fantasy figuring as the unchained unconscious. Dr. Hoffman's desire machines have instituted a state of chaos where the unconscious of human beings is manifested in the realm of the conscious. The gatekeeper, or the repressive mechanism to which Freud refers, has been overridden by Hoffman's machines so that now the conscious, preconscious and unconscious all function on the same plane. The Minster of Determination wages a war over reality, or reality determined by him, with Dr. Hoffman. Desiderio, he who desires, is both the protagonist and narrator in the novel. His memories are those that develop the surrealist landscape of the text.[6] The story begins with a slow but gradually mounting interruption of reality.[7] Desiderio reflects:

> Nothing in the city was what it seemed — nothing at all! Because Dr. Hoffman, you see, was waging a massive campaign against human reason itself .... We did not understand the means by which the Doctor modified the nature of reality until very much later. We were taken entirely by surprise and chaos supervened immediately. Hallucinations flowed with magical speed in every brain.... Dr. Hoffman's gigantic generators sent out a series of seismic vibrations which made great cracks in the hitherto immutable surface of the time and space equation we had informally formulated in order to realize our city [11; 17].

Into the mix of reality and fantasy Desiderio enters and sardonically assumes the role of hero, a hero whose actions will bring to an abrupt end the infernal desire machines of Dr. Hoffman.

The landscape Carter creates in *Dr. Hoffman* is one where reality and fantasy collide and coalesce. In Carter's novel, Dr. Hoffman's machines call into question the essence of reality and reason, proposing that reason is a sign by which reality is fixed. The intersection between reality and fantasy, each of which calls the other into question, is nicely evinced through recourse to a post-surrealism. Surrealism proposes an essence, or a kernel of truth that resides at the heart of all existence. This is why surrealism made recourse to symbols and not signs. Symbols assume an essence; they make recourse to the signified (concept); signs reject an essence and underscore signifiers (form). In other words, the power in symbols is seen to reside outside of the social and emerge into the social from another place. The sign, however, begins at the place of signifier. Its origins are in language with no particular essence attributed to it other than the shifting meaning affiliated with an arbitrary signifier (Barthes "Myth Today" 113 and "The Semiotic Challenge"). Hence Dali's underscoring of phantom meaning (signifier) as opposed to Breton's phantom object (signified). The sign is an arbitrary mark that is socially and historically located, while the symbol is an essentialized concept that bursts into the social and historical frame. In Carter's post-surrealist narrative the essence of things comes into conflict with arbitrary meaning: fixed meaning (symbol) opposed against fluid and shifting meaning (sign). She posits symbols in order to mark them as signs and, in so doing, underscores the mystified speech of symbols.

Between the two antagonists, the Minister of Determination (reality and reason) and Dr. Hoffman (fantasy and desire), stands Desiderio, the protagonist of the story. Desiderio, an agent of the Minister, is the son to which the two fathers wish to lay claim: his loyalty will guarantee the continuation of either of their systems. Desiderio, a young man born of a prostitute and a customer of Indian extraction, is a slip-up of business and a mix between races (16). This negative positing of Desiderio as male with only a female genealogy and carrying a "genetic imprint" of his unknown father locates Desiderio on the margins of the white, masculine and hegemonic power that rules the land. Like most heroes his parentage is in question, but unlike most heroes, royalty or godhood (King Arthur or Jesus) is not determined post-quest. It is Desiderio's insider and outsider status that both illuminates and challenges male subjectivity in the novel.

Desiderio is a cynical romantic, longing for something but bored with everything he finds. Throughout the movement of the text across differing landscapes Desiderio seeks his heart's desire, Albertina, daughter of Hoffman. She first emerges in his dreams, and throughout his quest he encounters her in a variety of guises. Each guise she takes is but a product of Desiderio's own desire. Often he does not recognize her, but when she does finally assume what might be her own form she is raped by the centaurs of nebulous time. Albertina claimed that the rape may have been the product of her unconscious (186) but what Desiderio knew was that it was a product of his.

Desiderio's desire, in equal measure, both sublates and subjugates Albertina. Albertina, like Beatrice of Dante's *Divine Comedy,* is but an ideation. Offered the bliss of fulfilled desire, his and Albertina's eternal embrace, Desiderio falters in the face of his desire. If he should consummate endlessly this desire with Albertina in a mesh cubicle powering the doctor's machines, he would become as nameless, as faceless, as those others in their cubicles. He would be feminized: an object of desire. Desiderio, instead, chooses to kill the Doctor and to brutally kill Albertina: to become a "hero" rather than a "lover." Having killed Albertina, Desiderio tucks a handkerchief stained with her blood into his breast pocket "where it looked like a rose" (218). Dead, she no longer threatens his male subjectivity; dead, she is the dream that fixes his desire. Desiderio can once again begin to long for Albertina as his heart's desire: "'And so I identified at last the flavour of my daily bread; it was and would be that of regret. Not, you understand, of remorse; only of regret, that insatiable regret with which we acknowledge that the impossible is, *per se*, impossible'" (221).

When we look for a delineation of male subjectivity in Carter's *Dr. Hoffman*, it becomes apparent that it is a slippery concept moving between the two proposed ideologies. Because Carter is concerned with gender and sex, one notes in the text how the female is an object to the male who is subject. It is this interplay she wishes to demystify. Albertina, as the Other of Desiderio's desire, figures as the something that fantasy projects in order that the male subject can locate himself in masculine hegemony. Lacan indicates that "Desire is a relation of being to lack. This lack is the lack of being properly speaking. It isn't the lack of this or that, but lack of being whereby the being exists" (qtd. in Silverman 20). In order to fill the gap, the hole which is the center of subjectivity, an object which is fictive and located as the motive of desire, is posited, so that both desire and the object can guarantee the reality of subjectivity. Fantasy, as Kaja Silverman states, "thus conjures forth a fictive object for a fundamentally a-objectal desire. It translates the desire for nothing into the desire for something" and that something is the self, the self as lack (symbolic castration) that recoups being through the object (that which mediates the passing of the phallus) and which then, as she states, "fills the void at the center of subjectivity with an illusory plenitude" (4–5).[8]

Throughout the text Albertina remains at a distance, far enough away so that she does not threaten Desiderio's subjectivity. At a distance she remains a fictive object of his desire. Once in the caves underneath the mountain behind the castle of Dr. Hoffman the reality of the fantasy became apparent. Desiderio would not receive the phallus from Dr. Hoffman mediated by Albertina: within the scenario of the imaginary realm, the unconscious, which Dr. Hoffman ruled, Desiderio's subjectivity as full was unmasked and he saw himself as lack, absence, merely a shadow upon the wall (as his name foreshadows). The "subject of the unconscious" (Desiderio in Dr. Hoffman's freed unconscious), as Silverman states, reading Lacan, "is 'acephalic' — that is 'headless,' or, to be more precise, devoid of 'self.' This subject, which Lacan calls the 'je,' is devoid both of form and of object; it can perhaps best be defined as pure lack, and hence as 'desiring nothing'" (Silverman 4). In order to reinstate fantasy in service of reality, rather than the reverse, Desiderio kills the father and the daughter, and captures the phallus ensuring again that his desire has a fictive object that will forever ensure his male subjectivity. His movement is the culmination of the positive Oedipal drama played out within the realm of fantasy and therefore upholding (masculine) reality. Desiderio returns a hero, the ideal of the masculine in patriarchal relations. As Desiderio realized, "'...perhaps I was indeed looking for a master — perhaps the whole history of my adventure could be titled 'Desiderio in Search of a Master.' But I only wanted to find a master, the Minister, The Count, the bay [the latter refers to the leader of the Centaurs], so that I could lean on him at first and then, after a while, jeer'" (190).

The Subject Contested

The subject contested brings us to the end of this paper. The mythic ground of subjectivity is called into question throughout Carter's writing. We note that both protagonists are marginal to their social systems. Marianne is the white daughter of the ruling, if not controlling, class of the professors while Desiderio lacks a male genealogy and is racially marked as indigenous in colonialist South America. We begin at the outset, then, with negative subjectivities attempting to find a positive subjectivity in a hegemony that already denies them "true" human status: racial, sexual, and class differences have set them apart. The myth of human nature, which establishes subjectivity, has already situated both protagonists as variant forms of the Other: only the white properly masculine Euro-western male can symbolize true human nature or the universal human, the capital "S" subject of Lacan's musings. Marianne and Desiderio reside in social systems that locate at their foundations the myth of human nature: a human nature that depends upon difference — sexual, racial and class — in order to guarantee its truth. Both Marianne and Desiderio struggle against this myth with greater or lesser success.

What Carter's novels do, then, is undercut an essentialized subject, the eternal human, and what they underscore is a constructed subject who in turn constructs a world. What is further made apparent is that the process of an idealized subjectivity depends upon the category of Other. In the struggle for subjectivity, then, the novels underscore the founding myth of the category of subject. This category relies upon the belief in a fixed human nature and it is this fixed human nature that is problematic to the Other who would claim it. To lay claim to subjectivity means laying claim to the Euro-western myth of subjectivity (white, masculine, European, middle and upper class) and consequently one must allow the already-there ideology to command her/his belief. However, Carter is not asserting that one lay claim to the position of object. Rather, she demystifies both subject and object locations and, in this, renders the binary structure of myth.

Her first move in *Heroes and Villains* was to propose reversal and dialectics to solve this problem, a bringing together of order and chaos in service of the social. These binaries emerged from the social and were shown as such, but problematically, the binary structure of myth was not fully demystified through this engagement. In *Dr. Hoffman* Carter drew upon semiotics in order to further uncover the mythic speech of binarism and reveal what Kaja Silverman (15–17) calls the dominant fiction; the phallus-penis equation that occupies absolute pride of place in Euro-western systems. "Indeed," writes Silverman, "that question is so central to the *vraisemblance* [verisimilitude] that at those historical moments when the prototypical male subject is unable to recognize "himself" within its conjuration of masculine sufficiency our society suffers from a profound sense of "ideology fatigue." Our entire "world," then, depends upon the alignment of phallus and penis" (15–16).

Throughout her work Carter does not resolve the dominant fiction of commensurability of the phallus and the penis. Rather, she demonstrates the linguistic, social and psychical operations of binarism that grounds the phallus in nature, i.e., the penis, in order to demystify the myth of subjectivity as propagated by a masculinist (Euro-western, white and elite) hegemony. Silverman emphatically argues that "'Male' and 'Female' constitute our dominant fiction's most fundamental binary opposition" (34–35). Carter, too, intent upon demystifying the mythic grounds of female subjectivity, male subjectivity and ultimately subjectivity itself makes apparent the mythic speech of binarism in order to cut out the ground from beneath the subject and illustrate the *bricolage* used to construct it.

Notes

1. At this junction "maybe" is used as Christine Delphy has argued that inherent to the very act of differentiation is valuation. According to the *OED*: "*binary system* (of classification): one by which each group and sub-group is perpetually divided

into two, the one with a positive and the other with a negative character, till individuals (or genera) are reached." In the binary system of numbers, 01010101, zero carries a negative value while one a positive value. This valuation, then, may well be transported into social understanding and at the outset establish a negative and positive valuation to even root binaries. And yet in the face of this logic one is not completely convinced. There is not an inherent negativity or positivity to the category of the female (or zero) or the male (or one). Rather, it is their relationality as different that allows the binary to be gathered up in a system of meaning related to valuation. Therefore, as with language wherein "a" or "e" carry no inherent value related to word use other than they are different from each other (de Saussure) so too on this level male and female are simply different. However, in the development of the binary system wherein associative concepts are linked to the root binary then value comes into play. It is at the level of exchange between binaries found in the metaphorical and metonymical relationships where value is introduced.

2. See G.E.R. Lloyd for a discussion of the Classical Greek thought and opposition.

3. See Claude Lévi-Strauss who fully develops this argument in his *Mythologiques*.

4. Eva Karpinski has argued, following Marina Warner, that the myth of Eros and Psyche is a "founding myth of sexual difference" (145).

5. The phrase "envaluated root binaries" emphasizes how female/male and out/in (root binaries) are already explicitly associated with secondary and tertiary binaries in the novel by Carter. Therefore, for example, "in" is associated with civilized while "out" is associated with barbarians, while "female" is linked to passive and "male" to active.

6. We read at the outset of the novel, "Because I am so old and famous, they have told me that I must write down all my memories of the Great War, since, after all, I remember everything" (11). But of course since fantasy has been engaged in the text the "I" of narrator is called into question: "...for I was a great hero in my own time though now I am an old man and no longer the 'I' of my own story..."(14).

7. "Interruption" is used intentionally as the effort is to capture both notions of "a breaking into" and "a break with" in order to express how Dr. Hoffman's machines affected "reality."

8. Carter comments in her essay "Femme Fatales" in *Nothing Sacred,* written in 1978, that "Desire does not so much transcend its object as ignore it completely in favour of a fantastic recreation of it" (120).

WORKS CITED

Barthes, Roland. *The Semiotic Challenge*. 1985. Trans. Richard Howard. New York: Hill and Wang, 1988.

_____. "Myth Today." *Mythologies*. 1957. Trans. Annette Lavers. New York: Hill and Wang, 1972. 109–59

Carter, Angela. *The Infernal Desire Machines of Doctor Hoffman*. 1972. New York and London: Penguin, 1994.

_____. *Heroes and Villains*. 1969. New York and London: Penguin, 1993.

_____. *The Sadeian Woman*.1979. London: Virago, 1982.

_____. *Nothing Sacred: Selected Writings*. London: Virago, 1982.

Delphy, Christine. "Rethinking Sex and Gender." 1993. *Sex in Question: French Materialist Feminism*. Eds. Diana Leonard and Lisa Adkins. London: Taylor & Francis, 1996. 30–41.

de Saussure, Ferdinand. *Course in General Linguistics*. 1959. New York, Toronto, London: McGraw-Hill, 1966.

Freud, Sigmund. "Resistance and Repression." *Introductory Lectures on Psychoanalysis*. Vol. 1. 1916–17. Eds. James Strachey and Angela Richards. Trans. James Strachey. London: Penguin, 1991. 327–343.

Gamble, Sarah. *Angela Carter: Writing From the Front Lines*. Edinburgh: Edinburgh University Press, 1997.

Karpinski, Eva C. "Signifying Passion: Angela Carter's *Heroes and Villains* as a Dystopian Romance." *Utopian Studies* 11.2 (Spring 2000): 137–51.

Kristeva, Julia. "From Symbol to Sign." *The Kristeva Reader*. 1970. Ed. Toril Moi. New York: Columbia University Press, 1986. 62–73.

LaFountain, Marc J. *Dali and Postmodernism: This Is Not an Essence*. New York: SUNY, 1997.

Lévi-Strauss, Claude. *Myth and Meaning: Cracking the Code of Culture*. 1978. Foreword Wendy Doniger. New York: Schocken, 1995.

_____. *Mythologiques: Introduction to a Science of Mythology*. 4 vols. New York: Harper and Row, 1969–1982.

_____. "Structural Study of Myth." *Structural Anthropology*. Trans. Claire Jacobson and Brooke Grundfest Schoepf. New York: Basic Books, 1963. 206–31.

Lloyd, G.E.R. *Polarity and Analogy: Two Types of Argumentation in Early Greek Thought*. Cambridge: Cambridge University Press, 1966.

Rubin, Gayle. "The Traffic in Women: Notes on the 'Political Economy' of Sex." *Toward an Anthropology of Women*. Ed. Rayne R. Reiter. New York and London: Monthly Review, 1975. 157–210.

Silverman, Kaja. *Male Subjectivity at the Margins*. New York and London: Routledge, 1992.

15

In the Spirit of Process:
A Braiding Together of
New Utopianism, Gilles Deleuze,
and Anne Carson

Jacqueline Plante

"Utopian" has become the academic term for that which is ineffective, naïve, impracticable and, at worst, certain to fail. Utopianism, regarded as such, has been restricted to literary forms that have minimal transformative potential; however, our approach to utopianism is itself under transformation. Recent feminist scholars, Lucy Sargisson and Elizabeth Grosz in particular, have begun to unravel common assumptions that have unnecessarily, and mistakenly, limited the potential uses of a utopian approach; efforts towards perfection of place, a blueprint for the future, are no longer appropriate. Rather, we approach utopianism as site of *becoming*, a process of conscious revolution, experimentation, and realignment of existing elements. Furthermore, literature provides a space in which *new* utopianism can be activated. Gilles Deleuze offers an experimental approach to literature in which the writer, reader, language and the book itself are taken up in a variable state of *becoming*. The following essay summarizes the initial stages of an experiment — a collision of Deleuzian concepts, feminist utopian discourse and the literary process — with intentions of reconceptualizing utopianism as a creative process in order to extend the subversive activity of literature. The essay will challenge the exclusive prescriptions of what we label "utopian," "feminist," and "science fiction" literature, with a brief introduction of Canadian writer and academic, Anne Carson. Working outside of categorical boundaries, Carson uses such vital creative techniques as hybridization, *rhizomatic* agency and becoming, and is, therefore exemplary of literature that both transgresses the conventions under fire within feminist discourse and is active in the creative domains of Deleuzian literary approach.

Every concept or genre is subject to simplification for the purposes of stabilizing a definition. Utopianism, not excepted, has been tied to common perceptions of its function and form. It requires, therefore, a continuous re-evaluation in order to release its transformative potential. Regeneration requires an exposure and unsettling of the resting standard conception of utopianism. "The myth of utopianism" or, "the colloquial uses of the term," formulate utopia as an ideal commonwealth whose inhabitants exist under perfect conditions (Sargisson 9). One thinks of the island in Thomas More's *Utopia*, the very birth of the term. Ideal political structures such as Plato's *Republic* and Francis Bacon's *New Atlantis* come to mind. Such expectations reveal two common, somewhat involuntary perceptions of utopia: it is a place, and it is perfect, reducing it to an *it*, a territory that is to be actualized or situated in space and time. Such perceptions provoke memories of rigidly authoritarian and hierarchical constructions (Grosz 133).

In a contemporary context where efforts aim at a transcendent perfection, as was largely employed in the modernist fantasy of objectivity, "utopian thought" is regarded as conducive only to oppressive unifying structures which are disempowering to all but those who constructed them (Sargisson 87). It is, therefore, considered an effort certain to fail and/or self-destruct. Quite suitably, considering, any form of the term utopia has become an academic "curse," an insult. "Utopian" in reference to a theory or theorist is synonymous with naivety and futility. Feminism provides perhaps one of the most severe rejections of utopianism, making venomous internal charges. Anxieties surround a belief that utopianism disregards the present situations of women in a preoccupation with delusions of an impossible future (Johnson 22). Between misdirected efforts toward a destination and the experimental efforts toward change that are being supported here, the rejection of both leaves little space for movement.

The standard view of utopia is fundamentally flawed with a definition that is unnecessarily and inappropriately exclusive and definitive (Sargisson

10). Reconsidered, as Elizabeth Grosz clarifies, utopia is quite literally trans-lated from the Greek as "no place is the good place" or "the good place is no place,"[1] that is, utopia is "beyond a conception of space or place," exist-ing only in the imagination (135). It is difficult for feminism(s) that are looking for solutions to concrete issues, for oppositions to the structures we are still inhibited by in everyday time and space, to accept a utopianism that prides itself in imaginative reflections of "nowhere" with little discus-sion of destination, or predictions of the future. But, *new* utopianism is, all the same, working with and in our situatedness; as Sargisson insists, utopian thought cannot exist independently from the real — it depends on and results from dissatisfaction with the present (49). According to Grosz it is to our benefit that the utopian space is one that cannot be accessed because it forces us to continue fighting in the real, for results we cannot foresee and certainly cannot reach consensus on (20). Rather than repeat-ing a tradition that advances "fantasies of control" in false "reassurances of a better future," we accept the unavoidable challenge of facing the unknow-able in the present, accepting risk (139).

Utopianism in this context becomes an action, a verb, a process or transformation, subversion, and experimentation, drawn from a desire for continuous movement toward unknown possibilities rather than self-contained, controlled bodies of academic effort working towards the justification of pre-existing beliefs. How then are we to understand this process? Where can it work? This exploration began in the manifestation of utopianism within literature. Although utopianism is not limited to fiction, literature provides a space in which we can explore the possibility of reinvention. The novel, as described by Eichler, Neysmith and Larkin, is "a natural vehicle for expressing the ontological paradox of utopias. Sci-ence fiction in particular provides the imaginative space for thinking beyond established boundaries" (11). It is also, perhaps, the only space remaining where utopia in its pure form is appreciated. However, within the confines of what is commonly labeled "utopian" or "science fiction," the novel is fixed to certain criteria — criteria that should be resisted. Although the author is given space to critique current social conditions while offering dramatic insights on possibilities of the future, further transformative potentials existing in the text are neglected. A renegotiation of the function of liter-ature alongside the re-definition — "the undefining" — of utopianism, will open new avenues of social change and possibilities for utopianism in the literary form.

How, then, do we move fiction, which the "myth of utopia" ironically confines to the same conventions that we are trying to overturn, into a place of agency in connection with a wider academic exchange? How can the writer write in movement with the forces of contemporary theory and how can the reader read in response to the writer's interaction with theory? Approaching utopianism as a process can serve to strengthen a feminist discourse which itself is continuously accelerating in its undefinability (Sargisson 14, 24). Utopian literature in this perspective, not only shifts and slides social codes regarding gender, sex and relationship, but also transfigures the concept of order itself, with a particular focus on modes of expression such as genre and narrative convention (Sargisson 201). The fictional novel becomes, as beautifully described by Grosz, "a passage or point of transition from one (social) stratum or space to another" (58). Grosz, appealing to the philosophy and literary criticism of Gilles Deleuze, reconfigures the agency of the book, describing it as a "thief in the night. Furtive, clandestine, and always complex," stealing ideas from all around, from the past and present, from outside familiar territory, to then "disseminate" them elsewhere (58). Utopianism, in such as approach, is left exposed, sitting in the laps of our minds — accessible for action without stable content. It is a site for continuous creation, an activity of unlatching and re-latching.

This brings us to the driving force behind this discussion: the thought of Gilles Deleuze (which will, by no means, be adequately unfolded here) creates a perspective, an inspiration that can activate this conceptualization of utopianism within literature and its interactions. We might explore the approach Deleuze has taken regarding the writer, in writing, the reader in reading, and the very structure of the book itself.

Perhaps one of the most crucial concepts within Deleuze for the project of activating new utopianism in writing is what is called *becoming*. Reductively expressed, *becoming* is to be continuously in-between one place and another, always in transit, nomadic. Consider, within the utopian action, the form of a book, the characters in the book, the writer and the reader, are always in a state of *becoming*. How do we conceive of such a paradox, the action of the inactive? The movement of written word? Deleuze answers:

> Writing is a question of becoming, always incomplete, always in the midst of being formed, and goes beyond the matter of any liveable or lived experience.... Writing is inseparable from becoming: in writing, one becomes-woman, becomes-animal or vegetable, becomes molecule to the point of becoming-imperceptible ["Literature and Life" 1].

He presents a form of book that, paradoxically, denies the restriction of form that is communicated through the vivid thought-image of the "rhizome." The rhizome "ceaselessly establishes connections between semiotic chains, organizations of power, and circumstances relative to the arts, sciences, and social struggles" having "no ideal speaker-listener" (*A Thousand Plateaus* 7). It grows outward, enabling indefinite connections with and extensions to its surroundings. An adherence to the expected unity of concepts or literary form is replaced with fragmentation and an allowance for connections with the seemingly un-connectable. In short, he creates an image of a book that is in constant motion, always in the midst, created from intermingling, offered to the task of intermingling. Such a book is unlikely to be placed within the confines of a genre, a particular discussion, or be marketable to a particular consumer.

This dissemination of previously existing elements in order to create new combinations necessitates a movement of language. The rhizome "puts language in a state of perpetual disequilibrium" (27). Deleuze challenges the writer to make "language stutter." Becoming a "stranger" or "foreigner" to one's own language, the writer resists its "major" uses to produce what Deleuze calls a "minor literature" ("He Stuttered" 24). The writer works to activate language by *showing* or *revealing*, rather than simply *saying* (27). She writes *with*, not simply *for* or *about* (*Dialogues* 42). Resisting the "major" uses of language to explore new possibilities amounts to resisting the dominant definitions of reality and its systems (Baugh 48). Exploring new possibilities of language is an effort that utopian literature should attempt as it not only provides the space, but calls for such efforts.

The utopian writer does not merely write from her life experience or "neuroses"; this would be a jarring of process. A writer is "bad" or "sickly" if she perceives only from behind one perspective or state of values — her own. The healthy writer is one who remains open to transformation depending on what is encountered, one who is dedicated to becoming. A writer with a 'delicate health' whose writing "stems from what he has seen and heard of things too big for him, too strong for him" makes *becoming* stir, making new utopian literature possible ("Literature and Life" 3). Healthy writing invents those who are missing: "literature begins only when a third person is born in us that strips us of the power to say 'I'" (3). The writer expands to something too immense for "I"-centered familiarities (3). However, the immediate world is not neglected; the writer engages in a "surveying," a "mapping," that extends to "realms that are yet to come" (Deleuze and Guattari 5). The writer provides reference points for an "experiment which exceeds our capacity to foresee" (Deleuze and Parnet 48). Writing is open to transformation depending on what is encountered, stemming from what the writer has seen and heard of things too vast and complex to hold, tracing lines that are not imaginary, because in reality writing involves us there (Deleuze "Literature and Life" 3).

The reader, in response to the writer, is also set in motion, ahead of herself, as an active, interested and concerned participant (Braidotti 167). Literature must be experimented with, combined with outside forces in order to extend its initial activity and use, to further activate its process. It is no longer appropriate to reduce a text to what it means, says or how it should be interpreted. Instead, the reader must ask: What does it do? (Baugh 35). A mere focus on the meaning betrays the functioning possibilities of the text. This consideration of literary action empowers reader *and* writer, rather than placing one in a position of authority that subjects the other to a confined response (Baugh 35). Deleuze rejects an approach to reading that is enveloped in the singular experience of the book: "We will ask what it functions with, in connection with what other things it does or does not transmit intensities, in which other multiplicities its own are inserted and metamorphosed" (Deleuze and Guattari 4). Such an approach allows an expansion beyond the elements within a single work, or even beyond the author's body of works. One can mingle the elements from one work with that of another, from one discipline or genre to another, or intertwine a work with that of one's own. Such an approach is evident within Deleuze, the authors and philosophers he discusses so allied and suppliers (47).[2] Deleuze's "method of AND," of "this and then that," encourages work with integrated with each other and with his own writing that there is a sort of *becoming* between literature that extends the relevance of one text to inform and explore another; the voice of one becomes an irreducible collective utterance (Conley 264). In this context, 'feminist' and 'utopian' aspects of literature become simply aspects, as opposed to all-encompassing categories. Such genres can be stretched further in each direction, on the molecular levels — experimenting with new connections that activate not only the creativity in new content, but the creation of texts that are transformative on several planes.

Although Anne Carson's *Autobiography of Red* does not comfortably fit within a "feminist," "utopian" or "science fiction" discussion for the conventional reader, in light of the open-ended and experimental sentiments expounded here, Carson's indistinguishable technique is exemplary of hybridization, *rhizomatic* agency and *becoming*. Her style has, thus far, played a crucial role in developing an understanding of utopianism as process. Comparable to Deleuze's 'method of AND,' Carson, being both a Classics scholar and a fictional writer, combines the influences of classical academia with fictional possibilities, as well as ancient thinkers and writers such as Plato and Stesichoros with contemporaries such as Keats and Stein. Playing with new arrangements she shifts speakers, time frames, and genres through a manipulation of the mythic form through essays, lyrics, narrative and non-narrative poetry (Rae 17).

Carson works toward a movement and reconfiguration of language. By drawing attention to words numbed by excessive use, and associating words with unlikely meanings, she uproots the predictability of language, allowing words, as much as possible, to realize new form, placing them as strangers in *action* together in an effort to refresh the reader's sense of understanding. The characters produced, particularly the protagonist of *Autobiography of Red*, who is not clearly animal, man, woman, ancient, modern or mortal, floats freely across each of these planes, exemplifying *becoming*. But no single boundary transgression in Carson is emphasized; as *Autobiography of Red* is homoerotic in its entirety, there is no apparent, or deliberate, effort to normalize the homosexual subject; Carson simply normalizes such subjects through a romance that happens to occur between what may be considered as two males, rendering such categories irrelevant.

The affectivity of her writing is that the form and content cross so many boundaries that she remains precariously indefinable. Carson's work is a pallet of mythos, fantasy, queer theory, poetry, novel, classicalism and postmodernity. And perhaps her lack of commitment to a particular agenda places her light-years ahead of the feminist effort in regards to transgressive writing. For these reasons, her work, as well as that of others who move on the periphery of literary genre, serves to stimulate and dislodge the fixities of those who write and read with an adherence to the categorical restrictions of genre, therefore denying the literary process its complexity of movement.

What can be learned from this braiding together of *new* utopianism, Deleuze and Anne Carson? The combination offers an approach to the theory and activity of the literary process that reflects the life force of utopianism: vitality through process. We have acknowledged that the desire to proceed with transformative literature, as is evident in the contemporary recapitulation of utopianism, necessitates that the literature *and* theory become themselves internally transformative. The dismantling of the organized organs of literature, language, content and form are crucial. But more crucially, failing fantasies of control and perfection have been exchanged with an indeterminably vast space for experimentation, movement and change. Influences on how we read or write "utopian literature" and "science fiction" which feed our desire to produce stimuli and change need not be limited to strictly "utopian" or "science fiction" genres or discussions; they may be received from outside, from theory and literature that is internally transformative, and therefore ahead of its time.

NOTES

1. Utopia, Moore's witty pun, is most frequently interpreted from its Greek roots: the adverb *ou*, meaning "not," and the noun *topos*, meaning "place," which is generally taken to mean "no-place." In addition, More plays with the Greek composite *eutopia*, meaning "happy," "fortunate," or "good" place or "no place is the good place"; the general consensus is that this good place is nowhere to be found (Grosz 135).

2. The names of philosophers (Plato, Spinoza, Kant, Nietzsche and Heidegger) appear alongside the names of literary figures (Melville, Whitman, Beckett and Carroll).

WORKS CITED

Baugh, Bruce. "How Deleuze Can Help Us Make Literature Work." *Deleuze and Literature*. Eds. Ian Buchanan and John Marks. Edinburgh: Edinburgh University Press, 2000. 34–56.

Boundas, Constantin V., and Dorthea Olkowski, eds. *Gilles Deleuze and the Theatre of Philosophy*. New York: Routledge, 1994.

Braidotti, Rosi. "Toward a New Nomadism: Feminist Deleuzian Tracks; or, Metaphysics and Metabolism." *Gilles Deleuze and the Theatre of Philosophy*. Eds. Constantin V. Boundas and Dorthea Olkowski. New York: Routledge, 1994. 159–186.

Carson, Anne. *Autobiography of Red: A Novel in Verse*. Toronto: Vintage Canada, 1998.

Conley, Tom. "I and My Deleuze." *Deleuze and Literature*. Eds. Ian Buchanan and John Marks. Edinburgh: Edinburgh University Press, 2000. 263–282.

Deleuze, Gilles. "He Stuttered." *Gilles Deleuze and the Theatre of Philosophy*. Eds. Constantin V. Boundas and Dorthea Olkowski. New York: Routledge, 1994. 23–29.

_____. "Literature and Life." *Essays Critical and Clinical*. Trans. Daniel W. Smith and M.A. Greco. London: Verso, 1998.

Deleuze, Gilles, and Felix Guattari. *A Thousand Plateaus: Capitalism and Schizophrenia*. 1987. Trans. B. Massumi. Minneapolis: University of Minnesota Press, 1998.

Deleuze, Gilles, and Claire Parnet. *Dialogues II*. 1987. Trans. H. Tomlinson and B. Habberjam. New York: Columbia University Press, 2002.

Eichler, Margrit, June Larkin, and Sheila Neysmith eds. *Feminist Utopias: Re-Visioning Our Futures*. Toronto: Inanna, 2002.

Grosz, Elizabeth. *Architecture from the Outside: Essays on Virtual and Real Space.* Writing Architecture Series — A Project by The Anyone Corporation. Massachusetts: MIT Press, 2002.

Johnson, Greg. "The Situated Self and Utopian Thinking." *Hypatia* 17.3 (2002): 20–44.

Rae, Ian. "Dazzling Hybrids: The Poetry of Anne Carson." *Canadian Literature.* 166 (2000): 17–41.

Sargisson, Lucy. *Contemporary Feminist Utopianism.* London: Routledge, 1996.

16

Dystopia in a New Land

Karen Huenneman

C. Peyton Wertenbaker observes that science fiction, as a subgenre, calls forth an innate human response to "things vast, things cataclysmic, and things unfathomably strange" (qtd. in Stover, *epigram*), but this appeal to our love of the preternatural often (although not always) masks a deeper sociological agenda. Science fiction, scientific romance, utopia, dystopia, tektopia... regardless of the label, the narrative combination of scientific observation and social commentary has created a tradition of alternative worlds stretching far into our literary past, long before the advent of Jules Verne and H.G. Wells, often considered the fathers of the form. James de Mille's *A Strange Manuscript Found in a Copper Cylinder* (1888), has been considered Canada's first novel in this genre.[1] It is, however, neither true science fiction nor fantasy, neither utopia nor unmitigated dystopia, but a complex and elusive amalgamation of elements of many subgenres. The result is a powerful discursive experiment, seemingly advanced for, and unique in, its time. It is not surprising, given the style and content of De Mille's text, that it was not put forward for publication in his lifetime, but published posthumously by his impoverished widow in 1888.

Although *A Strange Manuscript* enigmatically eludes classification, the focus of much criticism to date has been on defining the text — in terms of genre classification, in terms of De Mille's literary borrowings (how much of the novel is imitative, and what are its sources), and in terms of the novel's status as "finished" or "unfinished," given its seemingly

183

problematic conclusion. These are important issues, and must be addressed; interesting as others' investigations have been, however, no critic has yet delved sufficiently into *A Strange Manuscript* to answer the critical question of why the novel was not published when it was first written (although some give passing attention to the matter). An alternate reading of the novel, and a comprehensive investigation of the critical attention it has received, suggest that De Mille's novel was ahead of its time, both stylistically and satirically, and, as such, could not have been published comfortably by an author of De Mille's professional and social position.

De Mille's novel — its intent, genre, structure, content, and ellipses — has troubled critics since its publication. But their troubled approaches are an indication of what Linda Hutcheon defines as the difference between the "*modernist* search for order in the face of moral and social chaos" and the "*postmodern* urge to trouble, to question, to make both problematic and provisional any such desire for order or truth through the powers of the human imagination" (qtd. in Lamont-Stewart 33). More recent criticism has employed postmodern and postcolonial theories in unraveling *A Strange Manuscript*'s narrative complexities (Arnold, Gerson, Guth, Keefer, Lamont-Stewart, Milnes, Wilson). Gwendolyn Guth, for example, sees the frame narrative as "both an internal stylistic device and an external cautionary tale about the exercise of exegesis":

> As the later, it tacitly reminds readers that they are exegetes of the novel just as surely as the foursome on board the yacht are of Adam More, and as More is, in turn, of the Kosekins. Interpretation or exegesis thus unfolds itself in De Mille's novel in a series of [...] metaphysically disturbing frames: the reader reading the readers of a reader of a strange land [Guth 40–41].

Yet these critics do not draw the necessary connection between the content and structure of De Mille's novel, and the novelist's seeming unwillingness to offer it for publication (Parks, Editor's xxii). While Linda Lamont-Stewart observes that "[t]he gap between author and audience becomes an invitation to investigate questions of cultural production, and the text's troublesome generic instability becomes, ironically, the primary source of its aesthetic and intellectual value" (35), she nonetheless fails to recognize that De Mille's structure, combined with a biographical detail, constructs a reading of this "unfinished" novel that positions it firmly as an innovative work, an apparently solitary example of what could be termed the "Victorian pre-postmodern." The questions of genre, of allusion, of structure, weave together to enable a reading of *A Strange Manuscript* in which the narrative hiatuses leave the reader open to extrapolate upon the ethical issues the text presents. De Mille's concerns over where such contemplations might lead the discerning reader may have created the hesitancy on his part regarding publication.

In his introduction to the Carleton University Press edition of *A Strange Manuscript*, Malcolm Parks discusses De Mille's position at the time of writing *A Strange Manuscript*. Drawing on reliable contemporary report and biographical evidence, he describes De Mille as a member of "a small faculty of six professors and one lecturer" (Editor's xxiii), "witty and amusing" at times, but also "a quiet man who preferred to keep to himself" (xxiv). "There was little doubt," continues Parks, that De Mille "had more than a casual interest in [the evolution/creation debate] and that he would have been on the side of the anti-Darwinists" (xxix). While De Mille is presented as a firm member of the Anglican church, having converted from his father's austere version of Baptist piety in 1865 (Parks, "Strange" 68), Parks is successful in leaving us, like the readers of De Mille's *Helena's Household* (1867), with "no doubts about De Mille's Christian point of view and dedication to Christian belief" (70). At the same time, Parks establishes De Mille's abhorrence of what he termed "cant," quoting a letter from Herbert C. Creed to Archibald MacMechan, De Mille's biographer, that

> although De Mille was "doubtless a sincere Christian," he "took delight in ridiculing everything like cant, and even the ordinary words and actions of the 'pious' sort of people often brought to his keen eye and thin curling lip that peculiar sarcastic smile of his" [Parks "Strange" 68].

Placing De Mille carefully within his historical context, Parks also lays out a very credible argument for the date of production of *A Strange Manuscript*. Through investigation of the historic information in the text, combined with references to the correspondence of De Mille's family (discovered by Douglas E. MacLeod for his 1968 MA thesis at Dalhousie), Parks determines that De Mille cannot have written the novel before 1865, but that it was almost certainly finished, in more or less the current form, by 1867 ("Strange" 64). Parks' research also suggests that De Mille revised the text in 1879, most likely focusing on the ending, which, he "entirely agreed" with his brother Alfred, "could be re-written with advantage" (qtd. in Parks, Editor's xix). Parks' argument is sufficiently convincing to accept 1867 as the year in which the structure and content of *A Strange Manuscript* were solidified. This date is significant, in that when the text was first published in 1888, it was considered less of a novelty than it might earlier have been, given the publication of Samuel Butler's *Erewhon* in 1872, and —

of more immediate financial concern to the publishers — of H. Rider Haggard's *King Solomon's Mines* in 1885, followed by *She* in 1886, and *Allen Quartermain* in 1887. This situation greatly affected *A Strange Manuscript*'s popular and critical reception, despite the fact that De Mille had been dead for two years when Haggard's first novel, *Cetywayo and His White Neighbours* (1882), was published.

To the modern critical reader, the infringement of Haggard's success on De Mille's might seem inconsequential, but in the Victorian literary atmosphere, the similarities were striking. The comparison with Haggard made by most contemporary reviewers subsumed *A Strange Manuscript*'s satiric element in the obvious popular adventure tale. Yet, accompanying the myriad comments on the imitative qualities of *A Strange Manuscript* (Parks, Editor's xxxviii-xlii), one perceptive reviewer noted, in 1888, that "the motive of the book is entirely different from anything that Haggard, at least, ever wrote. [...] A vein of speculative philosophy runs through it, scarcely satirical, and yet presenting a sharp contrast to all our conceptions of life" (qtd. in Parks, Editor's xl). This brings us back to the first of the three issues critics deem worthy of their time: genre. *A Strange Manuscript* has been classified at times as either "science fiction" or "fantasy"; it is, strictly speaking, neither. Science fiction can be defined as "fiction in which the unfamiliar is brought about through scientific (most often technological) advance (in relation to the moment of production)," and fantasy as "fiction which denies the reader's consensus reality through the introduction of the impossible" (Didicher). While science fiction introduces alternative realities based on scientific advancement, fantasy "seems closer to legend and myth than realism; it describes heroic action in a world that is not our own" (Colombo, "Four" 30). According to these definitions, in both science fiction and fantasy proper, what is currently accepted as possible, according to known physical laws, is overthrown: in science fiction through the extrapolation of existing technological knowledge, in fantasy through a more nebulous recourse to the purely imaginative. While *A Strange Manuscript* does introduce science in the larger sense of the word (although the character Melick is adamant that there is "precious little science in it" [De Mille 226]), it does not deal with societal change as a result of technological or scientific advancement. And again, while it does have creatures not found in our modern (or even Victorian) world, it does not include mythological or strictly "fantastic" creatures, but rather creatures determined by Dr. Cosgreve to be survivors from the prehistory of our world (rather like the coelacanth). In fact, De Mille goes to great lengths, through the finders (thus readers) of the manuscript, to establish the possibility of veracity in More's accounts. Despite this nebulousness of classification, *A Strange Manuscript* is considered by many to be Canada's first "science fiction" novel.[2]

Critics have posited many classifications for De Mille's novel — popular fiction, science fiction, speculative fiction, fantasy, scientific romance, utopia, anti- or dystopia, prose epic, and the novel of ideas — and most agree, more or less, with R. E. Watters, that it is "deliberately all [or many of] these at once" (xvii).[3] Other narrative components that have been suggested (or that the text itself irrefutably illustrates) are the imaginary journey, the inversion narrative, the frame narrative, travel writing, and the imperialist adventure tale. Yet *A Strange Manuscript* eludes classification. How convenient for critics, who get to take the text and do what they like with it; it provides ample scope for seemingly dichotomous investigations. Yet, of course, the text itself constrains critical endeavor. While it contains elements of a multitude of genres and literary tropes, the final result points inexorably toward a reading of the novel as satire, as an intentionally elusive suggestion of the negative potentialities of dominant Victorian ideologies.

In terms of the second critical issue of import, *A Strange Manuscript* has obvious antecedents, carefully suggested and argued over by numerous other critics.[4] Some of these claims, given Parks's dates, are erroneous, but many still stand. Yet is it essential that all narrative elements in a text are unique? *Tropes* in literature, like Jungian archetypes, are so labeled exactly *because* they are both pervasive and mutually inter-referential. While James De Mille's *A Strange Manuscript Found in a Copper Cylinder* does contain passages that are not unique, why is he deemed "imitative of" or "indebted to" other texts, rather than merely sensitive to the human condition? His text is an aggregate of ideas and narrative tropes, some gleaned from other sources, fictional and non-fictional, some strikingly original. Some critics suggest that, as a professor of classics, history, rhetoric, and literature at Acadia and Dalhousie Universities (1860 to 1865, and 1865 until his death in 1880, respectively) (Lamont-Stewart 21), De Mille reveled in intellectual puzzles; these critics see *A Strange Manuscript* as an academic conceit, a "learned amusement" (Kime 302) as much a parody or satire of literary genres as of literary criticism (Beddoes 10; Gerson, *Taste* 55; Guth 43–44; La Bossière 52; New 104). If we accept this interpretation, even partially, we can see how De Mille was trying to cram into his narrative as many references — scientific, literary, religious, philosophical, philological — as he could, while still retaining the readers' interest in the adventure story. The structure of *A Strange Manuscript*— the academic and social gloss provided by the characters in the frame narrative — supports this reading of the text. De Mille presents us with a number of questionable scientific and sociological elements; the becalmed passengers on the *Falcon* critique More's tale for us; we are left to puzzle the external author's intent and effect according to our own subject positions: once again, "the reader reading the readers of a reader of a strange land" (Guth 41). De Mille has created a powerful metafictional relationship between himself and his reader; the same questions we are asking of De Mille's novel were asked by De Mille's readers of More's manuscript. Thus, comprehension of the text and its position within the canon of Canadian literature necessitates consideration less of what the novel *is* than of *how it functions* as a text.

The question of intent brings us to the third issue commonly addressed by critics: was De Mille's novel "finished" before his death? Again, critics hold diametrically opposed views. George Woodcock proposes that the erasure of Layelah and Kohen Godol from the story and the narrative gap which, if filled, might have explained "the circumstances in which, after his escape from sacrifice, More writes his narrative" ("De Mille" 100), point to an incompleteness of De Mille's text, and Patricia Monk concludes that *A Strange Manuscript* "is inarguably unfinished [and] remains a fragment as strange as its title suggests" (245). In the opposite camp, Guth posits "the simple truth about the end of De Mille's novel[:] it is finished in its incompleteness, it is completely (un)finished" (Guth 51), and Stephen Milnes reads De Mille's text in such an order — "manuscript, absence, letter" — that it can be perceived as "in an odd way, complete" (101), replete with the failure of More's imperialist power, read into the space between More's tale and its discursive production. Yet it seems that, once again, Parks's introduction provides the answer, in part, in a 1880 letter from De Mille's brother, Albert De Mill [sic], to Dr. John Pryor, De Mille's father-in-law. Albert notes that De Mille

> was never able to make a satisfactory *denouement* to the plot in it & consequently I do not think he ever offered it for sale. I read it over some years ago & told him that the concluding chapter could be rewritten with advantage and he entirely agreed with me [qtd. in Parks, Editor's xix].

While this communication seems to indicate that James De Mille was not satisfied with the ending of his novel, it also suggests that the novel was complete in content, if not polished in style; thus, we can proceed to evaluate its merits, incorporating its silences and ellipses as part of De Mille's intentional structure. While not relying on Parks's evidence, Milnes and

Guth come closest to recognizing the discursive power of De Mille's text; nonetheless, both fail to articulate a relationship between De Mille's intellectual productions and the situation within which he produced the text. If considered as incomplete, *A Strange Manuscript* gives rise to the modernists' critical dilemma previously described. Accepted as a carefully constructed whole, *A Strange Manuscript* can be explored as a literary aberration, a Victorian example of postmodern structure, in its expression of enigmatic philosophical relations and its refusal to present closure.

The Authors, the Readers, the Frame, and the Manuscript

Lamont-Stewart reminds us that "[t]he dual nature of [De Mille's] working life immediately opens the possibility, even the probability, that his fictional works will ironically exploit the gap between their intellectual author and the popular audience he is addressing" (21). Woodcock, in his attempt to classify *A Strange Manuscript* within a particular genre, observes that De Mille is a "bifocal novelist, whose works can be read at double levels of intent and meaning" ("De Mille" 101). While the reader of "popular literature" can read *A Strange Manuscript* on a superficial level, engaging solely with the traditionally constructed adventure narrative, the critical reader becomes involved in the text, evaluating its refusal to provide resolution to the ideological conflicts it creates. Klay Dyer, in *The Encyclopedia of Literature in Canada*, reveals that this narrative palimpsest was a trademark of De Mille, perceiving multiple layers of critical reflection in what De Mille called his "satirical romances": "a number of well-designed and well-executed comic novels that locate their author firmly in the tradition of Canadian parody" (Dyer 285). These comic novels were "at once entertaining (and marketable) fictions and self-reflexive commentaries on the popularity within Victorian culture of what was considered by many to be an intellectually and even morally corruptive form of 'light' fiction" (Dyer 285). If we consider the structure of *A Strange Manuscript*, we see the same technique at play.

The set-up for the novel's structure is as follows. De Mille's narrative ("the novel") opens in 1850, with four British travelers becalmed in their sailboat off the Canary Islands. In staging a paper-boat race to pass time, they retrieve from the ocean a "foreign"-looking copper cylinder, which contains, written enigmatically in English on an unknown, paper-like substance later determined to be papyrus, More's narrative ("the manuscript"). These four men — Featherstone, the host and an effete British aristocrat "weary of life in England" (De Mille 1); Dr. Cosgreve, his "friend and medical attendant" (1); Oxenden, the philologist, an "intimate friend of Featherstone" (1); and Melick, the sardonic *littérateur* from London, notably not labeled a "friend" (60) — take turns reading the manuscript and debating the authenticity of More's report. In doing so, they argue the veracity of his science, the level of his narrative ability, and whether the manuscript is (in Melick's view) "a transparent hoax" (61) or (according to Cosgreve and Oxenden) "a plain narrative of fact" (227). On these particular issues, Featherstone seldom weighs in.

Guth charts the novel's meticulous structure, the four sections of More's narrative alternating between movement and stasis, interspersed with critical commentary by the four men in the narrative frame. The whole is enveloped in the setting of the frame, within which More's narrative, its insinuations and its silences, is evaluated. The "strangeness" of More's manuscript appeals to the foursome on the *Falcon* on the same two levels as *A Strange Manuscript* appeals to readers (modern, and one can assume, Victorian): the exoticism of the world More describes intrigues the bored, becalmed yachtsmen and the adventure-hungry reader; at the same time, the unknown in More's narrative provides fodder for the Victorian drive to categorization, the reader's need to attach meaning to the "strange" and "unnatural" in De Mille's novel. Guth derides Cosgreve and Oxenden "for their glaring errors in exegesis: their penchant for the passive elaboration of knowledge rather than its active interrogation" (47), but Cosgreve and Oxenden are put forward as exemplars of one typical form of Victorian scientific endeavor. During the Victorian period, the development of systems of scientific classification, and the populating of those systems with facts, was as valid an activity as the investigation of the functioning of those systems; both contributed significantly to the knowledge base upon which our modern scientific activity is founded. Thus, the designation and categorization of More's discoveries is a useful addition to the foursome's — and the Victorian reader's — understanding of the land of the Kosekin. Cosgreve and Oxenden's descriptions call to mind the Victorian practice of anthropological classification; their explanations appropriate More's newfound land by familiarizing the unfamiliar. As Flavio Multineddu puts it, "More's descriptions estrange what in the words of Dr. Cosgreve and Oxenden becomes clear and known again" (65). Melick's derision of this activity is both of the technique — disclaiming that "there is no theory, however

wild and fantastic, which some man of science will not be ready to support and to fortify by endless arguments, all of the most plausible kind"
(De Mille 70) — and of the underlying assumption of More's text as factual. For Melick, it is not the scientific plausibility of More's tale (which
is tenuous at best), but the narrative technique, which reveals the artifice
of More's literary practices, that the text is an elaborate, although poorly
written, hoax. To discriminating Victorian readers, this familiar form of
intellectual debate lends veracity to the novel, inviting them to consider
the text in light of presented discursive possibilities. In this relation between
manuscript and interpreters, novel and readers, De Mille *cannot* prescribe
a solution to the questions he invites. To do so would have weakened the
satirical intent of his project, reducing it to what it is often derided for
being: a merely prescriptive, sensational pot-boiler.

Critics often comment on Adam More's nature as a "simple sailor" (De
Mille 227), although no one — except Melick obliquely in his observation
that "no sailor would express himself in that way" (65) — recollects that the
letters accompanying the manuscript are written in three languages: French,
German, and English (8); such linguistic ability is not an obvious talent
for the average "simple sailor." Critical focus falls more often on More's
fluctuation between intelligent observation and his obtuse lack of interpretive reflection. Lamont-Stewart perhaps puts it best:

> Adam More, the author of the strange manuscript, is an unreliable narrator,
> a good-natured fellow who at times seems reasonably intelligent, and at other
> times appears almost deliberately stupid. He describes Kosekin society in
> detail, but he is very slow in recognizing the significance of what he observes,
> and never seems to come to a real understanding of this strange people
> [23–24].

Lamont-Stewart's observation leads neatly into a postmodernist reading of
A Strange Manuscript. More is, as Guth points out, a stock character of
utopian fiction:

> Within the utopian frame, says Frye, one often find the *ingenu*: the "outsider"
> who "has no dogmatic views of his own, but ... grants none of the premises
> which make the absurdities of society look logical to those accustomed to
> them" (232) [Guth 42].

The absurdities are left to the four yachtsmen to interpret within the context of Victorian society, yet the issues they choose to discuss are the more
superficial of topics raised by More's narrative: the etymology of Kosekin words, the taxonomy of the strange beasts More encounters, More's

ability as a narrator and the possible sources of his narrative. Guth, in accordance with other critics, contends that

> [c]entral issues such as cannibalism, Kosekin society in general, and the love triangle between More, Almah, and Layelah are left unexamined despite the fact that the structure of the novel provides ample opportunity for — and in effect seems deliberately to court — such discussion [48].

In this situation, again, saying more would weaken the effect of De Mille's satire. By presenting More as an un-self-critical narrator, De Mille leaves the analysis of More's text to the four men on board the *Falcon*; they in turn leave the analysis of society — Kosekin and Victorian — to the reader. De Mille was unquestionably conscious of creating what may now be designated "post-modern" fiction: his narrative frame is a well-crafted vehicle of exegesis, although not solely a critique of the efficacy of exegesis. While it is important to follow Oxenden's warning of attributing to a text "motives and purposes of which the authors could never have dreamed" (De Mille 227), it is fair to say that De Mille's layering of his text is intentional, the sensational hiding the critical, the absurd masking a biting satirical commentary on his society.

De Mille's Society: Unprepared for Uncertainty

As more than one critic has lamented, the exegesis provided by the narrative frame does not address issues of race, gender, social mores, or imperialism. Guth continues to list ideological slippage in the text, noting that

> [h]igh on the list of omissions in the frame is Christianity, the implicit but absent moral referent that is obliquely brought to the reader's attention again and again. More's tale is replete with biblical echoes, almost all of which occur ironically, yet no mention is made of them [49].

Most obvious is the observation that the Kosekin belief system is, not an inversion, but a perversion of the Beatitudes. The discourse of idealism is taken to its logical, and horrific, extreme.

The manuscript does present these issues for consideration, and critics are wrong to claim that the analysis of the frame characters does not address them. In the chapter "Oxenden Preaches a Sermon," the focus of the discussion is the Kosekin love of death. Melick maintains that this morbid philosophy could be the strong spirituality of the Semitic race, carried out under exceptionally favorable circumstances to the ultimate results; for the Semitic race more than all others thought little of this life and turned their affections to the life that lives beyond this [De Mille 236].

Laying aside the questionable veracity of Melick's theology, if by "Semitic race" he means the Jewish peoples, the obvious extension of this thought is an acknowledgement that Christian history and eschatology stems directly from its "Semitic" basis. Before this theoretical discussion can be engaged in, however, Melick's discourse is ambushed, silenced by Oxenden's diatribe on other, non-Semitic religious beliefs (235–36). The reader's attention is thus diverted away from any contemplation of the more serious implications of Melick's — and by extension De Mille's — observations. This elision relates intimately to the novel's appearance as unfinished, and the period of rest between its production and publication. That "the degenerate morality of the Kosekin society is ironically accentuated by the silence of Cosgreve, Oxenden, and Featherstone on questions of Kosekin religion and values" (Guth 40), suggests that De Mille was hesitant to comment explicitly on what he perceived as the current level of "religious cant" pervading Victorian Canadian society. Oblique intimations of perverted beatitudes can be glanced over, but to have More's intellectual jury on the *Falcon* focus their critical eyes on these issues would reveal De Mille's satirical intent too overtly, injuring both the effectiveness concealed and the suggestion of innocuousness created by the narrative's seeming superficiality. To explain a joke deflates the humor; to provide a gloss for literary and social allusions negates narrative power. Scientific gloss in the narrative frame of *A Strange Manuscript* provides raw — and, to the age, relatively new — information, facts of which the Victorian reader might not have been aware. To condescend to moralize explicitly by explaining references to Christianity and social mores may have alienated De Mille's educated Victorian audience; it certainly would have bored his uneducated one. As Guth notes, "it does not take a particularly perceptive reader to note that the Kosekin ideal of right living is an extremist version of Christ's Beatitudes" (50), and what reader likes to have the obvious explained?

Given De Mille's social position — important member of society, resident of a relatively small community, respected academic, active member of the Anglican Church — it is conceivable that De Mille did not feel it appropriate (or expedient) to publish such an — albeit oblique — criticism of the fundamental tenets of his religion and society — or, as Guth adds, criticism of De Mille's profession:

It seems likely that De Mille, a professor of rhetoric, classics, and literature at Acadia and Dalhousie Universities, also envisioned *A Strange Manuscript* as a send-up of his own decidedly exegetical profession — perhaps even of scholarship in general. Such a satiric impetus might account for *A Strange Manuscript*'s not having been released into the sea of publication during De Mille's lifetime [Guth 46].

What differs between De Mille's more "marketable" novels and *A Strange Manuscript* is not the style, nor the intent (as much as we can determine that), but the object of the satire. Where satirizing popular literature and readers' literary taste was acceptable, *A Strange Manuscript* strikes closer to the heart of Victorian society, criticizing, in De Mille's oblique, open-ended style, the very foundations of Victorian culture: religion, ethics, morality, gender relations, and, as Stephen Milnes and Carole Gerson have so adeptly revealed, the imperialist project.

The Silence That Speaks

Both Gerson and Milnes approach *A Strange Manuscript* from a post-colonial perspective and in so doing contribute considerably to our understanding of the text within its historical context. Gerson focuses largely on the development of a colonial discourse within De Mille's metanarrative; her perception of the text as unfinished, however, steers her away from a reading, such as Milnes,' which interprets the conclusion of the novel in terms of its postcolonial implications. In the "ellipses between the point at which More's narrative is yawned off and the prefatory note accompanying the manuscript," Milnes constructs a critique of imperialism:

> The implied uncertainty generated by the narrative absence is provocative because it insinuates, through absence, More's decline, which, analogously, is the decline of colonial power. Perhaps this is what Lord Featherstone does not wish to read or have read to him [101].

Milnes is astute in his interpretation of the ending of De Mille's novel, and its discursive power as a critique of imperialism. Yet, in reading *A Strange Manuscript* as an imperialist text in which "More's language, style, images, and tropes [...] prepare the ground, so to speak, in readiness for his elevation as a supreme power" (89), Milnes denies some of the subtle undercurrents in De Mille's text. The text, however, can be read throughout as a *failed* imperialist narrative, a captivity narrative despite More's attestations that his "freedom is absolute" (De Mille 83). In the closing scene of

More's manuscript, where the "adventure reader" sees only More and Almah's imperial "elevation as a supreme power," it is already obvious to the critical reader that More has now, as he has had all along, little real power. The end establishes a seemingly imperialist hegemony, but it is, again, inverted: More becomes a supreme power, but of what? Kosekin society, which is to him abhorrent; he longs to "fly from this hateful land," but is trapped by his love of Almah who, having "quite adopted the Kosekin fashion, which makes women take the lead," smoothly assumes the role of empress (De Mille 268–9). She tempts More to retire to "rest and food," as Featherstone yawns and closes the manuscript: "It's time for supper" (269). More is trapped in his role of imperial magnate. There is a suggestion, here, of a resolution to the discrepancy between the manuscript reading's dramatic conclusion and the tone of More's letter. Milnes intuits that More's unread — unrealized — story is not one of power but of despair, reading into the silence "More's decline, which, analogously, is the decline of colonial power" (Milnes 101). The abrupt ending of the novel creates a stasis of thought which Milnes sees as intentional: Featherstone's yawn interrupts the narrative as it interrupts his listeners' and readers' thought processes. Almah has stilled More's dramatic power; Featherstone has silenced his listeners' critical powers. More is left in power/in Almah's power; his metafictional connection with the reader is severed; we cannot guess his future. In the same way that the four men on the *Falcon* do not discuss the ideological implications of Kosekin society, they are steered away from consideration of More's position as supreme ruler of the Kosekin. The readers of More's narrative once again leave the readers of De Mille's novel to extrapolate as much — or as little — as they are comfortable with.

Martin E. Marty observes that "[a]lmost every favorable feature of [St. Thomas More's] *Utopia* is the obverse of some social practice in the nation at the time" (62). Such is often the use of utopia in literature: to illustrate a more ideal society, following Dorothy Donnelly's observation that "the expression of the desire for a better way of being [centers], first and foremost, on redefining order" (qtd. in Marty 52). In *A Strange Manuscript*, order is not redefined; it is inverted, even perverted. The enigmatic aphorisms of Christ, the troubling ideas of Darwin, are both extrapolated to their literal extremes. De Mille refuses to provide closure for the controversial issues his text raises. His fictional *littérateur*, Melick, addresses this omission, asking of More, as we ask of De Mille, why he didn't "unfold [...] before us a full and comprehensive view of their philosophy and religion. [...] It must have been a strong temptation" (De Mille 238). The answer lies in the narrative gaps of De Mille's tale, in the critical silences of the narrative frame. It suggests why De Mille did not publish *A Strange Manuscript* during his lifetime; why it can be considered unfinished yet complete; and simultaneously why these answers do not inhibit — but rather augment — its position as a discursively advanced text of Victorian Canada, worthy of more profound critical consideration. Melick is the metafictional cornerstone, the link between the reader of the novel and the manuscript itself. By questioning the authenticity of More's narrative, recognizing the possibility of it being a constructed history, Melick "gestures beyond the fiction itself, towards De Mille" (Guth 47), and extends a fictional hand to the external reader. Melick's skepticism asks the reader to be more skeptical yet; the silencing of Melick is both De Mille's refusal to answer for his readers and his admission that perhaps the obvious answers were not messages that could be heard by his society. They can now be heard by ours.

Appendix A: Genre Considerations

The following quotations reveal the opinions of De Mille critics (and De Mille himself through the four men on the *Falcon*), regarding definitions of *A Strange Manuscript Found in a Copper Cylinder*. That these critics' opinions are contradictory, even at times self-contradictory, indicates the difficulty in attempting to categorize De Mille's novel according to traditional genre classifications.

Beddoes	"multi-directional parody" (10)
Brush	"nineteenth-century dystopia ... [a] dystopian and satirical construction of the land of the Kosekins" (239)
Cogswell	"anomalous" (112); "satire" (113)
Colombo, et al.	classified under "Science Fiction" (1); "A utopian adventure with satiric overtones, a classic in its field" (4)
De Mille	Melick: "transparent hoax"; "sensation novel" (61); "quiet satire" (226); "satirical romance" (226); "perpetual undercurrent of meaning [...] in every line" (227)
	Oxenden: "a plain narrative of facts" (227)
	Featherstone: "scientific romance" (226)
Dyer	"satire and utopian fiction"; "tale-within-a-tale" (285)
Gerson	"popular and utopian fiction" ("Contrapuntal" 224)

Guth	"tale-within-a-tale hermeneutic"; "complex interplay between romance narrative ... and frame story"; "satire" (39)
Hughes	"a positive Utopia which satirizes an aristocratic class that serves no useful function" (123)
Keefer	"fantasy" (130); "untopia" (132)
Ketterer	"this provocative philosophical work is not only the best nineteenth-century Canadian novel but one of the best Canadian novels *period*" (8); "dystopian appraisal [...] disturbed by flickering hints of a utopian subtext" (9); "satire" (11)
Kilgour	"utopian, dystopian writings, the anatomy and the 'symposium,' as well as adventure tales, travel narratives, and pure Swiftian satire" (22)
Kilian	"a Utopian satire" (61, 63); "an exotic adventure story" (61); "no Utopia" (64)
Kime	"travel narrative" (282)
La Bossière	"not a positive utopia ... nor ... an anti-utopia" (44)
Lamont-Stewart	"satire" (23); "utopian/dystopian elements and apparent satirical intent ... novel of ideas" (35)
Milnes	"a critique of colonial non-discursive and discursive practices" (89)
Monk	"satiric adventure story" (228)
Multineddu	"defies the attempt to make a single-genre account for itself" (62); cites an Italian critic, Proiette, who classifies it as "science fiction" (62)
New	"satiric send-up of academic discussion" (104)
Parks	"anti-Utopia" ("Strange" 64); cites J. O. Bailey in *Pilgrims Through Time and Space* who considers it "scientific" and "utopian" ("Strange" 66); "an amalgam of fantastic adventure and serious satire, or popular romance and moral philosophy" (Editor's xxvii)
Turcotte	"nineteenth-century Canadian gothic [...] a dystopian tale [...] a self-conscious work, aware of its textual process" (79)
Watters	"satirical anti-utopian commentary on contemporary life ...a swiftly paced narrative of travel, romance, and fantastic adventure" (vii)
Wilson	"parody" (129); "metafiction" (136); "satire" (138)

Woodcock   "a satirical view of our own world" ("Absence" 4); "the prose epic, the exotically sentimental romance, and the novel of ideas," "not a futuristic vision [...] not a work of science fiction [...] nor, in the strictest sense, is it a utopia or an anti-utopia" ("De Mille" 104)

APPENDIX B: A COMPREHENSIVE BIBLIOGRAPHY OF *STRANGE MANUSCRIPT* CRITICISM (SUPPLEMENT TO WORKS CITED)

Arnold, Angela. "To Seize, to Slay, to Conquer": Satirizing the Imperial Mission in James De Mille's *A Strange Manuscript Found in a Copper Cylinder.*" *Foundation: The International Review of Science Fiction* 30.81 (2001): 83–89.

Beddoes, Julie. "Inside out: Finding the Author in James De Mille's *A Strange Manuscript Found in a Copper Cylinder.*" *Signature* 3 (1990): 1–12.

Bevan, A. R. "James De Mille and Archibald MacMechan." *Dalhousie Review* 35 (1955): 201–15.

Bourinot, John George, Sir. *Our Intellectual Strength and Weakness: A Short Historical and Critical Review of Literature, Art and Education in Canada.* Montreal: Brown, 1893. 29, 83. *Early Canadiana Online.* Canadian Institute for Historical Microreproductions. 13 April 2004 <http://www.canadiana.org.proxy.lib.sfu.ca/ECO/ItemRecord/00205?id=92a30b8d3f7f3282>

Burpee, Lawrence J. "James De Mille." *Nation* 16 (1906): 138.

_____. "Recent Canadian Fiction." *Forum* (1899): 752–60. *Early Canadiana Online.* Canadian Institute for Historical Microreproductions. 13 April 2004 <http://www.canadiana.org.proxy.lib.sfu.ca/ECO/ItemRecord/17996?id=92a30b8d3f7f3282>

_____. "Who's Who in Canadian Literature: James De Mille." *The Canadian Bookman* 8 (1926): 203–6.

Cavell, Richard. "Bakhtin Reads De Mille: Canadian Literature, Postmodernism, and the Theory of Dialogism." *Future Indicative: Literary Theory and Canadian Literature.* Ed. John Moss. Ottawa: University of Ottawa Press, 1986. 205–10.

Colombo, John Robert, et al., comps. *CDN SF&F: A Bibliography of Canadian Science Fiction and Fantasy.* Toronto: Hounslow, 1979.

Crockett, A. J., and George Geddie Patterson. "Concerning James De Mille." In *More Studies in Nova Scotian History.* By George Geddie Patterson. Halifax, NS: Imperial, 1941. 120–48.

Douglas, R. W. "James De Mille." *Canadian Bookman* 4 (1922): 39–44.

Ketterer, David. "James De Mille: *A Strange Manuscript.*" *Canadian Science Fiction and Fantasy.* Indianapolis, IN: Indiana University Press, 1992. 8–12.

Kilian, Crawford. "The Cheerful Inferno of James De Mille." *Journal of Canadian Fiction* 1.3 (1972): 61–67.

Koopman, Harry Lyman. "Literary Men of Brown III: James De Mille." *Brown Alumni Monthly* 8 (1907): 27–30.

MacFarlane, W[illiam] G[odsoe]. "De Mille, Prof. James, M.A." *New Brunswick*

Bibliography: The Books and Writers of the Province. St. John, NB: Sun, 1895. 24–26. *Early Canadiana Online.* Canadian Institute for Historical Microreproductions. 13 April 2004 <http://www.canadiana.org.proxy.lib.sfu.ca/ECO/Item-Record/09418?id=92a30b8d3f7f3282>

MacLeod, Douglas. "A Critical Biography of James De Mille." MA. Halifax, Nova Scotia: Dalhousie University, 1968.

MacMechan, Archibald. "Concerning James De Mille." *Canadian Bookman* 4 (1922): 125–26.

_____. "De Mille, the Man and the Writer." *Canadian Magazine* 27 (1906): 404–16.

Monk, Patricia. *The Gilded Beaver: An Introduction to the Life and Work of James De Mille.* Toronto: ECW, 1991.

_____. "James De Mille." *Canadian Writers before 1890.* Ed. W.H. New. Detroit: Gale, 1990. 92–94. Vol. 99 of *Dictionary of Literary Biography.* 119 vols. to date 1978–.

Parks, Malcolm. "Some Animadversions Upon a Review of the CEECT Edition of De Mille's *A Strange Manuscript.*" *Papers of the Bibliographical Society of Canada* 28 (1989): 70–73.

Tracy, Minerva. "De Mille, James." *Dictionary of Canadian Biography Online.* University of Toronto/Université Laval. 24 October 2003. 13 April 2004 <http://www. biographi.ca/EN/ShowBio.asp?BioId=39065>

Turcotte, Gerry. "'Generous, Refined, and Most Self-Denying Fiends': Naming the Abomination in James De Mille's Strange Manuscript." *Seriously Weird: Papers on the Grotesque.* Ed. Alice Mills. New York: Lang, 1999. 77–88.

Vandervaart, Leonard. *Ideas in the Fiction of Victorian Canada: James De Mille, Agnes Maule Machar, and Robert Barr. DAI* 50.7 (1990): 2058A.

NOTES

1. Malcolm Parks notes that J.O. Bailey's *Pilgrims Through Time and Space* "unexpectedly includes *A Strange Manuscript* in its survey of "scientific" and "utopian" fiction" ("Strange" 67); David Ketterer observes that *A Strange Manuscript* is "as much an originator of Canadian SF as Frankenstein is of world SF" (12); and John Robert Colombo classifies *A Strange Manuscript* as "Science Fiction" (*CDN* 1) and considers De Mille the first Canadian-born author in the science fiction genre (*Other Canadas* vii), in fact, "the first native-born Canadian author to tackle a fantastic theme in a literary way" ("Four" 34).

2. Although the more purely utopian pamphlet *The Dominion in 1983* was published pseudonymously in 1883, five years before *Strange Manuscript,* it is a short, superficial pamphlet, holding little interest for the literary critic (although its existence is interesting to the literary historian).

3. See Appendix A for a list of critics and their claims regarding the genre classification of *A Strange Manuscript Found in a Copper Cylinder.*

4. Seventeen critics who consider *A Strange Manuscript*'s relation to other texts cite 46 texts by 44 different authors (an additional 12 references are to authors' works in general rather than to specific titles). Of these texts, six are written after the 1888

publication of *A Strange Manuscript*, and are therefore considered either as influenced by De Mille's work or as containing similar universal themes. A further 32 are written before 1867, and are therefore considered as influences on De Mille's work. Only five texts fall between Parks' composition date of 1867 and the publication date of 1888. These are the texts which have created such confusion for critics: Edward Bulwer-Lytton's *The Coming Race* (1870), Samuel Butler's *Erewhon* (1872), W. H. Mallock's *The New Republic* (1877), and H. Rider Haggard's *She* (1886–7) and *King Solomon's Mines* (1885) (although Rider Haggard's pre–1888 corpus, which includes *Allan Quartermain* (1885), is often discussed in general).

Of the 14 authors and 6 specific texts De Mille himself mentions — both in Adam More's account and the conversations on board the *Falcon* — only Daniel Dafoe's *Robinson Crusoe* (1719), Jonathan Swift's *Gulliver's Travels* (1826), and Richard Owen's works on geology and pæleontology (1854–8), are discussed by critics.

Considerations of the *Bible* have been left out; the *Bible* is such an obvious and transparent influence on this and most other Victorian novels that its inclusion would not contribute any significant critical information.

WORKS CITED

Brush, Pippa. "Romance in Dystopia: A (Re-)Evaluation of James De Mille's *A Strange Manuscript Found in a Copper Cylinder.*" *British Journal of Canadian Studies* 9.2 (1994): 238–48.

Cogswell, Fred. "Literary Activity in the Maritime Provinces, 1815–1880." *Literary History of Canada: Canadian Literature in English*. 2nd ed. Ed. Carl F. Klinck. Toronto: University of Toronto Press, 1976. 102–14.

Colombo, John Robert. "Four Hundred Years of Fantastic Literature in Canada." *Out of This World: Canadian Science Fiction and Fantasy Literature*. Ed. Andrea Paradis. [Ottawa, ON]: National Library of Canada, 1995. 28–40.

_____, ed. *Other Canadas: An Anthology of Science Fiction in Canada*. Toronto: McGraw-Hill-Ryerson, 1979.

De Mille, James. *A Strange Manuscript Found in a Copper Cylinder*. 1888. Ed. Malcolm Parks. Montreal, PQ: McGill-Queen's University Press, 2000.

Didicher, Nicky. "Children and Power." English 387: Studies in Children's Literature. Simon Fraser University, Burnaby, BC. Autumn 2003.

Dyer, Klay. "De Mille, James." *The Encyclopedia of Literature in Canada*. Ed. William H. New. Toronto: University of Toronto Press, 2002. 284–86.

Gerson, Carole. "A Contrapuntal Reading of *A Strange Manuscript Found in a Copper Cylinder.*" *Essays on Canadian Writing* 56 (1995): 224–35.

_____. *A Purer Taste*. Toronto: University of Toronto Press, 1989.

_____. "Three Writers of Victorian Canada." *Canadian Writers an Their Works*. Eds. Robert Lecker, Jack Davide, and Ellen Quigley. Fiction Series 1. Toronto: ECW, 1983. 194–256.

Guth, Gwendolyn. "Reading Frames of Reference: The Satire of Exegesis in James De Mille's *A Strange Manuscript Found in a Copper Cylinder.*" *Canadian Literature* 145 (1995): 39–59.

Hughes, Kenneth J. "*A Strange Manuscript*: Sources, Satires, a Positive Utopia." *The Canadian Novel: Beginnings: A Critical Anthology*. Ed. John Moss. Toronto: NCP, 1980. 111–25.

Keefer, Janice Kulyk. *Under Eastern Eyes: A Critical Reading of Maritime Fiction*. Toronto: University of Toronto Press, 1987.

Kilgour, Maggie. "Cannibals and Critics: An Exploration of James De Mille's *Strange Manuscript*." Mosaic 30.1 (1997): 19–37.

Kime, Wayne R. The American Antecedents of James De Mille's *A Strange Manuscript Found in a Copper Cylinder*." *Dalhousie Review* 55 (1975): 280–306.

La Bossière, Camille. "The Mysterious End of James DeMille's Unfinished Manuscript." *Essays on Canadian Writing* 27 (1983–4): 41–54.

Lamont-Stewart, Linda. "Rescued by Post-modernism: The Escalating Value of James De Mille's *A Strange Manuscript Found in a Copper Cylinder*." *Canadian Literature* 145 (1995): 21–36.

Marty, Martin E. "'But Even So, Look at That': An Ironic Perspective on Utopias." *Visions of Utopia*. By Edward Rothstein, Herbert Muschamp, and Martin E. Marty. Oxford: Oxford University Press. 49–88.

Milnes, Stephen. "Colonial Discourse, Lord Featherstone's Yawn, and the Significance of Denouement in *A Strange Manuscript Found in a Copper Cylinder*." *Canadian Literature* 145 (1995): 86–104.

Multineddu, Flavio. "A Tendentious Game with an Uncanny Riddle: *A Strange Manuscript Found in a Copper Cylinder*." *Canadian Literature* 145 (1995): 62–81.

New, William. *A History of Canadian Literature*. London: Macmillan, 1989.

Parks, Malcolm. Editor's Introduction. *A Strange Manuscript Found in a Copper Cylinder*. By James De Mille. Montreal, PQ: McGill-Queen's University Press, 2000. xvii–lix.

_____. "Strange to Strangers Only." *Canadian Literature* 70 (1976): 61–78.

Stover, Leon. *Science Fiction from Wells to Heinlein*. Jefferson, NC: McFarland, 2002.

Watters, R. E. Introduction. *A Strange Manuscript Found in a Copper Cylinder*. 1888. By James De Mille. Toronto: NCL, 1969. vii–xviii.

Weiss, Allan. "Politics and the Self: Themes and Techniques in Canadian Fantastic Fiction." *Transcultural Travels: Essays in Canadian Literature and Society*. Ed. Mari Peepre-Bordessa. Nordic Association for Canadian Studies Text Series 11. Lund, Sweden: Nordic Association for Canadian Studies, 1994. 89–99.

Wilson, Kenneth C. "The Nutty Professor; or, James De Mille in the Fun House." *Essays on Canadian Writing* 48 (1992): 128–39.

Woodcock, George. "An Absence of Utopias." *Canadian Literature* 42 (1969): 3–5.

_____. "De Mille and the Utopian Vision." *Journal of Canadian Fiction* 2.3 (1973): 174–79. Rpt. in *The Canadian Novel: Beginnings: A Critical Anthology*. Ed. John Moss. Toronto: NCP, 1980. 99–110.

17

Surfing the Singularity: Science Fiction and the Future of Narrative Media

Brian Greenspan

It's no secret that the ranks of science fiction enthusiasts are stacked with vanguardists eagerly awaiting the death of the currently dominant movement and the arrival of the next best thing, whether it be nanotech, hard science fiction, slipstream, cyberpunk or the new wave. Given such a yearning for innovation, it would be easy to show that hypertext represents "the future" of science fiction, were it not that this understanding of the history of forms as a linear succession of distinct movements is precisely what interactive digital media call into question. This urge to innovate seems especially odd given that so many favored science fiction stories are premised on either alternate histories and non-linear space-times that undermine the logic of singular progression, or technologies for guaranteeing the immortality of specific peoples and cultures. In his well-known polemic on "The Many Deaths of Science Fiction," Roger Luckhurst explains the rhetoric of death and apocalypse that has always accompanied science fiction and its various movements as a constitutive feature of the genre. Science fiction may be dying, he allows, but "it has been dying from the very moment of its constitution," exploring the premise that "[t]he history of the [SF] genre is the history of the attempt to die in the *proper* way"

(35, 43). Luckhurst argues that the serial deaths of each and every science fiction movement into yet another subgenre merely "become detours on the road to the proper death of SF," which is repeatedly imagined as a transcendent return to the mainstream respectability of "high" literature from whence science fiction originally emerged. He shows convincingly how science fiction seeks legitimation by appeals to its own generic markers, to its own history, or to science; however, in every case, Luckhurst limits his discussion to *literary* science fiction, never considering the genre's attempt to achieve legitimation by transcending the literary medium itself.

Veronica Hollinger has articulated a postmodern and post-literary version of the same narrative of science fiction's absorption by the mainstream. She argues that generic science fiction has lost its power to predict the future because that future itself no longer exists, having already collapsed into the present day. In Hollinger's view, science fiction survives this collapse of historicity not as a distinct genre, but as an everyday language, an utterly familiarized discourse lacking any potential for cognitive estrangement: "These days science fiction is everywhere, as a discourse of choice through which to describe a present which perceives itself as both technological and apocalyptic. In fact, this is a present which perceives itself *as already extending into the future*" (217). Yet, Hollinger elides the significant distinctions between the various media through which the generalized discourse of science fiction survives — literature, film, television and graphic novels (216), not to mention popular music, advertising and websites.

This tendency to shy away from the discussion of comparative science fiction media is surprisingly widespread, especially where hypermedia are concerned. Brooks Landon stands almost alone in his appeals to writers to produce science fiction in hypertext form. Writing in 1993, close to the onset of hyperfiction, Landon could still hold faith in the significance that hypertext held for the future of science fiction:

> Indeed, if SF, the fabled "literature of change," is to continue to deserve the cultural authority it has codified during the last few decades, it will almost certainly need to confront the changed status of writing made possible by hypertext technology. Or, to put this another way, science fiction, the literature with a special relationship to technology, will have to recognize that writing is itself a fundamental technology — one that is undergoing massive change ["Hypertext"].

Four years later Landon was still waiting for his prediction to come true, asserting that, "[o]ddly enough, the implications of computer technology for narrative are being explored mainly outside of SF" (*Science Fiction* 166).

To some extent, this view reflects the reality that hypertext fictions until fairly recently have, as Jane Yellowlees Douglas observes, tended to reflect a high modernist aesthetic of innovation that "seems to present itself as narrative fiction's next leap" into avant-garde respectability (8). Douglas contrasts artistic hypertexts in the tradition of Joyce (both James and Michael) with the sort of digital narratives one encounters through computer games and interactive fictions, which are often based on popular genres like fantasy or science fiction.

Even if we follow Douglas' lead and bracket out digital science fiction narratives, along with digital versions of print literature available from sources such as eReader.com or Project Gutenberg (or, for that matter, Cory Doctorow's *Someone Comes to Town, Someone Leaves Town*, a print novel that was first launched in the Second Life virtual environment), there remains a growing number of authors who are using digital media to explore and expand the future of science fiction narrative. Yet, the perception that hyperfiction owes more to Henry James than H.G. Wells remains widespread, perhaps reinforced by the fact that certain prominent writers of science fiction have rejected the idea of writing in a digital mode. In the "Acknowledgments" to *Snow Crash* (1992), Neal Stephenson admits that his original goal "was to publish a computer-generated graphic novel" in collaboration with the artist Tony Sheeder, but that the idea was too advanced for the technology at the time:

> I became intimately familiar with the inner workings of the Macintosh during the early phases of the doomed and maniacal graphic-novel project when it became clear that the only way to make the Mac do the things we needed was to write a lot of custom image-processing software. I have probably spent more hours coding during the production of this work than I did actually writing it, even though it eventually turned away from the original graphic concept, rendering most of that work useless from a practical viewpoint [440].[1]

Katherine Anne Goonan, too, originally conceived of *Queen City Jazz* (1994) as a hypertext novel "before such technologies were available to the public" (21). Given that the novel's episodes were written in non-linear fashion and in intertextual dialogue with popular artforms like jazz and comics, Goonan maintains that "[t]ransforming QCJ into a hypertext work (ignoring the massive cost of obtaining the rights to do so) would enhance the experience of this novel immeasurably."

While such confessions affirm the science fiction author's rhetorical commitment to the avant-garde of literary technologies, they might also be read as merely trendy nods to geek chic that warily position hypertextual science fiction as a future marvel not yet within our grasp. By relegating the potentially rich non-linear aspects of their respective works to the realm of a writerly path not taken, both Goonan and Stephenson draw on the power of hypertext and associated "popular" forms while insulating their narratives from them, ultimately expressing an unflagging dedication to print. Hypertext author and critic Stuart Moulthrop writes of Stephenson's "Acknowledgment,"

> Suppose that the abortive digital format for *Snow Crash* was not a series of printed panels intended for conventional bound publication, but instead a network of screens linked together by some graphic navigational scheme — in other words, an electronic hypertext. If this were the case, then the change of media, the reversion to the more traditional format of the book, might be very important indeed. It might suggest that *Snow Crash* is in more than one sense a defense of the book and its ethos: not just the story, but the *embodiment* of a New Deuteronomy [20].

Assuming Luckhurst to be correct, it seems that even the apparent proponents of hypertext can't genuinely envision the medium as representing the mainstream into which science fiction wants to be reborn. Despite critically acclaimed examples like Sarah Smith's "King of Space" (1991), Adrienne Wortzel's *The Electronic Chronicles* (1995) or Shelley Jackson's *Patchwork Girl* (1995), for most readers, hypertext science fiction remains a hybrid creature of pulp fiction and high technology, by many accounts no more than a half-working jinn that never quite reached the future, or a hideous progeny that has already become extinct. After all, hypertext betokens an even greater tragedy than the death of science fiction: namely, the Bradburian nightmare of the extinction of books of all kinds. Hardly ever has the topic of hypertext been raised without at least a token expression of concern for the books, libraries and literacies that it seems to place in peril, at least according to the dubious logic of what Paul Duguid calls "the notion of *supersession*— the idea that each new technological type vanquishes or subsumes its predecessors" (65). But what happens when the fear of media supersession intersects with the yearning for generic innovation?

This chapter considers the purported death of hypertext alongside science fiction's rhetoric of genre apocalypse in the attempt to understand both phenomena as registering at once a deeper cultural anxiety and a broader utopian impulse. Taking Luckhurst's metacritical account of the politics of genre a step further, I argue that assertions of the death of science fiction and hypertext alike rehearse an even greater tragedy: the imminent demise of literature's legitimating structures more broadly, including publishing houses, museums and libraries, funding for universities and humanities research, and the apparatuses of state capitalism that support these institutions. Far from signifying the impossibility of distance and estrangement in a present world already saturated with futurity, science fiction is increasingly migrating into new literary media and discursive genres, in anticipation of a future archive articulated to formations that are at once anarchic, communal and transnational.

Notably, in these depictions, the library and archive maintain their privileged place as the sites of future memory, culture and collective identity. Science fiction narratives in hypertext form reveal that it is impossible to imagine the contents of the science fiction library of the future without first considering the future of the library itself as an institution and a cultural technology. Mike Featherstone has written that the advent of hypertext and electronic archives "not only establishes a new relationship between the state and higher education, but also will produce a different relationship to the library, the archive and cultural repositories which stand behind the canon and syllabi. In short who will archive cultures in the future — the state, or the corporations, or the public? (167). Hypertext narrative and science fiction are privileged sites for exploring such questions about the present and future politics of information. By anticipating the future of new technologies for the inscription, storage, recall and reproduction of narratives, new media authors help us to imagine how these various residual and emergent institutions will negotiate control of the cultural archive, as well as to imagine what science fiction texts the libraries of the future might hold in store.

Alien Media and other Promising Machines

If the future of science fiction publishing seems to exclude hypertext, that may be because the metanarrative characterizing science fiction as a futureless genre is itself tied to a causal logic that has little to do with the dispersed, synchronic structure of new networked narratives. One science fiction text that explores the temporality peculiar to the hypertext medium is *Extreme Conditions* (1996), by the Columbian writer Juan B. Gutiérrez. A time-travel conspiracy narrative structured on several imbricated temporal paradoxes, *Extreme Conditions* exploits the tension between linear narration and the synchronic structure of a networked hypertext. The narrative is written for Literatronic, an adaptive, web-based hypertext environment created by the author (and software designer) to facilitate the reader's navigation through the text. As Gutiérrez explains, Literatronic "is a writing and reading form in which the links have different destinations depending upon what the reader has read before. An adaptive literary piece reconfigures itself for the reader, leading every time to a potentially unique book" (*Literatronic*, "What is adaptive digital narrative?"). Within this environment, the story itself unfolds in a non-linear progression, detailing the struggles of various "chrononauts" to influence the future of the human race by preventing an industrial accident in the past that gave birth to a new race of mutants better evolved to survive the planet's deteriorating environment.

In *Archaeologies of the Future* (2005), Fredric Jameson explores the paradox that the future can only be different if the seed of change already exists in the present; by corollary, the only future we can possibly imagine is a slightly estranged version of the present. Jameson understands the theme of apocalypse and disruption in general as part of this frozen dialectic, the "diachrony of synchrony." From this perspective, the repeated deaths of science fiction can all be seen as anticipations of a future, more radical break with history itself, and the emergence into a new temporality that marks the transition from the present social order to a genuine utopia (90). *Extreme Conditions* allegorizes this antinomy by foregrounding the tension between its own synchronic state as a network of hypertext nodes, and the many different configurations that the story can take when accessed in real time. A retrofuturist hybrid of cyberpunk motifs, graphic novels and conventional time travel narratives filtered through a bilingual, user-friendly interface that belies its technological innovativeness even as it complicates the temporality of reading in high modernist fashion, *Extreme Conditions* resists being positioned as the future of science fiction. The struggle between humans and mutants operates as an allegory of numerous present-day conflicts, especially those stemming from the Colombian economy, environmental issues and the hegemony of North America over Latin America, as Susan Pajares Tosca shows. For Tosca, Gutiérrez's choice of genre ironizes his choice of medium, since his political critique undermines common critical perceptions of hypertext as an essentially democratic and liberating technology: "[w]ith Gutiérrez, the polished postmodern avant-garde instrument [of hypertext] is dragged down to the sewers of science fiction" (275).

In advancing this reading, however, she exaggerates the text's difference from other "canonical" literary hypertexts, asserting that it "even neglects to make the meta-references that are nearly mandatory in the field." While certainly reveling in the grittier trappings of cyberpunk, *Extreme Conditions* is in fact replete with self-reflections on its own hypertextual non-linearity. The mutants in this future world are known as "avatars," a term that, in our world, denotes a user's virtual representative in a computer-mediated environment, and which thus encourages the reader to identify as closely with the subaltern class of mutants as with Gutiérrez's human characters. Numerous references to temporal paradoxes within the story — statements like, "It's not possible to change the past, even if we know it. It's impossible to change the future because we don't know it" — operate as metamedia commentaries on the experience of reading Gutierrez's interactive story, which allows the reader at every turn to choose between various proleptic and analeptic narrative paths. Such self-reflection makes it impossible to separate the more familiar elements of this post-apocalyptic cyberpunk narrative from its hypertextual medium: the mingling of digital effects with the traditional textualities of science fiction novels and comics come to stand for the possibility of a rapprochement between mutants and humans, between avatars and users. The innovative Literatronic interface itself thus plays a central symbolic role representing the future as an allegory of alterity, standing ambivalently for either the future humans who remain bound within the horizon of technological progress, or the mutated post-humans who live with the effects of progress. Gutiérrez' website makes these connections clear, describing his adaptive hypertext engine in post-human terms as "an autonomous entity" and "an artificial intelligence engine that designs a fiction book specific to every reader," and therefore one that is more familiar than the usual exploratory hyperfiction: "Rather than thinking in hypertext terms, which elements should be linked, the author considers levels of kinship, affinity, connection" (Literatronic, "What is this web site about?"). Construed in this way as an imaginary medium with real effects, the Literatronic engine enables a non-linear understanding of the adaptability that allows a human to understand, and even come to love, that which is most alien.

Jameson observes that, in science fiction narratives,

> temporal questions — the diachrony of synchrony, the matter of the transition to Utopia, the representational dilemmas in thinking historical time itself — seem fatally to lead in almost all cases to the rather different problem of whether alien life, radically different sentient beings, can be imagined at all [106].

Put differently, the daunting task of imagining a truly alien life is an oblique way of imagining utopia, itself an impossible goal. Jameson extends his "unknowability thesis" to include alien language and communications devices, stressing the "non-communicability between the absolutely alien and Other" (117). Oddly enough for a dialectical materialist, he pays relatively little attention to imaginary media, the material traces in which alien languages are embodied. Along with tractor beams, FTL travel and other *nova* that traverse many different science fiction texts and universes, alien or futuristic media like the communicator, vidscreen, holo, universal translator or ansible do not stand for any specific representations of alterity; they rather act as tools for inventing a multitude of possible languages, cultures and futures. Like the concept of utopia itself, alien media are, in Ian Buchanan's phrase, "promising-machines" that offer "the *promise* of a better future" while relieving us of "the burden of having to describe its peculiarly unpresentable content" (22–3).

Digital Archives and the Future State (of Narrative)

But if the content of the future society is impossible to imagine, it is ultimately no easier to imagine forms and implements for writing the future that are radically different from the media we already possess. That the unknowability thesis extends to media is perfectly illustrated in *Triple Helix* (2006), Ruth Nestvold's inaugural science-fiction hypertext. Nestvold notes the apparent dearth of science fiction narratives in digital form, but remains committed to the potential of hypertext, maintaining that "[s]cience fiction authors have participated in the electronic conceptually, experimentally and communally" (Lake and Nestvold). If printed text still provides the best background against which to present the futuristic interfaces that authors dream up, then *Triple Helix* inverts this figure and ground, using a hypertextual interface to foreground legacy document formats in novelistic fashion. The hypertext consists of interface to an archive of familiar genres *remediated* from print culture, including letters, diaries, interviews and glossary entries, from which the reader reconstructs a narrative of first contact. According to Jay David Bolter and Richard Grusin, remediation is the dialectical process through which digital media represent older, printed media; it also characterizes the reverse process through which science fiction novels in print can represent cybernetic or virtual reality interfaces. Remediation thus predicts that new literary interfaces, if they are to be intelligible, must remain trapped in the general paradox of future representation, falling back on the textual archive as the site of future memory. Jeff Noon's writings offer a case in point: his entire science fiction oeuvre is an intertextual library of literature, myth and folklore, remixed to create the peculiar form of iterative narrative that he variously styles as "dub fiction" or "metamorphiction." The collection *Cobralingus* (2001) offers the fullest explanation of his ludic process of composition by rules, which involves running classic literary texts through "filters" that execute textual commands like SAMPLE, MIX and REPEAT, transforming the source material into a new fiction. By remediating audio processing tools on the printed page, the "cobralingus engine" toys with new metaphors for instrumentalizing the process of textual creation. Noon, along with several of his fans, have also published Flash animations of the text of *Cobralingus* online, digital versions of his engine that further blur the distinction between narrative and software, and between Noon and his readers. Still, his output remains primarily a remediation of music sampling technologies in the form of printed narrative.

Other authors working in new media allow us to envision what the science fiction library of the future might contain, by anticipating the future of new technologies for the inscription, storage, recall and reproduction of narratives. As it turns out, in the library of the future, there is rarely any middle ground. In the ideal case, it contains the complete archive of all Earth culture and a universal repository for the entire history of printed literature, a dream that has underwritten hypertext system development ever since Ted Nelson's prescient Project Xanadu. Ironically, such visions of literary plenitude strike many as cause for concern: noting how new media are changing the ratios between *story* and *archive*, Randy Bass asks how literary scholars will respond to "the virtues of disciplinary abundance in the context of increasingly open digital (and hypertextual) access to cultural texts and materials. How do we make use of overrepresentation? By what *design* do we discover the expressive limits on representation?" (661). Such anxieties perhaps explain the proliferation in science fiction of the alternative scenario in which the future library is utterly destroyed, leaving behind only fragments and shards of our collective past, a popular motif ever since Wells depicted the future ruins of the British Museum Library in *The Time Machine*. In either case, representations of the future archive express anxieties over the present state of literary institutions.

The motif of the ideal database meets the theme of the archive's ruin[2] in Stuart Moulthrop's *Reagan Library* (1999), an online hypertext that mixes half-recognizable fragments from the insecure memories of an unnamed subject, who might be the late eponymous American president, with visual and textual glimpses of a mysterious, other-worldly landscape. The author describes his text as "an odd mixture of stories and images, voices and places, crimes and punishments, connections and disruptions, signals on, noises off, failures of memory, and acts of reconstruction. It goes into some places not customary for 'writing.' I think of it as a space probe" ("Author description"). Navigating through these eerie textual spaces gradually emulates the mental wanderings of a confounded subject exploring the library of his own ruined mind: "I awoke one inky midnight in the library. It was not what I expected, but here I was, poured out on the blank sands, my conviction duly registered, sentence indefinite.... The whole of the law is to keep your story straight — you must remember this." The reader's multicursal exploration of the text parallels the dilemma of the protagonist, who has forgotten the important secret he was supposed to keep hidden: "What does the President know and how does he know it? That was the real text." Different links return text in different fonts, interface styles and discursive registers, creating the sense of a radically fractured storage medium. In one lexia, numbered and bulleted notes resembling an official report tell us that "The man in the library has been condemned"; another offers an illusory sense of control by inaccurately informing us, "*You have now appreciated 35 percent of the text. Thank you for reading.*" Unlike the hyperlinks in Nestvold's "Triple Helix," each of which provides the user with a partial but incremental knowledge of the alien worlds described, the links in *Reagan Library* provide only the illusion of a growing understanding. Teaser links redundantly entitled "This is the real text" repeatedly promise revelation, while actually connecting to different lexia each time, enacting the impossibility of ever accessing the "real" text of memory. The hypertext reinforces the inaccessibility of the secret truth by instead returning trite revelations of faked lunar landings, or glimpses of the inside of an alien ship that evoke popular notions of false memory syndrome. Snatches of text that are fragmentary in one lexia return in others more completely, giving the sense of a gradual remembering; but these recollections are themselves just fragments of a larger discourse, lending weight to the observation that "[t]he universe would add up nicely if only we could find the other set of books...."

As archon of a disintegrating library, the president ultimately symbolizes the ruin of his culture and nation. Moulthrop's panoramic Quicktime landscapes depict the barely recognizable vestiges of monuments from the

National Mall and Memorial Park in Washington, DC. As an enactment of a mind suffering the throes of "archive fever," the text self-consciously demonstrates Jacques Derrida's theories of how electronic media are altering the historical connections between archives and state power. Derrida engages a "retrospective science fiction" to describe how electronic media are "on the way to transforming the entire public and private space of humanity, and first of all the limit between the private, the secret (private or public), and the public or the phenomenal.... [T]his instrumental possibility of production, of printing, of conservation, and of destruction of the archive must inevitably be accompanied by juridical and thus political transformations" (16–17). The constant innovation in archival technique is continually reinventing the future, reinventing what can be archived and, therefore, what can be written and disseminated in the first place: archival technique "conditions not only the form or the structure that prints, but the printed content of the printing" (18).

Douglas Barbour has explored models of futuristic archives in several science fiction novels in print, but texts like *Reagan Library* or *Triple Helix* do more than just represent the digital archive: they invite the user to query the textual database for public and private information about fictional characters and their worlds, and to experience directly its operating principles of vast storage potential, limited access and secrecy. These narratives exploit the tension between the structures of the narrative and database, which Lev Manovich refers to as "natural enemies" (226). In his view, a creative work in new media is less about creating a narrative than the construction of "one or more interfaces to a database of multimedia material": "[r]egardless of whether new media objects present themselves as linear narratives, interactive narratives, databases, or something else, underneath, on the level of material organization, they are all databases" (227, 228). While such a low-level description does not capture the experience of reading all digital fictions, it does go some ways to expressing the source of engagement in texts like *Triple Helix* and *Reagan Library*, which draw their interest from the tension between the archive and the database as cultural forms with historically distinct representational properties.

Communal Narratives and the Future

That digital archives are shifting the ratios of public and private information becomes especially clear in a web environment, in which networked narratives have at least the capacity to directly link fictional worlds not only to archives of real-time, non-fictional information, but also to actual reading communities. In modernist science fiction tales like E.M. Forster's *The Machine Stopped*, the digital library represents a fetishized alternative to human dialogue, as masses of data threaten to take the place of real community. But as technology has caught up with the predictions, prognostications of the resulting social anomie have proven overly alarmist. In fact, new media have enabled the formation of new kinds of literary communities. Douglas Rushkoff's *Exit Strategy* (2002) is a near-future artifactual hyperfiction about the politics of a high-tech startup that claims to have invented a new, global form of networked communication. Rushkoff explains his conceit: "Although the book takes place in the near future, the text itself only 'surfaced' online in the 23rd Century. The entire text is annotated with footnotes so that terms like "Microsoft" and "NASDAQ" make sense to the future reader who, presumably, lives in a world beyond such things." In what he calls an "Open Source Experiment," Rushkoff published the full text of *Exit Strategy* online for a year, during which time readers could contribute footnotes which were later incorporated into the printed version. His experiment in collaborative hypertext exemplifies the new dimensions of co-creation that web-based hypertext enables. Collaborative author forums such as *parallel-worlds.net, speculativevision.com* or *iSciFiStory.com* go further still in offering online publishing space, community feedback, even tools to help the busy aspiring science fiction or fantasy writer to craft fiction or poetry in Flash, or contribute episodes to collaborative interactive stories.

Such interfaces are not likely to gain critical recognition anytime soon, as they discourage the production of the sort of single-authored, coherent, realist narratives of determinate length that, as Lake and Nestvold point out, remain the gold standard of science fiction ("Electronic"). They also deny the cult of professional auteurism that has long dominated the field, which still measures an author's emergence from the date of his or her first "sale." For the first time in history, the popularity of web publishing raises the distinct possibility that amateur science fiction will soon be more widely read than works by professional writers. In *Convergence Culture* (2006), Henry Jenkins argues that science-fiction fan cultures have grown into genuine web-enabled "knowledge communities" that actively consume popular media texts and respond to them creatively by publishing their own fan fictions, songs, images and videos on the internet. These fans not only consume and produce fictional representations of utopia, but enact them through strategic alliances and tactical interventions into the mediasphere that reflect a deeper utopian temporality, a synchronicity promising glimpses of a lost communal reality. Transmedia texts thus operate not only on the level of representation, but also on the levels of performance, dialogue and community. Significantly, the central figure of these knowledge communities is the destruction of the corporate media archive, and the redistribution of popular cultural wealth by grassroots communities. The joint property of transnational media corporations and web-based global communities, transmedia artifacts allegorize the demise of nations and the rise of a new rooted in open knowledge structures.

For Katherine Hayles, such communities are characterized by the "entanglement of the bodies of texts and digital subjects" (7), operating through the logic of *intermediation*. An expanded form of remediation, intermediation includes not only the negotiations between different media, but also

> interactions between systems of representations, particularly language and code, as well as interactions between modes of representation, particularly analog and digital. Perhaps most importantly, "intermediation" also denotes mediating interfaces connecting humans with the intelligent machines that are our collaborators in making, storing, and transmitting informational processes and objects [33].

Intermediation need not take the form of science fiction, although, as a dialectical process that reflects the utopian desire for a new form of society, it frequently does. Science fiction already operates as an intertextual assemblage (Hayles 105) that is also intermedial, sharing concepts, discourses and properties across novels, comics, films and games. One example of intermedial science fiction is Diana Reed Slattery's *The Maze Game* (2005), a novel that shares Noon's interest in literary transformations and automatic story generation through mixed media. *The Maze Game* describes a futuristic universe in which humanity has developed the I-virus, which ironically guarantees immortality and near indestructibility. Like Swift's superannuated struldbruggs, those who are infected by the I-virus invariably learn the boredom and despair that accompanies eternal existence, ultimately living only for the thrill of gambling on The Game. A mixture of puzzle, dance and mortal combat, The Game is played by champion Dancers engineered from the genetic stock of four different castes, each with its own strengths and style: Bod, Swash, Chrome and Glide. Glide also describes the gestural and visual language of the game, which first emerged as a patois learned by Glide slaves from hallucinogenic lillipads, the source of all literature and mystical understanding in the novel's universe. To win The Game (which entails sacrificing oneself in the triumphal Dance of Death) involves a degree of mastery over the Glide ideograms and their semantic transformations, out of which the labyrinthine playing field is constructed.

The alterity of Slattery's fictional world is focused through the otherness of a post-human language, which we encounter through lexicographical illustrations of Glide poems provided in the text's margins. Deena Larsen notes that "[t]he meaning here is inherent in the actual motion: we discover a fluid thought process of morphing between the two glyphs [of a poem], a dancing state between the two static symbols of meaning" ("Transformations"). As a visual and gestural language built on ternary logic, Glide is genuinely difficult to visualize in all its transformations. To fully appreciate the semantic depth of glide and Slattery's narrative, readers must visit *The Glide Project*, a Flash-animated website that offers animations of Glide transformations, and even includes a downloadable lexicon and a "Collabyrinth" module in which users can write their own poems in Glide, a unique narrative interface to a linguistic database. Such interactive modules merge with the printed text to form a transmedia artifact, reinforcing the novel's utopian faith in a symbolic language that would unify the body, sense, music, dance and poetry in a millenarian narrative of liberation.

While *The Maze Game* and *The Reagan Library* both depend upon the reader's ergodic interactivity, neither constitutes a truly interactive fiction (IF), which Nick Monfort defines as "that type of computer program exemplified by the text adventure" (*Twisty* 2). In the classic IFs that Monfort describes, users are presented with a textual description of a fictional world with which they interact through limited high-level commands. The behavior of the story depends upon the user's input at any given turn. Monfort accurately characterizes such legacy fictions as rooted in a rhetoric of riddles and the structure of the adventure or quest (even if the high-profile exception of *Starship Titanic*, a computer game with artificially intelligent characters scripted by Douglas Adams, boasts a science-fiction setting); however, he has also acknowledged at least one departure from this tradition. Dan Shiovitz's *Bad Machine* (1998) is a fictional interface that intermediates natural language with computer code, allowing a user to explore the potential interactions between human and machine subjectivities. The user plays the role of a futuristic warehouse robot as it attempts to interact with other industrial machines, and must learn to manipulate the robotic avatar by issuing command lines. Faulty internal programming gives the avatar an emergent intelligence and autonomy, which reflects the player's experience of learning the code necessary to run it. While many science fiction narratives offer a window into the subjective perspective of machinic characters — Rudy Rucker's *Ware* series or Michael McCollum's *Life Probe* come to mind — what makes *Bad Machine* different is that the code that forms its protagonist's artificial mind is processual and executable. Reading the text of *Bad Machine* also means *writing* the text, issuing commands in an alien language that will provide access to the protagonist's database of stored commands.

Failed RAM chips and faulty programming libraries are a long way from the ruins of Wells's Porcelain Palace, the cultural memory of an empire. While this survey of futuristic interfaces is hardly exhaustive, it is nevertheless true that most science fiction writers remain more comfortable working in traditional print media. Writing "in defense of stone tablets," Gary Westfahl notes that, science fiction writers typically being about four decades behind any literary innovation, we can't expect to see the widescale adoption of hypertext until the year 2030 (122). Even so, he holds out little hope that interactive digital texts will displace traditional paper novels as the creative medium of choice, as "the joy of experience a genuine narrative lies in surrendering control to a masterful storyteller" (126). I believe that Westfahl's prognostication may be right, but for not for the reason he provides; nor is it just artists' lack of familiarity with the medium, or even the shortcomings of current authorware, that discourage authors from working in hypermedia. And given that most hypertexts are still single-authored, the reason can't be merely that hypertext transfers control from the author to the reader, as Niko Silvester has suggested ("The More"). Hypermedia by definition are beyond the singular control of an individual artist in a much more profound sense, since to use code as a narrative medium is perforce to participate in a developed network society and every contrary ideology it comprises, be it transnationalism, free-market capitalism, post-consumerism, technorealism or hacktivism. The assumptions that historically underwrite the printed text — publishing houses, gazettes and reviews, universities, public libraries and civil society itself — are by now largely transparent, and need not explicitly inform the writing or content of any given narrative. To author digital media, on the other hand, requires a constant awareness and negotiation of numerous extended collectivities, including web hosts and network specialists, freeware and groupware designers, open source communities, digital rights activists, online writers' forums, bloggers, Second Lifers and geocachers — communities that an author might well interact with and even influence, but can't possibly control. For the science fiction writer in particular, the artistic dilemma becomes that of representing a radically different future society — itself an impossible task, as we have seen — in a medium that already depends upon and instantiates so many overlapping and contradictory communities. By allegorizing, illustrating, digitizing, linking, tagging, migrating, operationalizing, compressing, completing, destroying or otherwise fetishizing the cultural archive, a public body of stored information removed from its immediate context, science fiction writers are tentatively exploring how new narrative media might represent or even connect to the networked communities of today.

NOTES

1. Katherine Hayles has since discussed the persistence of traces of digital composition in Stephenson's later novel, *Cryptonomicon*, arguing that the surface of the text reveals "contradictory enunciations of code/language and the conflicting historical vectors of mechanical past/informatic future" (119).

2. Of course, depictions of the future archive sometimes fall between these extremes. In Roland Emmerich's environmental catastrophe film, *The Day After Tomorrow* (2004), the New York Public Library becomes a refuge for survivors after the city is deluged by glacial storms following rapid global warming. Tragically, in the next ice age, books are apparently useful only as a fuel.

WORKS CITED

Barbour, Douglas. "Archive Fever in the Technological Far Future Histories *Appleseed, Permanence* and *Psychohistorical Crisis*." *Foundation* 94 (Summer 2005): 39–49.

Bass, Randy. "Story and Archive in the Twenty-First Century." *College English* 61.6 (July 1999): 659–670.

Bolter, Jay David, and Richard Grusin. *Remediation: Understanding New Media*. Cambridge, Mass.: MIT Press, 1999.

Buchanan, Ian. "Metacommentary on Utopia, or Jameson's dialectic of hope." *Utopian Studies* 9.2 (1998): 18–30.

Douglas, J. Yellowlees. *The End of Books — or Books without End? Reading Interactive Narratives*. Ann Arbor: University of Michigan Press, 2001.

Duguid, Paul. "Material Matters: The Past and Futurology of the Book." Geoffrey Nunberg, ed. *The Future of the Book*. Berkeley: University of California Press, 1996. 63–102.

Featherstone, Mike. "Archiving Cultures." *British Journal of Sociology* 51.1 (January/March 2000): 161–184.

Goonan, Katherine Anne. "Consciousness, Literature, and Science Fiction." *Iowa Web Review,* August 2005. Available at: http://www.uiowa.edu/~iareview/main-pages/new/aug05/ documents/goonan.pdf.

Gutiérrez, Juan B. *Extreme Conditions.* 1996. Available at: http://www.literatronic.com/src/Pagina.aspx?lng=BRITANNIA&opus=1&pagina=1.

_____. *Literatronic: Adaptive Digital Narrative.* Available at: http://www.literatronic.com/src/initium.aspx.

Hayles, N. Katherine. *My Mother Was a Computer: Digital Subjects and Literary Texts.* Chicago: University of Chicago Press, 2005.

Hollinger, Veronica. "Future/Present: The End of Science Fiction." David Seed, ed. *Imagining Apocalypse: Studies in Cultural Crisis.* London: Macmillan, 2000. 215–229.

Jameson, Fredric. *Archaeologies of the Future: The Desire Called Utopia and Other Science Fictions.* New York: Verso, 2005.

Jenkins, Henry. *Convergence Culture: Where Old and New Media Collide.* New York: NYU Press, 2006.

Lake, Jay and Ruth Nestvold. "Electronic Community and the End of the Lone Writer." *Internet Review of Science Fiction* 2.5 (June 2005). Available at: http://www.irosf.com/q/zine/ article/10156.

_____. "What Happened to Hyperfiction?" *Internet Review of Science Fiction* 2.7 (August 2005). Available at: http://www.irosf.com/q/zine/article/10174.

Landon, Brooks. "Hypertext and Science Fiction" [Review of Gareth Branwyn, Peter Sugarman, et al. *Beyond Cyberpunk: A Do-It-Yourself Guide to the* Future]. Science-Fiction Studies No. 61, 20:3 (November 1993). Available at: http://www.depauw.edu/sfs/review_essays/land61.htm.

_____. *Science Fiction After 1900: From the Steam Man to the Stars.* New York: Routledge, 1995.

Luckhurst, Roger. "The Many Deaths of Science Fiction: A Polemic." *Science-Fiction Studies* 21 (1994): 35–49.

Manovich, Lev. *The Language of New Media.* Cambridge, Mass.: MIT Press, 2001.

Montfort, Nick. *Twisty Little Passages: An Approach to Interactive Fiction.* Cambridge, Mass: MIT Press, 2003.

_____. "A Bad Machine Made of Words." Available at: http://tracearchive.ntu.ac.uk/print_article/index.cfm?article=116.

Moulthrop, Stuart. "Deuteronomy Comix" [Rev. of Neal Stephenson, *Snow Crash*]. *Postmodern Culture* 3.2 (1993). Available at: http://www.infomotions.com/serials/pmc/pmc-v3n2-moulthrop-deuteronomy.txt

_____. *Reagan Library.* 1999. Available at: http://collection.eliterature.org/1/works/moulthrop__reagan_library.html.

Nestvold, Ruth. *Triple Helix.* 2006. Available at: http://www.ideomancer.com/main/vol5issue2/ nestvold/one.html.

Noon, Jeff. *Cobralingus.* Daniel Arlington, ill. Michael Bracewell, intro. London: Codex, 2001.

Rushkoff, Douglas. "The Open Source Experiment." Available at: http://www.rushkoff.com/ bull.html.

Silvester, Niko. "The More Things Change: Science Fiction Literature and the New

Narrative." *Strange Horizons* 25 November 2002. Available at: http://www.strange-horizons.com/ 2002/20021125/change.shtml.

Slattery, Diana Reed. *The Maze Game.* Kingston, NY: Deep Listening, 2003.

Stephenson, Neal. *Snow Crash.* New York: Bantam, 1992.

Tosca, Susana Pajares. "*Condiciones Extremas*: Digital Science Fiction from Columbia." Edmundo Paz-Soldán and Debra A. Castillo, eds. *Latin American Literature and Mass Media.* New York: Garland, 2001. 270–287.

Westfahl, Gary. "In Defense of Stone Tablets: Isaac Asimov Explains Why Science Fiction Is Skeptical about 'New Information Technologies.'" *Science Fiction, Children's Literature, and Popular Culture: Coming of Age in Fantasyland.* Contributions to the Study of Science Fiction and Fantasy 88. Ed. Donald Palumbo. Westport, Conn.: Greenwood, 2000. 121–128.

About the Contributors

Robert Boschman is an English instructor at Mount Royal College in Calgary, Alberta, where he teaches literature and composition.

Lee Easton teaches English and communications at Mount Royal College. He has a Ph.D. from the University of Toronto. In addition to interests in science fiction, he works in the areas of gender and sexuality studies and media studies. He is at work on a book about videogames.

Steven Engler is a religious studies instructor in the Humanities Department at Mount Royal College. Pastimes include listening to jazz, improvising at the piano, and reading, for more than thirty years now, science fiction. He has a Ph.D. in religion from Concordia University in Montréal and has taught philosophy and religious studies at colleges and universities in British Columbia, Québec, and Alberta. Current research interests include theory of religion and relations between science and religion. He was a visiting research professor (2005–2006) at Pontifícia Universidade Católica de São Paulo, Programa de Estudos Pós-Graduados em Ciências da Religião, Brazil, sponsored by a fellowship from the Fundação de Amparo à Pesquisa do Estado de São Paulo (FAPESP).

Gail de Vos is a professional storyteller who specializes in telling tales to young adults. She is an adjunct professor at the School of Library and Information Studies at the University of Alberta where she teaches, among other courses, storytelling and graphic novels and comic books in libraries and schools. She is the author of seven books on storytelling and folk literature for young adults.

Brian Greenspan is assistant professor in the Institute for Comparative Studies in Literature, Art and Culture and the Department of English Language and Literature at Carleton University, Ottawa. He is a research collaborator in the Cybercartography and the New Economy Project.

Richard Harrison is the author of six books of poetry, among them *Hero of the Play* and *Big Breath of Wish*, which have won or have been shortlisted for several regional or national honors, among them the W.O. Mitchell/City of Calgary Book Prize and the Governor-General's Award. His essays on a range of cultural topics, from religion to hockey, and from poetry to comic books, have been published in Canada and the United States. He holds degrees in philosophy (Trent) and English (Concordia). He teaches English and creative writing at Calgary's Mount Royal College.

Mary Hemmings is the English literature librarian at the University of Calgary. She is also co-ordinator of the newly acquired Gibson Collection of Speculative Fiction at the university.

Linda Howell teaches English literature and composition at Mount Royal College in Calgary. Science fiction in general and cyborg fiction in particular are two of her longstanding research and teaching interests.

Karyn Huenemann has lived and studied in England, India, and the United States, as well as her native Canada. Combined with an interest in science fiction and fantasy, Karyn's academic focus on Victorian and Canadian studies makes De Mille's *A Strange Manuscript Found in a Copper Cylinder* one of her favorite novels both to teach and recommend to friends. Karyn is a literature instructor at Simon Fraser University, Burnaby, British Columbia.

David Hyttenrauch teaches English at Calgary's Mount Royal College. His research specialty in medieval English Arthurian romance complements his teaching and study of modern fantasy. He is a student of Tolkien's fiction and of its medieval Norse and English sources and analogues. In addition to teaching and researching Tolkien, he has served as production dramaturge on two professional stage productions of *The Hobbit*.

Marie Jakober's historical fantasy, *The Black Chalice*, was shortlisted for the Sunburst Award and ranked among "The Year's Best" by the Science Fiction Book Club. The novel has been translated into French, and a German edition is forthcoming. Ms. Jakober has published six other novels in the fields of SF and historical fiction. Her novel of Union spy Elizabeth Van Lew, *Only Call Us Faithful*, received the Michael Shaara Award for

Excellence in Civil War Fiction in 2003. She has also won the Georges Bugnet Award twice. Marie Jakober lives and works in Calgary.

Darlene M. Juschka is associate professor of women's studies and program coordinator and adjunct professor, religious studies, at the University of Regina. She has a number of interests which are derived from her background in religious studies and women's studies. She is working on a triprovincial longitudinal research project that tracks the lives of women as they emerge from abusive relationships, "The Healing Journey: A Longitudinal Study of Women Who Have Been Abused by Intimate Partners." She is working on a monograph entitled *The Semiotics of Gender: Political Bodies/Body Politic*, while recently published articles include "Spectacles of Gender: Enacting the Masculine in Ancient Rome and Modern Cinema" in *Religious Studies and Theology* (2005) and "Gender" (2005), in John Hinnells (ed.), *The Routledge Companion to the Study of Religion*, 225–238. She edited and annotated *Feminism in the Study of Religion: A Reader* (2001).

Christine Mains is a Ph.D. candidate at the University of Calgary, completing a dissertation on narrative representations of the genius in popular culture. She has published on fantasists Patricia McKillip and Charles de Lint, and on the television shows *Stargate: SG-1* and *Stargate: Atlantis*.

Todd C. Nickle is a geneticist and educator. He teaches in the department of chemistry and biology at Mount Royal College.

Jacqueline Plante completed her masters of arts in gender studies at the University of Northern British Columbia. She has recently completed a contract for international relief in Indonesia.

Ruby S. Ramraj teaches in the department of English, University of Calgary. Her interests are science fiction and fantasy, postcolonial writings, and Victorian novels. She has been working on Canadian science fiction, in particular Robert Sawyer and Nalo Hopkinson. Her article on Hopkinson's *The Salt Roads* appears in *Foundation*.

Randy Schroeder teaches in the Department of English at Mount Royal College. He often fantasizes that his fiction — much of it published under the unlikely pseudonym A.M. Arruìn or the hopelessly unrealistic Alexandra Merry Arruìn — provokes real social change.

Ken Simpson teaches in the Department of English and Modern Languages at Thompson Rivers University in Kamloops, British Columbia.

Index

aesthetic experience 100
AI 2, 17, 78, 137, 138n.4
Albrecht, Donald 144
Aldiss, Brian 113, 125, 126
Alice in Wonderland 19
alien 16, 18, 83, 111, 131, 143, 208, 209, 211, 216
alterity 208, 209, 215
America 24, 66, 102, 105, 106, 126, 127, 128, 139, 158, 167, 170, 207; *see also* United States
American South 28
Amis, Kingsley 116
archetypes 52, 53, 93, 187
artificial intelligence 138n.4, 208
Asimov, Isaac 17, 123, 132, 135, 138n.2
Astounding Stories 140, 145
Atwood, Margaret 24
The Avengers 105, 106

Bain, Dena C. 69
Bal, Mieke 50, 51, 54
Barbour, Douglas 59, 212
Barthes, Roland 160, 161, 163
Batchelor, Stephen 14
Baudrillard, Jean 24
Bear, Greg 17
Bhabha, Homi 138
binarism 14, 15, 16, 18, 24, 59, 161–163, 165, 166, 171, 172
the body 17, 67, 74, 93, 94, 164, 215
Brave New World 12
Brin, David 138n.2

Britain 86
Butler, Octavia 8, 138n.2

California 22, 25, 55–8, 61–69, 217
Campbell, Joseph 45, 48, 50, 53
Canada 1, 2, 3, 84, 124, 127, 131, 181, 183, 187, 189, 196, 198, 199, 200, 220
capitalism 55, 130, 206, 216
Captain America 105
Captain Marvel 104
Caribbean 131, 132, 133, 134, 135, 136, 138
Carson, Anne 12, 174, 175, 179, 180, 182
Carter, Angela 160, 162, 163–171
Clarke, Arthur C. 112
colonialism 28, 131, 133, 135, 136, 138, 194, 195, 197, 201
comic books 24, 83, 92, 93, 95, 96, 97, 98, 99, 101, 102, 103, 104, 220
computers 6, 65, 71, 105, 120, 135, 203, 204, 208, 215
constructivism 8, 9, 11, 12
Crichton, Michael 121
Cultural Studies 7, 8, 10, 13, 21
cyborg writing 7, 143
cyborgs 7, 138, 140, 141, 142, 143, 146, 148, 153, 154, 155, 157, 220

Daredevil 92, 95
DC Comics 103
deconstruction 14, 15, 18
Delaney, Samuel R. 8
Deleuze, Gilles 12, 15, 174, 177, 178, 179, 180

demythologize 162
Derrida, Jacques 12, 13, 15, 24n.2, 212
digital fictions 212
disability 13, 73, 76, 77, 79
Disch, Thomas 1
Disney, Walt 86
discourses 7, 71, 72, 73, 78, 79, 214
DNA 119, 120, 121
Doležel, Lubomír 45, 46, 49, 50
dominant discourses 12, 75, 81
Donawerth, Jane 88, 91, 142, 143, 150, 155
Donawerth, Paul 143
dualism 17, 21, 23, 128, 161
dystopia 132, 183, 187, 196

Einstein, Albert 9, 14, 122
epistemology 11, 161, 162
estrangement 90, 155, 166, 203, 206
Europe 24, 88, 110, 126, 127, 128
extrapolation 7, 12, 186

Featherstone, Mike 7, 206
female subjectivity 163, 164, 165, 171
femininity 150, 151, 157
feminism 176
France 126, 127
Frankenstein 87, 140, 143, 150, 154, 155, 156, 199n.1
Frye, Northrop 51, 191

Gaiman, Neil 92
GATTACA 13, 70, 71, 72, 73, 74, 78, 79, 80, 81, 121, 124
gay 74, 75, 76, 79, 81
gay gene 76
the gaze 164
genetic code 119, 120, 121
genetics 2, 72, 76, 120
Germany 28, 126, 127, 128
Gibson, William 17
Goodhew, Linda 19, 20
graphic novel 8, 23, 24, 92, 98, 99, 100, 101, 103, 104, 105, 106, 203, 204, 207, 220
Grosz, Elizabeth 174, 175, 176, 177, 181n.1

Haiti 133
Haraway, Donna 10, 11, 13, 143, 153
hard science fiction 202
Hawke, Ethan 71, 81n.1
Hayles, Katherine N. 214, 217n.1
hegemony 56, 80, 133, 164, 168, 169, 170, 171, 195, 207
Heinlein, Robert 112, 123

Hellboy 92, 96, 97
Herbert, Frank 113
heteronormativity 15, 81
heterosexuality 70, 73, 75, 79, 81, 155
Hinz, Christopher 111, 113
Hollinger, Veronica 70, 203
the Holocaust 28, 105
homoerotic 80, 143, 180
homosexuality 72, 75, 76, 78, 79
homosocialization 77, 78, 79, 80, 154
Hopkinson, Nalo 8, 12, 131–138
human gaze 153
human genome project 120
hybridity 7, 14, 21, 22, 23, 134
hybridization 175, 179
hyperfiction 203, 204, 208, 213
hypertext 202, 203, 204, 205, 206, 207, 208, 209, 210, 211, 213, 216

ideologies 7, 8, 10, 12, 13, 17, 18, 20, 24, 56, 72, 88, 109, 137, 144, 151, 152, 153, 157, 160, 162, 163, 169, 171, 187, 216
imagination 33, 47, 48, 49, 51, 52, 65, 87, 129, 139, 176, 184
individuality 18, 32, 44, 66, 73, 81, 92, 93, 98, 100, 109, 110, 115, 116, 121, 127, 128, 129, 133, 137, 163, 216
infinity 118
interpermeation 20, 21, 23
intersectionality 6, 18, 20, 21, 23
intersubjectivity 16
intertextuality 24, 204, 210, 214
Iron Man 105, 106, 107
Iser, Wolfgang 12

Jackson, Peter 19, 32–42
Jamaica 132, 133
Jameson, Frederic 7, 21, 25, 55, 56, 207, 208, 209

Kirby, David 72, 73, 74
Kirby, Jack 106
Kurzweil, Ray 5, 6, 8, 22, 118, 119

Lacan, Jacques 169, 170
Lee, Stan 106
Left Hand of Darkness 16, 25, 59, 69, 157
Lessing, Doris 125
Linster, Murray 145
Loy, David R 19, 20

machine 38, 78, 101, 120, 121, 140, 142, 143, 145, 148, 149, 152, 153, 215
male subjectivity 163, 168, 169, 170, 171
Marvel Comics 106

Marx, Karl 101
Marxism 21, 108
masculine gaze 148
masculinity 73, 77, 78, 79, 80, 82
medieval Europe 110
Mignola, Mike 92, 96, 97
militarization 146
modal logic 45
modality 46
modernity 69, 84, 96, 97, 108, 109, 110,
    111, 114, 115, 116, 121, 138, 180, 186, 190,
    192, 221
molecule 120, 177
Montgomery, Charles 107
morality 7, 18, 33, 44, 73, 85, 88, 100,
    101, 106, 137, 184, 192, 193, 194, 197
mutations 11, 29, 119, 125

nanotechnology 2, 119, 121
narratology 54
Nazi Germany 28
neo-Marxism 15
Neuromancer 10, 17
New York 3, 24, 25, 26, 31, 54, 69, 82,
    87, 98, 106, 107, 116, 117, 124, 138, 172,
    173, 181, 199, 217, 218, 219
1984 12, 18, 25, 26, 135
Nussbaum, Martha 5, 6, 9, 22

objectivity 11, 58, 63, 164, 175
oral tradition 103
Orwell, George 16, 18, 135
the Other 14, 15, 16, 18, 30, 37, 53, 85,
    111, 132, 165, 169, 170, 171, 209
otherness 12, 14, 131, 165, 215
Otherworld 45

patriarchy 56, 60, 73, 132, 133, 165, 166,
    170
Piercy, Marge 56, 57
Plato 101, 102, 107, 175, 180, 181
postcolonialism 133, 138*n*.2, 184, 194
posthumanism 6, 146
post–Marxism 8
postmodernity 8, 10, 18, 55, 56, 180, 184,
    189, 191, 203, 207
post-structuralism 8, 10, 11, 14, 15, 23,
    24*n*.1, 166
post-theory 8, 22
prediction 6, 70, 118, 123, 124, 176, 203,
    213
Prigogene, Ilya 11, 22
propaganda 88, 145, 154
Propp, Vladimir 45, 48, 50, 53*n*.1
protein assembly 120

psychoanalysis 161
pulp magazines 83, 84, 85, 87, 88, 90,
    145

quantum 9, 122, 135
queer 2, 13, 16, 74, 78, 80, 81
queer theory 15, 180

racism 28, 88, 131, 150, 170
reification 14, 17, 18, 20, 21, 23
religion 8, 61, 65, 76, 100, 108, 109,
    110–115, 116, 128, 129, 187, 193, 194,
    195, 220, 221
ribosomes 119
RNA 120
RNA interference 120
robot(s) 5, 119, 120, 149, 152, 155, 215
Rogers, Steve *see* Captain America
Ronell, Avital 139, 156, 158
Russ, Joanna 56
Russia 55, 128

Saussure, Ferdinand de 172
saviour 132
Sawyer, Robert J. 2, 111, 118, 132, 135,
    137, 138*n*.5
secularization 114
semiotics 221
Schwartz, Julius 106
Shelley, Mary 87, 127
Simak, Clifford 145
singularity 2, 3, 5, 6, 8, 14–18, 20, 21,
    22, 73, 118, 119, 120, 121, 122, 123, 124
slavery 28, 132, 133, 136
Slonczewski, Joan 56, 57, 113
Snow Crash 111, 112, 204, 205
Stapledon, Olaf 6, 125, 126, 127, 128, 129
Star Trek 1, 111, 117, 143
Stark, Tony *see* Iron Man
Stengers, Isabelle 11, 22
Stephenson, Neal 111, 112, 204, 217*n*.1
Sterling, Bruce 6
Stockwell, Peter 134, 137, 138*n*.3
storytelling 27, 47, 54, 92, 93, 94, 95,
    96, 97, 100, 101, 102, 220
structuralism 9, 17, 18, 23
subjectivity 12, 14–16, 17, 20, 56, 58,
    163, 165, 166, 169, 170, 171, 173, 215
superhero 24, 101, 102, 103 104, 105
Superman 24, 101, 102, 103
Swift, Jonathan 126, 214

tachyons 122
Taoism 17, 56
technology 43, 82, 107, 112, 113, 116, 158

television 92, 105, 128, 129, 139, 140–142, 144, 146–148, 150–153, 156, 203, 221
thermodynamics 121, 123
Tichi, Cecilia 139, 144, 146
Todorov, Tzvetan 148
Tolkien, J.R.R. 32, 33, 44
trauma 103, 139, 140, 142, 144, 146, 147, 149

United States 84, 85, 127, 128, 220
utopia 12, 51, 56–62, 64, 65, 66, 68, 109, 135, 175, 176, 183, 187, 195, 197, 198, 207, 208, 209, 217

Vinge, Vernor 6, 112, 119

the Wasp 106
weapons of mass destruction (WMDs) 126, 129
Weird Tales 83, 84, 85, 86, 87, 88, 89, 90, 91
Wells, H.G. 10, 126, 183, 204, 210, 216
the West Coast 57, 58, 59, 60, 61, 68
Whitehead, Alfred North 5, 22
Williams, Raymond 12
Wilson, Edward 26
Woolf, Virginia 88, 142
World War II 139, 140, 144, 157